PENGUIN BOOKS

Ordinary Joe

Joe Schmidt was born in the Far North of New Zealand in 1965, the third of eight children of a district nurse and a post-master. As a young man, he played on the wing for Manawatu in the National Provincial Championship, and worked as a schoolteacher, administrator and coach at schools around the North Island – and, for a year and a half, in Co. Westmeath.

After making a name for himself as an innovative schools rugby coach, he worked as an assistant coach with Bay of Plenty, the Auckland Blues in Super Rugby, and Clermont-Auvergne. In 2010 he became head coach of Leinster, where he won two Heineken Cups in three seasons. As Ireland coach from 2013 to 2019, he achieved unprecedented success, including three Six Nations championships in six seasons, and was World Rugby Coach of the Year in 2018.

He and his wife, Kelly, have four children, and live in Dublin.

Ordinary Joe

JOE SCHMIDT

PENGUIN BOOKS

PENGUIN BOOKS

UK | USA | Canada | Ireland | Australia
India | New Zealand | South Africa

Penguin Books is part of the Penguin Random House group of companies
whose addresses can be found at global.penguinrandomhouse.com.

First published by Penguin Ireland 2019
Published in Penguin Books 2020
001

Typeset by Jouve (UK), Milton Keynes
Printed and bound in Great Britain by Clays Ltd, Elcograf S.p.A.

A CIP catalogue record for this book is available from the British Library

ISBN: 978-0-241-98109-2

To Kelly and our kids, Abby, Tim, Ella and Luke, with thanks for your patience and support

Contents

Prologue

November 2016

Not long after our win over the All Blacks in Chicago, an email arrived at the Irish Rugby Football Union:

> *Our two brothers have been having a dispute over whether Joe Schmidt is the same Joe they used to play rugby with after school in their home-town of Te Aroha. We are talking around 45 years ago and they played against Joe and his brother. PLEASE CLARIFY THIS FOR US, it will really help stop this family debate!*

> *Thanks, Aly*

Aly was Alyson Gwynne. There was a house between the flat-roofed, Art Deco-styled Gwynne residence and ours in Te Aroha but no fences between the grassy backyards, which offered plenty of space for running about. My elder brother, Kieran, and I would combine with Aly's brothers, Brent and Clark, to play marathon rugby 'test matches' after school until we couldn't see the ball or each other. Aly's note brought me right back to those barefoot battles we'd had when I was just four or five years old.

I wrote back to Aly, confirming that I was the same Joe Schmidt from Aroha View Avenue who used to play back-yard rugby and kick the ball around with her brothers. Still the same, and very ordinary, Joe Schmidt.

PART ONE
Kicking Off

1. Looking Back

When you finally go back to your old home,
you find it wasn't the old home you missed but your childhood.

Sam Ewing

I began life in a small maternity hospital in the very small town of Kawakawa. It was September 1965 – springtime in the Far North of New Zealand.

We shifted to Te Aroha, a small town in the Thames Valley, when I was very young, so my earliest memories come from there. Catching chickenpox and not being able to go to the birthday party next door; going to athletics on summer evenings at the club just across the bridge; swimming in the thermal pools on Sunday evenings. We'd be packed into the family Mark II Zephyr, each of us jockeying for position to avoid sitting close to the hole in the floor, where stones would fly up and sting your legs if someone shifted the cardboard that covered it.

I went back to Te Aroha recently and was struck by how little had changed since my early childhood. The town is nestled at the base of the Kaimai ranges, and the immense Telecom tower that sits at the very top of the ranges was just as impressive as I remembered from when I used to look out my bedroom window at its flashing red lights. Boyd Park at the end of Aroha View Avenue, with its multiple rugby and soccer fields, was as expansive as I recalled, as were the wide streets with their generous grass verges. Plenty of space for youngsters to run and breathe.

The house we lived in was still there, and it still backed directly on to farmland; but the back lawns were now divided by fences. Looking at the chimney – a metal funnel that doesn't really fit with the stucco of the house – I thought back to the day that the house felt like it was going to be shaken apart. The original brick chimney toppled over and thundered down the sloping roof during a powerful earthquake. My mother was usually unflappable, but earthquakes were one of the few things capable of unsettling her and the noise of the chimney made it sound as if the roof was about to collapse in on top of us.

My formal education started under the watchful eye of the nuns at St Joseph's Primary School. I would set off for school with cheese-and-jam sandwiches and home-baked treats, especially the peanut brownies that my mother still bakes better than anyone else I know. We quickly learned to be vigilant in the classroom, conscious that a sudden smack across the knuckles could occur at any time if we were caught being sloppy in our exercise books. Sometimes it was the flat side of the wooden ruler that would be used, but most often it was the narrow harder edge, which delivered a painful, sharper blow.

At break times, we'd play tag, leaping up steps and across tyres in the school's 'adventure playground', then launching ourselves down slides and hurdling seesaws. The monkey bars were officially out of bounds for the new entrants but, as a lightweight kid, they were great to use as an escape route, swinging hand over hand to get away. One day my hand slipped and the momentum of my legs swung them higher than my flailing arms. I fell to the ground with my left arm extended. The impact hurt, but what really upset me was how crooked my left forearm looked.

I still remember one of the nuns scolding me for being on the monkey bars, because I was only five years old. Then she softened a bit and took me to the sick bay, where I waited for my mother to collect me and take me to Waikato Hospital.

By the time I was seven years old we had shifted to the lower North Island town of Woodville, where my dad took the position of Postmaster. That meant that he supervised the Post Office's banking and mail operations, as well as managing the telephone exchange. The Post Office occupied the lower floor of a large old two-storeyed building, while we lived on the floor above. It was handily positioned just across the road from the primary school and had a good-sized backyard.

Woodville was wedged between the steep hills and jagged peaks of the Ruahine and Tararua ranges. It was even smaller than Te Aroha, with a population of about 1,600 people. There were seven kids in the family at that point. My elder brother, Kieran, and sister, Anna, are twins. I was third, followed by a sister, Mary, two brothers, Andrew and Jamie, and finally a sister, Lucy. The youngest of us, Helen, was born after we shifted to Woodville, and once she started primary school my mum became the district nurse.

With eight kids in the family plus the odd stray youngster that my mum would bring home after her nursing rounds, meal times could be a bit cramped and chaotic. But before mealtimes the kitchen was usually quiet, with mum reading a book while cooking dinner. She would have the book open on the benchtop, reading passages in between checking the oven or whatever was on the stove. Her other ritual was successfully completing the crossword on the back page of the *Dominion* newspaper every morning, during or immediately after breakfast. Her speed and efficiency at both were impressive.

In an effort to keep some sort of order at mealtimes, our parents would enforce the need for basic etiquette, such as keeping our elbows in, or holding the knife in the right hand and the fork in the left, and you had to finish your food before you'd be allowed to excuse yourself. The bright evenings in summer meant that we'd head back outside after dinner. In the winter, there was television, reading or board games, or possibly a bit of homework might get done. At bedtime, the four boys were stacked into two sets of bunks for easy storage in a shared bedroom, while the girls were spread between two rooms.

I was always keen to be active and would play whatever game was being played at school. During lunchtimes on fine days we most often played 'Bullrush', where a line of players would try to get from one side of a pitch to the other without being tackled. If you were tackled you had to join the tacklers in the middle for the next charge from the players still 'free'. When the grass areas were deemed to be too damp to be played on, Four Square or padder tennis tended to dominate. After school, it was backyard cricket when we got home or basketball with an old hoop up on the garage or a game of tennis down at the public courts. Because Woodville was a farming community, a lot of my mates would have to catch the school buses to get home after school, so we would be a bit short of numbers for larger-scale games.

Inside the classroom at Woodville Primary School, it was a different era. Classrooms were quieter in the 1970s than they are now and learning was largely an individual responsibility, in contrast to the shared learning opportunities that are often promoted in classrooms today. On one occasion, when I was nine, we were doing maths and the teacher had said that there was to be absolutely no talking. A friend of mine sitting at the desk in the row next to me asked in a whisper how to work out a question. As I was whispering back, my name was called out and I was ejected from the classroom.

While I was waiting in the corridor, one of the girls came out to go to the bathroom and told me that Mr Schofield had said that he was going to strap me. Surely, I thought, I wasn't going to get strapped just for talking? Even when Mr Schofield stepped out into the corridor with the leather strap in his hand, I thought he was going to threaten me with it, not use it.

I was wrong: he deemed that my disobedience had earned me two strikes with the strap. After asking me which hand I wrote with, he told me to hold my left hand out to my side. 'Higher,' he said – then the wallop. I almost fell over from the blow, but gathered my balance and absorbed the shock to stay upright. My hand was hot and felt twice its normal size. 'Higher,' Mr Schofield said again, and then the second blow: the same sensation but not quite as bad. The teacher mumbled something about doing as I was asked in future, and I was sent back into the classroom in a bit of a stupor.

The memory of being strapped; the beige cardigan with big buttons and heavy-rimmed glasses that Mr Schofield always wore; the feeling that my hand had swelled so much when it was still the same size; the empty corridor and silence from inside the classroom as the other kids waited to hear how many strikes I got – it all still seems vivid despite being so long ago.

The pain had not been too bad, I thought afterwards, but

what really worried me now was that my parents would find out. With so many brothers and sisters, the news was bound to leak out. I loitered on the way home, anxious to be really clear in my mind about how I was going to explain to my mum what had happened. The truth seemed like a good option: the teacher had said no talking but my friend couldn't do the equation and I was just trying to help him.

'What happened to you today?' my mother asked when I arrived in the kitchen. She knew what had happened, that was plain. I got halfway through explaining why I'd been strapped when she interrupted, saying, 'You didn't do as you were asked: get to your bedroom and you'll get another two from your father when he gets home!'

I felt pained by the injustice – being punished once didn't seem fair, but to be punished a second time? I knew that I had to convince my dad that I'd only been trying to help a friend. It was the waiting that was always the worst when I was in trouble. By the time my dad got home, I think he felt that I'd stewed long enough and that constituted sufficient punishment. He gave me a stern warning and said that I could leave my room when I was called for dinner.

Dinner happened as it always did, though I was very keen to find out who'd got home from school ahead of me and told mum that I'd been strapped. Funnily enough, no one admitted to having 'narked'. I absorbed the lesson that I had to take responsibility for the choice I made but, even now, when something happens that seems unjust, it frustrates me and tends to linger more than it should.

When the All Blacks went on tours of the northern hemisphere, I used to love getting up in the early hours of the morning with my dad to listen to the matches or watch the staccato footage on our old black and white TV. The commentary from Bill McLaren was my favourite: I loved his rhythmic Scottish lilt, which added an almost musical quality to the action. I'd sit there happily, with a little bit of chocolate and a cup of tea. It was great to share the time with my dad and sometimes one or two of my brothers.

It wasn't just about rugby. As a Kiwi kid, I was inspired watching John Walker win Olympic Gold in the 1,500 metres and Dick Quax get the silver in the 5,000 metres, or the hockey team winning gold, or the rowers, or seeing the Kiwi number one, Chris Lewis, play in the Wimbledon final. Like so many others, I harboured dreams of wearing a black singlet or jersey one day.

The reality was that I was a long way from the top of any sport, but Saturday-morning rugby was a good place to start. Barefoot and full tackle from the very beginning, it was a bit of a baptism by fire for a weedy little kid among robust farming stock, but you got wise pretty quickly about how to bring bigger boys down and how to avoid being crushed by them when you had the ball.

Once we got to ten years old we were allowed to wear boots and had set positions, which we thought made us real rugby players. It was not long after that transition that I copped my first, and what would be my only, sending off in a match.

We were playing against Pahiatua, a town more than twice the size of Woodville. There was a keen rivalry between the teams and we'd gotten to know each other pretty well over the years. They had a good scrum half, Ewan Steminger, who was a bit more robust than I was and we would sometimes exchange a few terse words on the pitch. Playing against him was always competitive.

We were playing at home on the Woodville School main pitch, two twenty-minute halves. It was one of those frosty mornings when the grass was white and prickly and the cold gnawed away at the feeling in the ends of your fingers. On those mornings, if someone kicked your hand or stood on it, the pain was magnified by the cold. At some point, when we'd been playing long enough for things to get testy between Ewan and me, Ewan picked the ball up to clear it. One of our players barged through the middle of the ruck at the same time, flailing a boot and clipping Ewan's fingers and the ball at the same time. He yelped in pain.

I blurted out, 'Serves you right!'

The whistle shrilled. Time started to slow down as the referee looked directly at me while pointing his finger in the direction of the sideline: 'That's not in the spirit of the game, you're off!'

'Whaaat?' I protested. 'I didn't say anything bad, I didn't even swear!'

The referee then said, 'You're off, not just to the sideline but you can walk home as well!'

My shoulders slumped. It was bad enough being sent off. To be sent home as well was even worse. But the fact it was my dad refereeing was the ultimate shame for a ten-year-old in front of his mates. It was a lonely trudge back across the playing field and a pretty sad walk home, made worse by cold feet on the gravel footpath as I carried my socks and boots with me to avoid scuffing my sprigs.

I still have some good friends from my years at Woodville Primary School, and while I seldom have the chance to get together with them, it's incredible how quickly and comfortably we knit back together.

We all lived in fear of the school Principal, Jack Salt, whom I only ever really saw at full school assemblies or, sometimes, from a distance on the sports field. So I was taken aback, as a very small ten-year-old, to read my school report. On the back of the report, Mr Salt wrote: 'One of the best young footballers I have encountered and a good scholar as well.' I thought, 'Wow, really?!' I was far more focused on the first part of the message than on the second. (It was great to meet Jack Salt about a dozen years after I left primary school. He was just ahead of me in a supermarket checkout and introduced himself. At that stage, I was playing in the First Division of the National Provincial Championship (NPC) for Manawatu and it was nice to chat to him and to feel that his assessment of the ten-year-old player he'd watched long ago hadn't been completely off the mark.)

As much as I dreamed about playing sport at a high level during those early years, I was always conscious that I was in a small pond. Coming from a place like Woodville, you never really think that you'll match up to the players from the big towns who play in the big teams. We thought it was incredible one time when we had a student teacher, Brian Morris, who was playing for Manawatu. They held the Ranfurly Shield from 1976 to 1978 and went on to win the National Provincial Championship in 1980. They had a good number of current All Blacks as well. Living close by, on the other side of the Manawatu Gorge, we'd support Manawatu as well as our home union of Wairarapa Bush, who were usually in the second division.

'Mr Morris' would throw the ball around with us and kick goals from halfway at lunchtimes: we thought he was phenomenal. I even convinced my dad to take me to watch him playing in a Ranfurly Shield defence against Wanganui, which wasn't easy with so many other kids in the family needing to be ferried to different places.

My siblings and I learned the value of work early on. It was inevitable in a big family: if you wanted anything extra, such as a new basketball or rugby boots or a cricket bat, you'd have to buy them for yourself. In my final two years of primary school I did a paper run on my bicycle six days a week. I would often time myself from when I picked up the newspapers to when I got back to the house, and sometimes I'd try to beat my best time, mostly in an attempt to stay warm in the winter. It was hard to get below seventy-five minutes, because I had to get off the bike and hand-deliver some of the papers, and there were some long distances between houses. Also, there was a racecourse in Woodville, and the horses making their way to the track for workouts were another complication: the jockeys and stable hands would get grumpy if you rode past too quickly and spooked the animals.

It certainly kept me fit! It also gave me a work ethic and an appreciation for punctuality and reliability; plus, it kept me afloat financially, with pay of almost $5 a week.

2. Small Pond, Simple Ambitions

When I started secondary school, I worked during the holidays in a tree nursery: planting, potting, pruning and weeding. They were long days, starting at 7.30 a.m. and finishing at 5.30 p.m., and the days I spent planting pine trees on angular slopes were particularly arduous.

I also did the more stimulating job of 'runner' on the seven race days Woodville hosted every year. After each race I would run up the steps and along the rooftop of the main stand, to get the photo and confirmed results from the judge. Results and photo in hand, I'd run back across the roof, down the steps, then down the zig-zag of the internal stairs to the secretary's office underneath the stand. I'd wait for the results to be signed off by the Secretary before running across to the main tote so that all the calculations could be completed and impatient punters could be paid out. The final leg brought me back to the Secretary's office to pass on a copy of the dividends and total turnover.

I developed a love of horse racing that I still have. The wild-eyed beasts had intimidated me on my paper run a few years earlier, but I was mesmerized by the speed, power and excitement generated by those half-tonne athletes as they galloped along at speeds of 60–70 kilometres an hour.

In the classroom at Tararua College, I think I was more of an observer than a worker, and I didn't have much of an idea what I would do beyond secondary school. Thankfully, I did enough to get the grades I needed and qualified to go to university. There was the odd hiccup along the way, the occasional scuffle or clash with authority, including once when the cane was used to modify my relatively harmless behaviour. We'd been clowning around, spraying each other with 50ml syringes full of water on the way to mathematics class, and I had got the worst of it. Just after we'd sat down in our classroom, I attempted to get some payback. Murray McLean, a good friend, had done the most damage to me but as I turned to spray him, he anticipated the reprisal and blocked the jet of water with his hard-covered textbook. The water deflected up into a very visible fountain, just as our teacher walked in. Mr McKnight had a golf handicap of just 5 and used a two-handed swing with the cane that ensured the bruising was visible for over a week. I was thankful to my English teacher during the following class: she allowed me to stand rather than sit through the lesson.

When I went back to speak at the school assembly a few years ago, Mr McKnight was one of the few staff still there from my time as a student. We had a chuckle about the incident with the cane. He said that his golf handicap was nowhere near as low as it used to be and that he had obviously not used the cane since the abolishment of corporal punishment in New Zealand schools almost thirty years ago.

I had broken my left arm for a second time in my last year of primary school, and wasn't allowed to play rugby that year, so I filled the time playing soccer. I also took up basketball, which was great fun. I played in the local league on Sunday evenings with a bunch of schoolmates for a season. Alan Thrush, who ran the basketball in Woodville, asked me to play for the senior men's team the following season, and it was in that environment that I really started to appreciate more about strategy and working hard off the ball to get into space or to create space for others.

We would play in weekend tournaments around the central North Island, and we also played each Wednesday in the Senior Men's league in Pahiatua. Cutting through the tight confines of the key in one of my early games with the team, I turned to offer myself as an option; but before I could look up the ball crashed straight into my nose, which immediately started gushing blood. I was subbed out to wash the blood off. When Alan came off the court, I asked, 'Why did you throw the pass when I wasn't looking?'

'You were in space, so look!' he said.

You learn that way, I guess, and quickly, because if you don't you're likely to get a few more bloody noses, along with the same sort of blunt feedback. Playing with adults as a young teenager is a great way to absorb their tactical acumen. Alan Thrush developed my understanding of the various moving parts in a team sport, including the way opponents can be manipulated as well as an appreciation for the interdependence teammates share. I was also lucky that Alan balanced high expectations with patience and enthusiasm – an ideal mix when working with young players. We respected his game intelligence and competitive grit but also his sportsmanship, something that's easily lost in competitive situations.

In a small pond, it was great to be successful competing in a range of sports, but I focused mostly on basketball and rugby during my time at secondary school. With so many bus pupils, like myself, rugby training was held at lunchtimes on Tuesdays and Thursdays. Playing for the First XV, we worked hard to be competitive, but there was also plenty of socializing and we probably didn't get the balance right often enough. At the same time there were life-long friendships formed and plenty of great stories that we bring back to life whenever we're back together.

Many years later, at a NZ Rugby conference for coaches from Super Rugby and the NPC, Professor Bruce Abernethy from the University of Queensland gave a presentation on 'The Development of Expert "Game Sense" and Decision-Making in Players'. He went through evidence collected from the National Football League in America, the Australian national cricket team and Australia's National Rugby League competition. He discussed a number of characteristics of what he called 'experts', such as their ability to anticipate play and to make good decisions more often than other players.

It's a challenging area for coaches, as coaching programmes often focus on skill acquisition more than tactical understanding. This can create a bias towards looking for improvements that can be measured and quantified. There is no doubt that skill development is important, but I think coaches are also very aware of the need for players to accumulate 'game sense'. The question is how to facilitate this in training.

Game scenarios and small-sided games or conditioning games tend to work reasonably well, but can be a bit artificial. The best opportunity to really develop game sense is in organic environments where as many as possible of the moving parts from the actual game are present, along with as many as possible of the pressures that exist in match situations. With rugby, one difficulty is factoring in the contact. You can't use full contact in training too often because of the physical attrition involved. The challenge is to try to create enough pressure, albeit a bit artificially, so that players are forced to cope with the threat of contact while making good decisions and executing skills effectively. This is more easily said than done.

Professor Abernethy – a former professional Australian rules footballer – presented various studies that demonstrated the 'Birthplace effect' (Ericsson et al., 1993; Côté et al., 2003 and 2006), whereby athletes who come from smaller towns appear to have a greater sporting aptitude. In small places, kids are more likely to play unstructured games with different age groups to make up the numbers; they're also more likely to get structured opportunities to play with older players or adults, as I did with Alan Thrush and the other men of the Woodville senior basketball team. These sorts of experiences appear to contribute to game sense. Abernethy also spoke of 'expert players' often playing multiple sports until they specialize in their early to mid-teens. He contended that the number of hours of deliberate practice needed to acquire expertise was 'inversely related to the number of other sport activities undertaken prior to specialization'.

These insights made sense to me – and yet they are the reverse of what so often happens in elite team sports, where young players are encouraged to specialize earlier on the basis that they will build greater skill competency. I think early specialization can stifle the ability to understand and anticipate complex game environments. It narrows young people's opportunities to experience situations where they have to adapt and act based on reading various cues in a game that they don't yet fully understand. I know there have been some highly successful child prodigies who specialized from a very early age, but they tend to be in individual sports such as tennis (Andre Agassi or the Williams sisters) or golf (Tiger Woods or Rory McIlroy).

So often people marvel at the skill and speed of New Zealand rugby teams, and they imagine that this is the result of a sporting monoculture. Rugby is one of the most popular secondary school sports for males in New Zealand, but it is common for youngsters to compete in a range of sports.

For me, the opportunity to play a variety of sports, sometimes alongside older and more expert players, was pivotal in developing game sense. Allied to this was the enjoyment and the contagious enthusiasm that we shared for sport, which led us to train more often or commit more fully because of our collective motivation.

It can be similar in the classroom: a teacher's enthusiasm can ripple through a group of students. Genuine enthusiasm and passion can be contagious and it was one of the reasons why I applied for teacher training college when leaving school.

The major reason was because I didn't really know what I wanted to do, but it was also because of a teacher I'd had: Jim Cairns. 'Big Jim', as we'd call him when speaking quietly among ourselves, was a giant of a man, allegedly measuring 6 foot 7. He came into our classroom as a part-time English teacher, halfway through my third year at Tararua College, which was the year level where students were required to sit their first State Examinations. Students who did not achieve a minimum pass mark of 50 per cent in at least three subjects, including Maths and English, would have to repeat third year. Relying on 'Big Jim' to teach us what we needed to know to get through our English examination, I was amazed at how such a big and feared man could get so excited about small words on a page. He loved Shakespeare's *Julius Caesar* and phrases still rattle around in my head, such as 'Yond Cassius has a lean and hungry look; He thinks too much: such men are dangerous.' I still remember how animated he got about what this revealed of Cassius's ambition and intellect and the dangerous combination they presented for Caesar.

I left secondary school after four years because I had accumulated the qualifications required for university and doing the final year was of limited value. Also, being one of eight kids, we were expected to make our own way in the world as soon as we were qualified to do so. During the year, I decided to apply for teacher training college in Palmerston North but was told that I was too young, having not yet turned seventeen, so I decided to work in the Pahiatua branch of the Bank of New Zealand. My dad was keen on this: banking was the sort of solid and safe career that he had opted for himself. But when the representative of the college contacted me part way through the year, encouraging me to reapply for a place in their programme, I decided to opt for teaching.

In my first year at teacher training college I lived in a hostel reserved for first-year trainees. I was allocated a shared room with a guy called Paul Gibbs. He was a small-pond cricketing star from Marton but was good at pretty much any sport he played. He had a whippy arm action that allowed him to generate lively pace as a bowler, and he was also well able to bludgeon the ball about the park when batting. We both enjoyed watching and playing sport, though Gibbo was much more patient than I was and could spend hours fly fishing. We got on really well from the outset and remain close friends.

On the first day of my English tutorial, I met Kelly. She was attractive and had the sort of energy and autonomy that I found interesting. She was good company but headstrong and fiercely independent. I think we're a little bit similar, so we've had some robust discussions over the years!

While I was completing my three years of teacher training

at college and then finishing my final year at Massey University to gain my degree in Education, I worked during the holidays at the butter factory in Mangamutu. I worked 'six days on, two days off', with every second six days being night shift. My job was to test the butter for moisture, a role which, like the 'runner' at the Woodville races, has long since been replaced by more efficient electronics. The job consolidated my readiness to be independent and to take responsibility for myself. I also learned to fit in with a variety of people.

From a sporting perspective, rugby tended to dominate. In my second year of teacher training I joined the bulk of the other teacher trainees at the Palmerston North High School Old Boys Club, where I played on the wing for the senior team. I played two years in the Manawatu U21 team before graduating to the Manawatu Senior Representative team in 1988. That was also my first year teaching. I started off at Monrad Intermediate School, where I gained certification as a fully qualified teacher.

Playing both club and representative rugby often meant that I had club training on Tuesday and Thursday, and representative team training on Wednesday and Sunday. I think we trained more on the pitch than current professionals do, and I remember feeling pretty tired before the ball was even kicked off when graduating to play my first senior NPC match against Counties in Pukekohe. I was a massive 68 kilos chasing shadows as Lindsay Raki and Sean Lineen wreaked a bit of havoc.

I got the message about my lack of size very clearly from one of the coaches at Manawatu. Mark 'Bullet' Donaldson, a former All Black half-back, took over in 1990, which was also my first year teaching at Palmerston North Boys' High

School. 'Bullet' was adamant that I was too light and not robust enough – and he was right! I learned plenty from him tactically and technically, but I just didn't have the time to commit to pushing weights in the gym as well as doing the on-pitch training. I found the gym to be repetitive and, being a young English teacher, preparing assignments and marking essays was incredibly time-consuming. I would read all the essays, slot them into piles with provisional grades from A to E, and make any comments or corrections in pencil. I'd then go back through them confirming the appropriate grade with a ballpoint pen. With a class of thirty students, even if they're writing just a page each, the evenings were regularly long and studious.

The year before 'Bullet' took over the Manawatu team, we'd been coached by Garth Thelin and Donny McCaskie, who did a fantastic job galvanizing the group. They had a contagious positivity about them and created a competitive but highly connected environment, where people mattered and players performed. The players were relatively young, and Garth and Donny would focus on positive actions and offer encouragement before fault-correcting. They were also inclusive and would invite wives and girlfriends to post-match gatherings before it became common practice to do so. It's something that I regularly reflect on now. As good as a coach is technically or tactically, it's building that shared purpose and enjoyment within the group that forms the platform for the coaching to stick and for the players to stick together.

I was, at the same time, doing my own coaching and learning plenty on the job. When first arriving at Palmerston North Boys' High School, the Rector, Dave Syms, met with me. We discussed my teaching responsibilities as well as the requirement to be involved in the 'co-curricular life of the school'. PNBHS is a traditional New Zealand single-sex boys' school with plenty of activities outside the classroom on offer, and these demand a lot of effort from teachers. I wasn't sure what exactly was expected of me, but I volunteered to coach basketball.

I still enjoy the interactive coaching that basketball allows, where substitutions and time-outs can be used to alter tactics during the game. Another bonus is that basketball is played indoors, which was part of my strategy to avoid the breezy and damp winter weather in Manawatu. In response to my offer, Dave Syms replied that the basketball league was played on Friday nights, so that was ideal because it wouldn't interfere with my rugby coaching on Saturday mornings!

We've looked back at that meeting a few times and laughed at the way I was directed into rugby coaching. Dave still tends to laugh about a few other moments when I was unsure of myself in my first year at the school. One particular time was the evening that Kelly and I turned up for the school ball. Staff were encouraged to come along to help with supervision and we dutifully turned up, but got turned away at the door. The parent on duty at the entrance was convinced that we were students and that we needed to present our tickets. After we explained that I was a staff member, he went in search of someone more senior. When Dave Syms stepped into the hall foyer, he laughed – as did the parent when he realized that I was in fact a teacher.

Dave was pretty intimidating, so I complied with the dual-coaching requirement, spending Friday evenings at the basketball centre and Saturday mornings shepherding my U14 rugby lads. A couple of training sessions needed to be factored in for each of the teams, so the days were busy and the evenings were as well.

Kelly and I had got married on Easter Monday in 1990 and decided that before we got too settled we'd head off, as so many Kiwis do, on an 'Overseas Experience'. We had planned to teach in the UK, but fate intervened: Mark Donaldson passed on to me an offer he'd received to play and coach in Mullingar for the 1991–2 season. We had no idea where it was, but decided to take the opportunity all the same.

A few months later, having successfully gained leave of absence from our teaching positions, we headed for Ireland. I remember that we took four different flights to get to Dublin, with the first stop being in Perth, Australia. While waiting in the transit lounge, Kelly and I exchanged some pretty nervous reservations about the step into the unknown that we were taking. Then, after finally arriving in Dublin, we were given fresh cause for worry. Everyone else who'd been on our flight claimed their baggage, leaving Kelly and me scanning the carousel hoping to see our bag appear. Meanwhile the representatives from Mullingar who had come to welcome us and to bring us to Mullingar had seen all the other passengers file through and began to fear that we'd made use of the tickets they'd sent us and absconded en route.

After about half an hour, the airport staff spotted our derailed bag on the far side of the carousel. They retrieved it for us and we finally walked through arrivals. A relieved Eddie Holland and Ray Billington welcomed us and guided us to the car for the journey to Mullingar. Winding our way through small towns and relatively narrow roads, I asked if it was quicker to get to Mullingar on the back roads as opposed to using the main highway. Eddie Holland, who was driving, explained that this *was* the 'main highway'. It's so different now, with the motorways making travel so much more direct and efficient. Eventually, we arrived at Con's pub on Dominick Street in Mullingar and a Guinness materialized in front of me. It didn't really inspire me on first tasting, but I've long since acquired an appreciation for it.

The first training at Mullingar RFC was an education. An incredibly diverse bunch showed up, and that was just the rugby balls, of which there were about half a dozen. A couple of them were flat and soft and pretty much unusable so, with thirty to forty players turning up at the early-season sessions, getting some new balls was an immediate priority. The players were as diverse as the rugby balls had been, but they were brilliant craic and very quickly they helped me settle in. I was their new coach, but I was also one of the younger members of the senior squad and I learned a lot from them. I thoroughly enjoyed their company and the challenge of trying to help get them organized.

Coaching on Saturday mornings at the club, there were swarms of youngsters thoroughly enjoying the games and the opportunity to hone their skills, and some of them were very good. I was constantly on the move from group to group, and I have the utmost admiration for those volunteer coaches who give up their Saturday or Sunday mornings to coach kids, which can sometimes resemble herding cats.

The first match I played for Mullingar was at Edenderry. The pitch was a hay paddock, and the Mullingar lads told me not to say anything or the Edenderry lads would know I was a foreigner and kick the living daylights out of me. Robbie McDermott, who played for Edenderry that day, is now on the Leinster committee and we've often chuckled about the game.

I did a bit of part-time teaching in a couple of different schools, and started coaching alongside one of the teachers at Wilson's Hospital School in Multyfarnham. Joe Weafer was the coach of the senior team and a great bloke. His enthusiasm for whatever he was doing, whether out for a run, coaching the lads or even driving the bus, was inspiring. He was great company and made a difference with minimum fuss and maximum effort.

We had a fantastic time, and I still occasionally catch up with some of the lads from the team we coached. We qualified for the final of the Section A Schools Cup for the first time in the school's history. The multi-talented Joe Weafer drove the bus into Donnybrook Stadium, where the pitch was a bit worn but the surface was firm.

The whole school arrived in a fleet of buses and, for the first time, I experienced a Leinster Schools Cup atmosphere, albeit in the second division. Chanting and raucous, the students from the two schools offered genuine support as the Wilson's Hospital lads beguiled the St Conleth's team. Playing with width and enjoying themselves in their first final, Nicholas Drion on one wing scored two tries, while on the other wing Raymond Bell scored one. The fullback, Liam Plunkett, had a great game chiming in from the back with two tries of his own. Andrew Thompson, who went on to be a Shannon stalwart, was imperious at out-half and ran the game superbly. The referee was John West, and the former international whistle-blower still gets along to watch matches at all levels. It's always great to chat with him about current matches, but we still occasionally reminisce about that Section A final, played almost thirty years ago.

Back at Mullingar, we slipped up to Edenderry in the Midland League but managed to win the following season. The Provincial Towns Cup, however, eluded us when we were beaten by the eventual winners, Carlow, in the quarter-final. Kelly and I were lucky enough to get along to the 1991 Rugby World Cup games that were played at Lansdowne Road, where Gordon Hamilton's try to put Ireland ahead of Australia with just a few minutes remaining is still a highlight for me. We drove around Ireland and the UK and toured through Europe on a Contiki Tour holiday. We spent a sweltering day at Wimbledon for the tennis and got to the Barcelona Olympics for twelve days of amazing athletics. Fantastic life experiences and an 'OE' that has connected us to Ireland and Europe ever since.

Kelly and I were only due to stay for one season, but we enjoyed our time so much that we stayed on for a good part of the following season as well, helping my replacement, Kerry 'Sharky' Whale, settle in. Sharky and I had played provincial and club rugby together and he was a quality, uncompromising back-rower. His temper could sometimes get the better of him, as it did when we played together for Manawatu against the touring French national team. After being held down in a lineout by the big French No. 8, Devergie, Sharky unleashed an uppercut that jolted Devergie's head back and left blood splattered on his face and the front of his jersey. It's not so long ago, but it was a very different era.

We have some great friends from the sixteen months we spent in Mullingar. Jas and Marian Gillespie, who adopted us when we first stayed at their bed-and-breakfast in Multyfarnham, have become pseudo-grandparents to our children, especially our youngest, Luke. Len Ethel is a Kiwi surfer and successful rugby coach now landlocked on a farm in Multy-farnham. We've had many rugby discussions and our families remain friendly.

Many others, such as Eddie and Aideen Holland, remain good friends, but we've also lost some of them unfortunately. Joe Weafer lost a battle with cancer far too young, and Paddy Keogh slipped away a few years ago. We lost Ray Billington more recently but remain friendly with his family. Ray did a great job looking after us, and these people along with many others made Mullingar a wonderful place to be.

I returned from Mullingar at the start of 1993 to continue in my teaching position at Palmerston North Boys' High School. I also returned to playing rugby at the start of the club season – but only very briefly, because in the third game back I ruptured my Achilles tendon. Dave Syms had asked me to coach the First XV rugby side when I'd arrived back from Ireland. I'd initially declined, but when I phoned him from the hospital to say that I wouldn't be in school for a few days but that I would coach the First XV rugby team, he was happy enough.

It was the beginning of what became an accidental coaching career.

3. Competitive Edge

I finished the 1993 rugby season hobbling around on crutches, coaching the senior team at the High School Old Boys club. The team had been struggling, but we put up some improved performances towards the end of the season, and I learned a fair bit about the differences between coaching my peers and coaching youngsters.

I remember one particular game against College Old Boys, who were on top of the table and had hammered us earlier in the season. We played nothing but short lineouts and quick ball from scrums, trying to get real tempo into the game. Hamish Adams, who captained the side, played and led well. What struck me was that the players really seemed to enjoy having a plan, a specific strategy that helped them anticipate where their teammates were going to be and what they were likely to do. It also unsettled the College Old Boys players that we did something out of the ordinary, something that they hadn't really got themselves organized to combat. We didn't win the game, but it took them until the final few minutes to get their noses in front. Like me, Hamish ended up working in Irish sport, firstly in rugby, then as CEO of Irish rowing, before moving on to be CEO of Athletics Ireland – a long way from the rugby pitches of Manawatu.

With the PNBHS First XV, I took over an experienced side and they were pretty set in their ways. I was learning on the job and it meant that we weren't as consistent as we could have been. I remember sharing a post-match drink with the manager of the team, Steve Kissick. We'd been beaten by Gisborne BHS and I was gutted. I thought that we could have won the game.

They'd dominated the scrum with their big tighthead, Michael Noble, doing plenty of damage. The ground was puggy and we'd not been able to get the tempo to stress their bigger pack. Their coach, Kim Harris, explained his tactics to me afterwards. That only made me feel worse, because we could have done a better job of closing them down if I'd anticipated their approach to the game. Steve Kissick reassured me, saying that there would be tough days but that I was doing a good job. I wasn't so sure, but I spent the remainder of the weekend thinking about how to do it better.

I decided that we'd film every game that we played. We had an editing suite at the school and I was well versed in how to use it, having taught the senior Media Studies class. On Sunday evenings, I'd head into the editing suite with a videotape of the previous day's game. I'd select a few coaching clips – some good and some not so good – and copy them on to a backup videotape. The following day, I'd meet the squad in my classroom at interval or lunchtime to show them the clips and discuss what we'd done well, what we could improve upon and what we could do at training to try to make the improvements.

Being part of a wider school network, I'd often look to scavenge tapes of opposition teams from people who'd already played them. Sometimes I'd just chat to other coaches to see what they thought of a particular team, looking to find out who their key players were and what strengths or possible weaknesses they had. The players gained confidence from feeling that they had a bit of a head start in a match because they already knew a few things about their opponents.

I also enlisted the aid of the former All Black hooker Bruce Hemara, whom I'd played with in the Manawatu team. He took over the scrum and made it work. When Bruce moved on to coach overseas, Gary 'Boof' Nesdale, a former Manawatu prop, came in to replace him. Bruce and Boof did a great job getting the most out of our pack of forwards, who were often smaller than the opposition but operated well as a collective.

At the time, it might have seemed over the top to be so invested in a schoolboy rugby side, but the players got better and the team improved. We became more consistent and began to win games with collective endeavour or decisive plays that would tip the balance in our favour. When you are competitive and you see improvement, it spurs the effort to keep working hard, and I didn't mind working hard.

While becoming more involved in coaching, I also took on the responsibility of 'Third Form Dean', managing up to 400 young men embarking on their first year of secondary school. Add to that the birth of our first daughter, Abby, followed by the first of our sons, Tim, and life was busy – sometimes too busy.

One day we played at Ongley Park in an U21 club match against Feilding. Prior to kick-off I would nominate players to various roles if they weren't in the starting XV. One would need to 'run the touch' as a linesman, a couple would run water, one would be in charge of the gear stacked on the sideline. After Tim was born, I tried to help Kelly by looking after Abby, and so one sub got a particularly challenging job: minding a toddler . . .

It was a close game against Feilding. They were bigger and

older, but we were just a little bit fitter and kept our cohesion. We made a few substitutions during the game as their bigger boys wore us down. The player looking after Abby was called into service, but the player being replaced didn't realize that he had a new job to do and Abby, a confident two-year-old, wandered off.

We hung on to win, but satisfaction turned to panic at the end of the game as I looked around for Abby. Thankfully, one of the mums had noticed her ambling into the rose garden next to the pitch and had followed her. She answered my panicked post-match calls. I felt that I'd been well intentioned, leaving Kelly to look after the baby and keeping Abby with me, but I tend to lose myself in the game. From then on, I always enlisted one of the mums to help supervise Abby, because I am not good at multi-tasking when I'm coaching.

We grew in confidence, and in 1996 we worked our way through the National Knockout competition to make the Top Four play-offs. The semi-finals were held in Auckland at Western Springs Stadium, followed by the final at Eden Park as the curtain-raiser to the Auckland v Otago NPC clash.

We were drawn to play Rongotai College from Wellington. They were huge! They had the national shotputt and discus champion in their back row, along with a number of other very good athletes throughout their team, but even more intimidating was their ability to play rugby. It was one of those games where the better team played well but were unlucky and didn't get the result. I still remember how well organized they were and how positively they played. We were struggling, chasing a nine-point deficit with six minutes to play.

We got a penalty and our No. 10, Fraser Hodgson, kicked a superb ball to the corner. The drive and score by Shane Ratima still left us with plenty to do. Fraser had not been goal-kicking well, but he nailed the sideline conversion and we trailed by just two points with three or four minutes remaining. Grabbing the kick-off and playing back at them, we managed to work our way into their half and won a long-range penalty. I wasn't too confident, but Fraser was and again he sent it between the posts.

There was time enough for the kick-off, and after it slipped through the fingers of our No. 8, Grant Webb, Rongotai still had time to get back in front with a scrum well inside our 22. Thankfully, we managed to hold on and, somewhat luckily, scrambled into the final.

On the day of the final, I delivered a few last words in the team room at our hotel before we headed off to Eden Park. I focused on a couple of priorities and how we wanted to start the game. I was leaning on a trestle table when the whole thing flipped up and I landed on my backside, with the table clattering on to my head. It must have looked hilarious, but there was silence . . . until Isaac 'Cookie Bear' Cook started to chuckle and we all burst out laughing. I guess we can all take ourselves too seriously at times, and it eased the tension as we headed out to get on the bus.

We were up against another huge opponent, Kelston Boys' High School from West Auckland. They had a number of future Samoan internationals as well as a future All Black, Kevin Senio, in their team. It was a great occasion and we somehow managed to lead at half-time, based on a dominant scrum and some good game management, but in the second half Kelston ramped up the intensity and powered their way to a deserved win.

The following season we worked hard again, with our sights set on trying to get back into the Top Four. On a bizarre evening, Kelly got a phone call to say that she'd won a biscuit-wrapper competition. She would sometimes send away entries to competitions, and actually won a few of them, but this one was the best: the prize value was $10,000. For two young schoolteachers with two toddlers it was an exciting windfall. Kelly is not a biscuit fan – she prefers chocolate – so I felt that I'd at least contributed by eating sufficient biscuits so that she had the three wrappers to send away . . .

Later that same evening, we received another phone call, encouraging me to apply for the vacant assistant-coach position with the NZ Schools Rugby Team. I was flattered, but I hadn't coached at regional level and had only worked with a provincial U16 team at one tournament. I wasn't going to apply – but then, almost as an afterthought, I decided that I would. I heard back a few weeks later that they wanted me to assist with the team selection and coaching for a three-match Australian tour at the end of the season.

Some days, things just seem to fall your way.

At PNBHS, we battled our way through to the Top Four tournament again, this time being played in Pukekohe, just south of Auckland. In an extra-time thriller, we managed to topple Southland BHS, who were spearheaded by a young Mils Muliaina showing the qualities that later saw him accumulate over a hundred All Black caps. Wesley College were too strong for us in the final, with one of the most impressive secondary school athletes that I'd seen on a rugby pitch: their No. 8, Sione Kepu.

After the match, the NZ Secondary Schools team was announced, and the following day we assembled. After two days of getting to know each other and a couple of brief trainings, we headed to Auckland International Airport for our flight to Australia. The tour didn't start very well, as two of the players didn't get the right-sized jackets. I volunteered to run back to get replacement jackets, which had been sent to the airport. The plane was just about to board as I raced from the departure gate back to the security area, where the jackets were to be picked up from. I got back to the gate panting but with the two jackets under my arm. I scuttled on to the plane and took my seat just as an attendant came past. I was sweating and thirsty and asked him for some water or a soft drink. He apologized saying that he only had beer on his platter but that he'd get a soft drink for me.

He must have got distracted, because when he came back past me and I repeated the request, he apologized again: he'd not yet collected any other refreshments, so the beer was still the only drink on his tray. My mouth and throat were dry so I said, 'That's okay, I'll just take the beer in the meantime, if that's okay?'

The attendant looked from me to the head coach, Paul Cathersides, who was sitting next to me. 'If I make an exception and serve this player, I'll have to serve them all,' he said.

To which Paul Cathersides replied drily and without hesitation, 'Yes, fair enough, he is the captain, but best not to make any exceptions.'

I couldn't believe it. I'd always looked a bit young, but I was in my early thirties! It was funny, absolutely, but I was parched, and worse still, a number of the boys heard the exchange and started laughing. Some of the players from that tour still enjoy bringing it up when our paths cross.

After a couple of wins against selected sides, we ran into a good Australian schools side. The future NRL stars Ryan Cross and Craig Wing combined successfully with future Wallabies Phil Waugh, David Lyons and George Smith to get the better of us. It was tough to take, because NZ had not lost for a few years against Australia, and the last time they'd played in Australia Jonah Lomu had been utterly dominant and had scored four tries. Our side was led by Jerry Collins and Tom Willis and had a massive front row, with a young Carl Hayman formidable at scrum time, but we were only allowed to push a metre so our scrum advantage was minimized.

It was a very different environment compared to the weekly rhythm of coaching players that were well known to me. It was also a fantastic learning opportunity. Helping to meld a group of young men from around the country, with a couple of alpha males who were very keen to impress on the pitch as individuals, was a challenge. The players certainly shared a willingness to work hard, but we also had to work smart, with very little preparation time. Getting the setpiece organized, along with a defensive structure and a few attacking plays, was very different from the continual fine-tuning and cohesion that's built into the training week with a school 1st XV.

I had not been looking to shift jobs, but when Ross Brown, the Principal of Napier Boys' High School, mentioned an Assistant Principal position that they were looking to fill, I thought it would be a good challenge. While it was a promotion, it was really the new challenge that most motivated me, and it was in a school that I already knew a bit about due to the regular sporting exchanges we had with them. I also knew Ross because he had been the hostel manager when I'd first arrived at PNBHS. Kelly, Abby, Tim and I moved to Napier halfway through 1998. It's a great spot on the coast in sunny Hawkes Bay. The job was incredibly busy and varied, and there were plenty of learning experiences during the two and a half years I spent at the school.

Kelly had to leave her job at Highbury School in Palmerston

North when we shifted, so she suggested that this was a good opportunity to add to our family. I wasn't sure that we needed to make any further additions but certainly wouldn't change it now. Ella arrived on 18 May 1999 and has kept us entertained ever since. She was born in the late afternoon, so I went into school as usual the following day, but my office door was locked and there was a note stuck to it, telling me to go home and spend the time with Kelly and the kids. Ross Brown turned up later in the day with a gift and a bottle of champagne. It's what good leaders do, I guess. They appreciate important milestones and invest in people, not just in 'workers'.

In my second term at the school, I was in my office when the receptionist called out to me down the corridor: there'd been an accident in the metalwork room. We arrived to find an horrific scene. The metalwork teacher was holding a bloodied cloth on the groin of a student, who was lying barely conscious in a pool of blood. Apparently he had been chasing another student out of the classroom when the door had been slammed shut in front of him, dislodging the glass panel in the upper half of the door. A heavy shard of broken glass had dropped like a guillotine, cutting deeply into the student's thigh, severing his femoral artery.

The guidance counsellor had called an ambulance, while the first-aid-trained staff member checked the student's vital signs. The Deputy Principal was outside ushering students out of the way and clearing a path for the ambulance we were hoping to hear and see as soon as possible. The receptionist and I kneeled either side of the student, but he became unresponsive. A minute or two later, with the pulse so faint it was barely detectable, I called the ambulance again. I emphasized the urgency and the location, as the ambulance had gone to the wrong entrance of the school.

The boy's pulse was now imperceptible, while his breathing seemed to have stopped completely. I exchanged glances with the trained first-aider and the receptionist, and frantically thought through what I should do. The boy wasn't breathing, so one of us had to breathe for him. We had to keep what blood was left moving as best we could. I carefully clasped his nose, tilted his chin and exhaled a slow breath into him, watching his chest rise at the same time, and we kept him ticking over for the minute or so that it took the ambulance crew to arrive.

They gave me two bags of saline to hold up while one of the guys got the intravenous line working and the other tried to make sure that the pressure on the wound was maintained. It's a blur now, but I remember being bundled into the back of the ambulance still holding the almost empty bags of saline. In less than twenty minutes, during which two further units of saline as well as one of whole blood were administered, we arrived at the hospital.

Staff were on hand to make the hurried transfer to the theatre in the emergency department, with the priority of stabilizing the patient as best they could. I watched for a minute or so, stunned. A nurse noticed me and guided me to the waiting room, saying that the family were on their way and that the vascular surgeon would come by as soon as he had an idea of what needed to happen next.

By the time the surgeon came in, some of the family had arrived. The surgeon explained the gravity of the situation, but also expressed his confidence that the student was young and strong. He said that he hoped to be able to repair the wound over the next two hours. In fact, it was more than twice that long before the surgeon returned to explain that there had been a large piece of glass embedded in the wound and it had complicated the surgery. He was hopeful but we'd have to wait and see.

I'd been calm throughout, but it had been tough waiting with the family, especially as the time dragged on. The Principal drove to the hospital, and on the journey back to the school I told him about events at the hospital. When I got back to my office, I dialled home – and suddenly felt that I wasn't able to talk. I'd never experienced delayed shock, and I tried hard to contain myself, but suddenly sobbed. The Deputy Principal spoke to Kelly on the phone and explained that I'd be home soon. I was embarrassed and frustrated because I couldn't rationalize why, after having coped during the crisis, I'd suddenly broken down.

Thankfully, the young man survived. I went back to the hospital to see him after a few days. He was almost unrecognizable. He'd suffered an immense haemorrhagic shock and had lost pretty much all of his body hair as a result. He eventually made a full recovery, but it took a few months.

While working as Assistant Principal at Napier Boys' High School I spent two years coaching the 1st XV. We had two really positive years, culminating in winning the Super 8, which was a tremendously competitive league comprising the eight big boys' schools in the middle of the North Island. We had a great mix of players, and a number of them went on to play first-class rugby.

I remember spending a hard-working weekend crutching at Otupae Sheep Station before the season started. We raised thousands of dollars from the weekend, but it was also a great team-building exercise. Many professional teams look for an edge by paying money to do team-building activities, but working hard together is a great way to do it and get paid!

We had enough farm boys who knew what they were doing and parents who helped out using the hand pieces to do the actual crutching, while the others herded the sheep into pens or dragged for the lads crutching or scurried around cleaning up. There was plenty to keep everyone active.

In my second year with the team we were drawn to play away to Hastings Boys' High School, just fifteen minutes down the road. Hastings were coached by a former Manawatu teammate of mine, Bevan Lynch. We were good mates but keen to get the bragging rights all the same.

The sidelines were lined three or four deep with spectators jostling for viewing space. The pre-match haka was spine-tingling. Our boys launched into the school's traditional Tika Tonu haka, borrowed from the Ngati Kahungunu tribe. They showed great energy and unity laying down the challenge to the stony-faced Hastings players. When the Hastings boys responded to the challenge with their own stirring haka, the intensity was incredible.

As impressive as the pre-match was, the match itself didn't disappoint either. In the best traditions of schoolboy rugby, both teams played with pace and skill. The willingness to attack from the deep, and to link up through the tackle, and a real desperation in defence, were all evident throughout the first quarter.

Unfortunately, some of the traditions that make schoolboy rugby special in New Zealand can get contaminated with more modern exhibitionist stunts. I'd seen the State of Origin game where the NSW second-rower, Bryan Fletcher, had done the 'hand grenade' try celebration. It was a bit of fun, but at Queensland's expense – and they still haven't forgotten or forgiven the insult, judging by the comments Queensland legend Darren Lockyer made in a recent interview.

The first half ebbed and flowed but we got away to win by a couple of scores in the second half. Our sharp-stepping fullback, Glen Horton, scored the bonus-point fourth try and bounced up while many of the team crowded together nearby. I watched cringing as Glen bit the imaginary pin out and lobbed the ball into the cluster of players, who feigned being blown apart. While they jumped up quickly and made their way back to the halfway, one of the Hastings supporters stormed on to the pitch threateningly. His entry on to the pitch was defused by the referee, but it took some very humble apologies from our captain after the match to appease those assembled in the after-match function.

I apologized to Bevan Lynch after the match and explained that I was totally unaware that the boys were going to pull a stunt like that. He laughed and said that he thought it was funny but also added, 'What goes around, comes around . . .' I was embarrassed and, as I flogged the players at training the following Tuesday, I explained to them why it was important to respect their opponents. What goes around, goes around and around, when you have to do a lap for every player in the grenade cluster.

I guess you grow based on the sum of your experiences and how you react to them. The challenge is to keep thriving. Or, as Eric Butterworth wrote, 'Don't go through life, grow through life.'

4. Leading and Learning

We celebrated the turn of the millennium on Marine Parade in Napier surrounded by 30,000 other people, with the east coast of New Zealand being one of the first places to welcome in the New Year. By that stage Abby was five years old, and on her first day at Onekawa Primary School she'd skipped off and left us without hesitation. It's probably fair to say that she's been skipping off independently ever since.

A few weeks later, we were headed for Tauranga, in the Bay of Plenty. Again, I hadn't been looking to shift to a new position, but Graham Young, the Principal at Tauranga Boys' College, chatted to me after our Super 8 rugby fixture against them and encouraged me to apply for the position of Deputy Principal. He explained the position and the added responsibility that it would entail for me. He was also clear that it was because of the work I did in the school and not my rugby coaching that he was keen for me to consider the shift.

Kelly and I discussed it, and I travelled up for the interview and to have a look around the school and surrounding area. It's a beautiful part of the country and is attached to the golden sand beaches of Mount Maunganui. We bought a house two blocks from Tauranga Boys' College, with an enormous copper beech tree and lush hedge that enclosed the front lawn. Abby made full use of the climbing frame provided by the tree and Tim regularly dragged me out to play soccer or cricket on the lawn.

At the College, being responsible for 1,600 young men

certainly presented a challenge, and it didn't take long before I wasn't sure that I was managing things quite as well as they should be managed.

A student came to me and said that he'd seen another student with marijuana in his lunchbox. Obliged to follow it up straight away, I located the student and removed him from class. Once we got back to my office, I asked him to show me what he had in his lunchbox. He was hesitant but slowly withdrew a clear-topped lunchbox from his bag, through which I could see fresh green marijuana leaves. I asked the student where he'd got the leaves from. He said that he had found them, and that he hadn't been sure what they were. I confirmed to him that the leaves were marijuana and that I would need to call his mother to come in and collect him.

I phoned the student's mother and explained the situation. I informed her that I was suspending her son from the school pending a disciplinary hearing in three days' time and that she needed to come and collect her son. She stormed into the office about ten minutes later, seized her son, glanced at the open lunchbox and stated that the whole process was a disgrace. Then she snatched up the suspension letter, declared that I'd be hearing from her lawyer and stormed back out again.

I phoned the police, as they were required to come in and collect the marijuana, and then I was left to wonder which part of the process I'd got wrong. It tormented me for the next three days.

I made sure that we had our school lawyer, our board chair and the Principal at the suspension hearing at 7.30 on the Friday morning. Our guidance counsellor waited outside the boardroom ready to greet the student, his mum and their legal representative.

When the knock on the door came and the guidance counsellor poked his head in, I felt a sense of foreboding. But the mother and her son were alone – there was no lawyer in tow. Once they were seated, the board chair explained the process for the hearing and she asked if there were any questions before we started. The mother of the student said, 'No, I'd just like to thank Mr Schmidt for the way that he dealt with the incident and to say that my son is somewhat naive but very sorry for what happened.'

Wow! I didn't know whether to stand up and curse the woman for causing my three days of ruminating self-doubt or to exhale in relief, knowing that I hadn't made some mysterious but monumental error.

When I got home that evening, a bunch of flowers had been delivered along with a card. The message on the card was something along the lines of 'Dear Kelly, I know that it's been a bit of a tough start for Josef and that he may have been a bit difficult to live with over the past three days' – at which Kelly chuckled, 'That's nothing new!' But the card also said, 'He did a good job, which is much appreciated, so please enjoy a meal out together.' It was signed by the Principal, Graham Young, and inside the card was a voucher for a local restaurant.

That acknowledgement is something that still resonates. The empathy and support helped my confidence and consolidated my loyalty. When you feel that your efforts are recognized, you're always prepared to work a bit harder.

And I worked hard! There was always plenty to do. I spent long days counselling wayward students, supporting staff and helping them to develop positive management strategies. I also squeezed in the time to teach a senior English class myself, as well as trying to be accessible to parents. In break times, I would try to be visible and vigilant regarding student behaviour and the school environment. And I was coaching the 1st XV rugby team.

Assisting students with their sport, art, drama or music is an incredibly effective way to develop positive relationships with them. They appreciate the effort you make and the time you commit for their benefit. One day, when a tricky situation arose, the investment paid off.

Mid-morning on 14 June 2002, I received a phone call from the deputy head at Tauranga Girls' College. She said that hundreds of girls had walked out of the school in support of teachers who were seeking better pay. The Girls' College was just four blocks from us, and the deputy head had called me to let me know that the masses of girls who'd walked out were heading our way.

It was about twenty minutes before the interval. My first thought was to cancel the interval break and get teachers to keep their classes indoors, but I knew that messages about the girls' protest would have been received on any number of phones and that the boys would be incredibly restless. It would be very tough on staff to hold them in the classroom.

I grabbed the available deans and headed straight for the Physical Education Department, which was located on the south-western edge of the campus. The Girls' College was about 1.5 kilometres to the south-west and the girls would be coming from that direction along the main thoroughfare, Cameron Road. They would be able to make their way across the school playing fields before encountering the disused roadway of 14th Avenue, which separated the playing fields from the teaching campus. The boys would be prevented from joining them by the hip-high wire-netting fence that separated the teaching campus from the road. I spoke with Daryl Boyd, the head of Physical Education, and we got the staff primed to hold the line. The deans and physical education staff spread out along the far side of the 200-metre length of the fence, ready to move up and down the disused roadway to persuade the boys to stay on the campus side of the fence.

The bell to signal interval was a few minutes away when hundreds of girls started flocking across the playing fields. I stood on the unused roadway as they accumulated on the fields but they didn't cross into the school. There were shin-high wooden barrier fences intermittently spaced along the edge of the playing fields to stop vehicles from driving on to the fields, and they settled on the far side of them.

The boys arrived with impressive speed when the interval bell rang. They quickly clustered three or four deep along the fence line, while the girls called to them. The staff encouraged the boys to show restraint, emphasizing that they didn't need to join the girls and punctuating their affirmations with steely glances to confirm that there would be consequences if any of them did.

It looked as if about half of the 1,600 students from the Girls' College were assembled at the edge of the playing fields, urging the boys to join them. I was about two thirds of the way along the line, up towards the smaller of the two school gymnasiums, when there was a roar. I swung around to see a solid-looking, fair-haired young man land over the fence.

I was a long way off but knew immediately who it was and yelled his name with as much force as I was able. He stopped, looking at me from about 100 metres away – too far for me to read the expression on his face. I shouted: 'Get back over the fence.' At that distance, the instruction had to be simple and at full volume. The young man continued to look back at me.

Encouragement from both sides of the fence and the opportunity to be heralded by the boys behind him and welcomed by the girls on the other side of the road, just a few metres in front of him, must have held huge appeal.

I was walking toward him along the fence line. Not so fast as to appear concerned, but fast enough to shorten the distance between us. He hesitated for a few moments, looking longingly at the crowd of girls, and I feared that the dam was about to burst – but then his shoulders slumped and his head dropped.

He slowly turned and heaved himself back over the fence as I closed the space between us.

We knew each other pretty well. I also knew his parents and I'd invested time and effort in helping him on a number of occasions. We had a good relationship and he understood that he would have been held accountable if he'd gone through with the decision to break the line.

The minutes ticked by and the bell sounded to end the morning interval. As the boys tore themselves away from the allure of the girls assembled on the playing fields and trudged back to class, I commended the student for his positive choice. His response was that he didn't think he had much of a choice!

I breathed a sigh of relief and, along with a few of the Girls' College staff and their prefects, we cleared the playing fields, corralling the girls back in the direction of their own school.

The deans and the physical education staff did a great job in holding the line. They knew the students well and had invested their time in them, both inside and outside of the classroom. The boys respected them and were less inclined to revolt as a result.

As a teaching staff, we have a responsibility for the safety of students on their way to and from school, which is difficult to manage, but we need to make every effort to ensure that they're safe during the school day. If the boys had left the school grounds and any accident had occurred or they had caused any problems, the school would have been questioned about it. As well as that, a mass walk-out would have set a precedent that wouldn't be ideal. At assembly the following day I commended the students for their restraint. I also thanked them for showing their support for teacher salary issues and, more importantly, for the support that they showed for the staff who had asked them to remain in the school.

There were plenty more challenges in my three years teaching at Tauranga Boys' College, but my time there was incredibly rewarding. I still call in most years for a visit, and it's great to see the staff there still doing a great job in a complicated profession. More and more responsibilities that were once the sole domain of parents or community/sports groups, such as the teaching of life and social skills, have been added to a very crowded curriculum. Even more taxing has been the introduction of the National Certificate of Educational Achievement, with the continuous cycle of 'achievement standards' or 'unit standards' needing to be graded, moderated and recorded.

During my time at Tauranga Boys' College, I studied extramurally and was also the assistant coach of the NZ Schools rugby team for two years. A requirement laid down by the NZRU was that coaches involved with national underage teams had to undertake the Rugby Coaching

Practicum, a challenging coach education paper offered by Massey University.

Wayne Smith, dubbed 'the professor' due to his rugby knowledge and analytical approach to the game, gave a presentation at one of the practical sessions. His belief in 'query theory' – focused on asking better questions and trying to get players to problem-solve, as opposed to delivering direct instructional feedback – influenced my thinking. So did the simplicity of a drill he did on attacking space, where he manipulated different game-based situations and encouraged players to work out which cues were most important so they could best exploit any attacking opportunity.

Dave Hadfield, a mental-skills coach who worked with many NZ rugby teams as well as working in other sports, touched upon ideas that I was interested in and motivated to learn more about. He stressed the importance of building character, clarifying purpose and maximizing preparedness through the development of mental skills. I have continued to seek his counsel on occasions and he became a great sounding board and resource as I tried to develop my own understanding of how best to develop individuals, while also building a positive team culture.

With the Practicum contributing to a Diploma in Sports Management, which in turn could be fleshed out to complete a Masters in Management, I continued to study, looking to better understand management theory and practice as well as delving into the areas of sports psychology and physiology.

I enjoyed linking back up with the NZ Schoolboys team and the challenge of getting such a talented but diverse group organized in the space of a week or two. Steve Kissick, the manager, and head coach Gerry Davidson, who was teaching at St Bede's College in Christchurch, were great company. We spent plenty of time together at provincial and regional tournaments to ensure that selection was as thorough as we could make it despite the geographical distances. The provincial tournaments were during the holidays, which put an extra burden on Kelly with the kids in tow – something that I probably haven't thanked her for often enough.

We got our revenge against the Australian Schoolboys in 2000. The match was in the balance right up until the final minutes. They were spearheaded by star backs Morgan Turinui and Mark Gerrard, and a barnstorming Lei Tomiki made life difficult for our forwards. Cooper Cronk, who would go on to be a Rugby League star, was also among their cohort of talented players.

The hard-hitting Sam Tuitupou was at the forefront of our attack, and out wide we had Joe Rokocoko and the precocious talent of Ben Atiga. The Australians did a great job curbing the impact of Thomas Waldron, who had run amok in the lead-up games, and we struggled to get momentum. With a rowdy atmosphere and fast sunny conditions in Sydney, we finally got the lead late in the game. An illegal clean-out from our flanker Nili Latu almost offered them a crucial opportunity to strike back, before Nili redeemed himself with an excellent try in the corner to put us out of reach in the final few minutes.

Next, in January 2001, we assembled an U18 New Zealand Secondary Schools squad for an eight-match tour of the UK and France. We trained for a few days prior to New Year and flew out on New Year's Day. Future high-fliers Luke McAlister, Stephen Donald and Jimmy Gopperth joined the backs, and the forwards boasted some exceptional prospects, with Liam Messam, Jerome Kaino and John Afoa all in the early days of what would be highly impressive professional rugby careers.

The wet and icy conditions that prevailed during the tour caused some havoc with training and match venues, but the opportunity to experience the hospitality of rugby people on the other side of the world and to learn to cope with different challenges along the way was ideal – for the players and coaches alike.

5. Study and the Steamers

With just five papers to finish in my Masters of Management at Massey University, I applied for an educational scholarship whereby I would be given paid leave from Tauranga Boys' College for the duration of the university year. Around the same time, the Bay of Plenty Rugby Union CEO, Jon Brady, called to ask if I had time to chat to him.

I presumed Jon wanted to discuss the outstanding young player we had in the school, Tanerau Latimer, who had been included in a national sevens training squad but was only seventeen years of age. That meant that the NZRU would need to speak to the school, as well as getting parental permission, if he was to be signed up to play in the sevens tournaments.

The meeting was a career changer.

Jon asked if I was interested in assisting Vern Cotter with the Bay of Plenty team in the National Provincial Championship. The Steamers had finished at the bottom of the ten-team competition for the last three years and had survived promotion–relegation matches to maintain their place in the top flight.

During the previous pre-season, I'd been invited in twice to do skill sessions with the Steamers, and a few weeks before Jon's call Vern Cotter had chatted to me in passing at a big schoolboy match we'd played against Rotorua BHS. We'd played well in the match against the big Rotorua side, who ended up sharing the National Title with Napier BHS at the end of the season. They bullied us into submission in the final quarter but the game had been close until then.

I presumed that Vern's chat with me and the two skill sessions from the season before had served as an evaluation of sorts. I checked with Kelly, who was now expecting our fourth child. We thought that it should be feasible provided I got the scholarship and the paid leave, because I could control my own work schedule for the papers I had to finish for my Masters. The coaching would be mostly concentrated into a four-month window starting toward the end of July, with a couple of pre-season games leading into the NPC.

In the lead-up to my discussion with Jon Brady, I'd had some angst about an upcoming interview for the Rector's job at Palmerston North BHS. It's a great school and I'd had a few discussions with Dave Syms, my former boss, about what the job entailed. I also chatted to the Board Chairman, Craig Hart, who had contacted me about the job. One thing Dave Syms was adamant about was that if I was not going to accept the job, I should withdraw before the interview and not waste people's time. I knew that taking the job at PNBHS would effectively lock me into the education system. That didn't unduly concern me, but there was a 'what if' that was nagging me. What would a semi-professional rugby environment be like and how well would I cope in that environment? Finally, I decided that there would be other opportunities in education but there might not be in rugby. The day prior to the interview, I withdrew. My application for paid study leave was accepted, and I opted to accept the Bay of Plenty Steamers role while finishing my Masters.

My first meeting with Vern is still pretty clear in my mind. It was in a quiet corner of the Welcome Bay Tavern, which was owned by the Steamers' manager, Craig Morris. Vern encouraged me to take the role, and then looked at me directly and demanded my loyalty. I think loyalty is something we all need from our fellow coaches and management, but usually we hesitate to be quite so direct. Not VC: he did *direct* without hesitation, and I liked the clarity of that.

The remuneration for the assistant coach role was $1,000 worth of petrol vouchers for the travel I would be required to do between Tauranga, Rotorua and Whakatane. The provincial cities were about an hour apart and were the centres for the three regions that made up the province of Bay of Plenty. It didn't qualify as a 'professional' coaching role, but I felt the pressure to be as professional as I could be.

I spent the first six weeks of the school year in 2003 working furiously. I was full-time and full on at Tauranga Boys' College before my study leave started towards the end of March. The study was time-consuming, with six-hour road trips to Palmerston North for courses, then six hours back again, but it was also quite flexible, with most of the work being done independently and online. My Masters research project led me to consider the 'cost of poor recruiting', and I still find some of what I learned to be useful. If an organization skimps on recruitment, it increases the risk of not getting the right people. If that happens, then apart from the direct impact on the efficiency and growth of the organization, there's also the possible loss of clients as well as the potential that the performance of other staff members will be adversely affected. Added to that might be the direct financial cost of any redundancy package if the poorly selected staff member has to be let go, and of re-advertising the position and repeating the selection process.

That season with Bay of Plenty was a whirlwind. A

pre-season win over the touring Italian national team offered some confidence, and further momentum was gained from our narrow first-round win over a dangerous North Harbour team, boasting backs of the calibre of Nick Evans, Luke McAlister, Rudi Wulf and the Gear brothers, Rico and Hosea.

In the lead-up to the match against Italy, we trained at the Rotorua International Stadium, where the match was to be played. During a defensive session, a line break happened and the outside backs raced across the pitch, deep into our right-hand corner, to cover the break. Directly from the ruck a cross kick to our left found sufficient space for our training opposition to score.

From half the pitch away, VC roared: 'Get your bloody backs sorted to cover that space, Schmiddy!'

Feeling aggrieved because the backs had raced across the field to cover the initial break into the right-hand corner, I yelled back at VC, 'They can't be in two places at once!'

A brief but reasonably loud debate ensued between the two of us before Vern cut it short, saying that we'd sort it after training.

I've never been keen on separating the performance attributes of the forwards and the backs in general play. It can create a 'them and us' partitioning of the team, which can lead to a bit of a blame culture between the two units. We discussed the line-break situation in further detail after training, using a flip chart and drawing a myriad of arrows. We didn't really get the clear resolution we were looking for, which left me brooding somewhat. We decided to leave it, and VC said I should call into his place on the way home for a coffee.

I had travelled to Rotorua with Kevin 'Herb' Schuler, who

had been drafted in as our defence coach. Herb and I had played a few years together for Manawatu, and he had recently returned from a long rugby-playing and coaching career in Japan. We were both pretty intense when it came to detail and problem-solving any flaws in a performance. After the difficult conversation with VC, Herb told me to get over myself, and we stopped for coffee at VC's farm, high up on the hills behind Te Puke.

VC's a great host and we pretty quickly laughed off the disagreement but resolved not to confront each other at training in the future. VC was head coach and very good at what he did, and I should have held my tongue, but at least it meant that we cleared up the expectations we had of each other.

The following day, I missed training. I was backing out of the driveway when Kelly's mum, who'd come to visit because the baby was almost due, called out to me. It was happening. We lived about 800 metres from the hospital, so it didn't take long to get there, and Luke didn't take long to arrive either.

At training the next day, there was plenty of good humour and I was fined for missing the previous day's session, while at the same time being congratulated on the arrival of Luke. Ironically, VC, who had validated the fine, missed the captain's run a few days later. This time it was him rushing to the same hospital for the birth of Holly, the first of his and Emily's three children.

In the second round of the NPC, we were away to perennial big guns and Ranfurly Shield holders Canterbury. One of our reserve backs, Nathan Strongman, injured his calf in the warm-up and we had no extra reserve players: our B squad had travelled with us to Christchurch, but they were playing about half an hour away from Jade Stadium. VC said to me that we had no alternative but for me to go on to the bench. Panic was thankfully replaced by relief as Ray Mac-Donald, who had played at No. 10 for the B team, was quickly ferried to the stadium just in time to take his place on the bench. Phew! I hadn't played in ten years and if I'd been required to take the field, I'm sure it would have been ugly.

Narrow away losses to Canterbury and Otago were followed by a home win against Taranaki. Next up, we travelled to Wellington, who had inflicted a 74–12 home defeat on Bay of Plenty the previous season. After Glen Jackson scored under the posts from a nicely timed double-around set play, we led 10–0 and probably deserved to, at that point.

Unfortunately, our hooker, Ngarimu Simpkins, was sin-binned soon after, and Wellington started to get a supply of ball to their All Black legends Tana Umaga and Christian Cullen. A virtually unknown youngster, Conrad Smith, timed his angled running to perfection to scythe through our defensive line a couple of times, and we trailed 11–10 at half-time. The end result – a 33–13 defeat – wasn't a disaster, but it certainly dented our chances of qualifying for the semi-finals.

After an away win in a high-scoring match in Northland, a turning point arrived with a home match against Auckland. We hadn't beaten Auckland for twenty-three years, and it didn't start well as Ben Atiga scorched over for an early converted try. Auckland were defending champions and had an intimidating coaching team of Graham Henry, Wayne Pivac and Grant Fox. On the pitch, they oozed confidence and class. We fought our way back from the early setback and, while a late try from Auckland got them to within a score, we held on for a memorable win.

A big loss to our nearest neighbour, Waikato, meant that

to qualify we'd need an even bigger bonus-point away win in the deep south, plus a few other results to fall in our favour. Southland, playing in front of their home supporters, leaped out to a two-score lead early on but we surged back, scoring some impressive tries, to get the big bonus-point win that we needed. It was fast and frantic throughout but, despite the win, other results did not go our way and we missed the play-offs, finishing fifth on the league table.

The season seemed to have passed incredibly quickly. I'd enjoyed it and learned a lot. There was a buzz about the team and in the community. But I had no intention of continuing in the role: I just didn't have time to coach and to help run a school the size of Tauranga Boys' College. I had no regrets either. I was happy to have been involved.

I also had plenty to do straight after the season finished, with a thesis to complete and a few examinations pending. At the same time, I tried to help out with the kids at school. St Mary's Primary School enjoyed an idyllic setting alongside the estuary, along with a very supportive band of parents. I remember being parent help during kayaking lessons for Abby's class, standing out in the warm and shallow water, at the edge of the kayaking zone. We had a social basketball team made up mostly of parents from the school. Kelly and I had plans drawn up to extend our house and we had settled comfortably into the community. We certainly weren't looking to move anywhere else.

Things got complicated when David White, the Auckland Rugby CEO – no doubt encouraged by my former boss Dave Syms, who was now the Auckland High Performance Manager – asked if I was interested in a full-time position as assistant coach of Auckland. I confided in Kevin Senio, a quality individual, who said I should definitely have a look at the job, but that I should stay with the Bay all the same. He was an Aucklander and knew plenty about the Auckland set-up and the depth of their resources but he was playing for the Bay and we'd enjoyed the season working together. He also believed that Bay of Plenty could be just as competitive the following season if we all stuck together.

I was due to fly to Christchurch to catch up with my brother-in-law and a couple of friends, so I booked to fly from Auckland and prepared for the meeting with Auckland Rugby. But I wasn't sure, and after plenty of discussion with Kelly we decided that we'd stay where we were. I phoned David White to tell him of my decision, but he encouraged me to come for a chat at Eden Park because my flight was leaving from Auckland anyway.

I arrived at Eden Park to see Steve Hansen – whose Wales team had just been knocked out of the Rugby World Cup by the All Blacks in a high-scoring quarter-final – getting into a taxi. When I got upstairs, Graham Henry and David White welcomed me in and plied me with questions. I was a bit star-struck. I remember some astute questions from Graham Henry, one in particular that I answered clumsily, and I thought they'd certainly be questioning the wisdom of including me in such an elite coaching team. I was taken aback when they put a contract for the position of backs coach in front of me at the end of the discussion.

I flew to Christchurch and met with Steve Hansen for a chat at the races. He had been offered the role of forwards coach and we were both trying to work out what we would do next. It was New Zealand Cup day at Riccarton and he had a couple of horses running in some of the other races on the programme. I felt a bit out of my depth. Primarily because Steve had accumulated some impressive experience, but also because I struggled to finish my pint before he was halfway through his second one. I was a lightweight!

Events in Sydney that evening changed the landscape incredibly quickly. Stirling Mortlock's interception, Elton Flatley's kicking boots and George Gregan's 'Four more years' sledge saw the All Blacks lose 22–10 to the Wallabies in the Rugby World Cup semi-final. A few weeks later, the national coaches, John Mitchell and Robbie Deans, had been replaced by Graham Henry and Steve Hansen, who added Wayne Smith to their coaching team to complete an impressive triumvirate.

At least it simplified my decision-making, because two thirds of the coaching team that Auckland had been trying to put together was no longer available. At the same time Bay of Plenty decided that they should start a Rugby Academy. In light of my background in education, and after the competitive season we'd had in the NPC, they asked if I'd do both the Academy and assistant-coach roles. I wasn't sure, but the Tauranga Boys' College Principal, Graham Young, was as understanding as always. He suggested that I try it for a year and he would keep my position open at the school. I changed careers with the comfort of a safety net I'd happily collapse back into.

We had a great bunch of first-year Academy players, predominantly from Rotorua Boys' High School. We created a training course alongside their study or apprenticeships, liaising with Bay of Plenty Polytechnic in Tauranga and Wairariki Institute in Rotorua, which have since merged to form Toi Ohomai Institute of Technology.

As part of my coaching role, I tracked players in the club competition, liaised with our strength and conditioning coach, Keith Roberts, and helped VC with pre-season sessions. I really enjoyed attending club trainings and sometimes was drafted in to do a segment or two on various elements of the game. Players were receptive and I got to know them better. I think the investment in getting along to see the preparation work they did and to help them with some of it was beneficial for me, and they seemed to get something out of it as well.

Bay of Plenty centurion Damon Kaui had hit the line hard and straight and had been indomitable as the last defender during the 2003 season. At the same time, as is often the case in strong teams, there was a real contest for the No. 15 jersey with ex-All Black Adrian Cashmore's return from playing club rugby in Japan. Rua Tipoki also arrived towards the end of the club season and added an extra edge to our midfield. In addition to the newcomers, eleven of our players had secured Super Rugby contracts, after having had just two the previous season.

Despite the slight increase in our depth of playing resources, one dismissive pundit from the *NZ Herald* declared that the 'reality check is in the mail'. Chris Rattue believed that we'd overachieved the previous season but that the natural order would be restored and that we'd finish towards the tail of the competition.

We travelled north to Auckland on Sunday, 15 August, for our Round 1 clash, which doubled as a Ranfurly Shield challenge. Despite the predicted 'reality check', we defied 103 years of history to claim the Shield for the first time. Glen Jackson kicked us into a one-point lead with a drop goal in the final quarter. Then, late in the game, Rua Tipoki scythed through a gap. The Auckland defence condensed and the ball was whipped wide to Ants Tahana, who scored in the corner.

Glen Jackson, who scored in every manner possible during

the game, then slotted the sideline conversion. With just a few minutes to go in the match, we led by eight points. When Auckland were awarded a penalty with seconds remaining, I stood to shake VC's hand and to congratulate him. The Auckland captain, Angus MacDonald, unsure about the time left, mulled over taking the kick into the corner, then settled on the three points from the penalty goal to grab the losing bonus point, but the Shield had slipped from their grasp.

Paul Tupai, who featured in his 100th game for Bay of Plenty in the Shield match, became temporary custodian of the Shield. The celebrations were raucous and uninhibited, with plenty of celebratory snapshots on and off the field. The Red Fox Tavern on the journey back to Tauranga was jammed with supporters. Ex-players celebrated, their frustrations from past Shield losses assuaged somewhat. The Shield has a galvanizing quality and it was on its way to the Bay of Plenty for the first time.

I have a vivid image in my mind from later that week as my son Tim walked to school trying to carry the Shield under his arm. He was only eight years old at the time, and his little arms didn't extend far enough to clasp the Shield securely, but he was so excited to have it in his possession and was looking forward to telling his class about it. We have some great photos including one of Luke, just one year old, sleeping soundly with the Shield resting at one end of his cot. These memories, where my family share in the enjoyment on successful days, are particularly special.

The whole week was a sustained feel-good celebration around the Bay of Plenty. As described by the *Sunday Star-Times*, 'In Tauranga, Rotorua, Whakatane, Te Puke and Taneatua, they came out in their hairnets and dreadlocks, gang patches and school uniforms.' The cross-section of people looking to see or touch the Shield was incredible. The ability of sport to evoke emotions and to energize a community is brilliant: it creates a connective tissue where people share a pride in effort and performance and sometimes, on special occasions, a small piece of history being made.

The players spent Monday and Tuesday celebrating the victory. I joined them intermittently, but in between times I tried to look at how we might cope with a high-powered Ranfurly Shield challenge from Waikato in a few days' time.

When interviewed about the players, VC lamented that 'we are two days behind with our recovery after a very physical game.' We were both concerned by the prospect of having the shortest Ranfurly Shield tenure on record, but felt that the players needed to get the celebrations completed before we turned our attention to defending the Shield.

By the time we did the captain's run on Saturday morning, we had started to gain a bit of rhythm again. We'd decided that we couldn't sit back and wait to repel the dangerous attacking force that Waikato presented, with the likes of Byron Kelleher, Sitiveni Sivivatu and Liam Messam, among many others. We'd been clobbered by them the season before and we were going to have to get on to the front foot. Effectively, our preparations were focused not on defending the Shield, but on winning the game.

We needed to attend a civic reception early on Saturday afternoon, followed by a parade. I was in a convertible sports car with our tighthead prop, Ben Castle. We slotted in towards the rear, trying to keep a low profile. The week had been a blur so, for me, Saturday evening was spent trying to relax despite intrusive 'what if' and 'if we can just do this or do that' scenarios buzzing around in my head.

The next day, we built a commanding lead with the wind

behind us in the first half but had to withstand huge pressure in the second half. What mattered most is that we held on, and the 26–20 victory ensured that we'd hold the Shield for another two weeks. I remember the former Bay of Plenty prop Peter Kennedy coming into the changing sheds after the game, struggling to keep his voice steady and emotions in check. He'd played over a hundred games for the Bay and had been denied a late try against Canterbury in a closely fought 1984 Ranfurly Shield challenge but, finally, he had the Shield in his hands.

We couldn't lose the Shield playing away to Taranaki the following weekend, but there was plenty that we did lose. A 58–14 hammering was bad enough, but the loss of our half-back, Kevin Senio, for the remainder of the season with a broken ankle, plus the broken leg suffered by midfielder Jeff Ierome, left us reeling. The emotional energy expended over the first two weeks of the NPC had taken its toll and we'd looked brittle and one-paced.

Boarding the bus the following morning, Keith Roberts was buoyant and a cheer went up as he announced that Grant and Cherie McQuoid had just had their first baby back in Tauranga. I'd known Grant since first coaching him in the NZ Schools team. He and Cherie were such good people and everyone got a boost from the news. Later that morning, we were shocked to hear that they had lost their baby. There was a mournful hush for the remainder of the trip back to Tauranga and for the week that followed.

The Canterbury Shield challenge diminished in importance as we attended the funeral. The shoebox-sized coffin being carried out of the church by Grant still evokes the same heavy sadness that dominated the week. Convinced that he needed to do something active to provide a positive distraction, Grant decided late in the week that he would play. And he played a super game, culminating with a central role in the spine-tingling finish.

In a match that see-sawed against the All Black-laden Canterbury side, the final play saw Adrian Cashmore break through the tackle of Dan Carter and blast into the open. Grant McQuoid swooped outside him in support and Nili Latu punched through on the inside with space in front of him. A converted try would seal a Shield-saving draw. When 'Cashie' kicked ahead, I thought that Grant was going to win the race to ground the ball. The crowd rose and roared, just as we did in the coaches' box, desperate for a miracle finish to a harrowing week. But sporting fairytales are few and Ben Blair at full stretch narrowly got the first hand to the ball as it bobbled around in the in-goal. The final whistle blew and the players looked absolutely spent. They had given all that could be asked of them. The Shield was on its way back to Christchurch, where I felt it weighed substantially less on the shoulders of the Cantabrians than it did on those of our first-time holders.

There were plenty of accolades regarding the quality of the match and the resilience of our players, but there was little time for reflection. We quickly turned our heads toward the win we needed against Otago the following week. The NPC is relentless and Otago were our fourth 'big city' opponents from a Super Rugby franchise base in five weeks. The players responded superbly with a dominant 44–16 win. We gained our revenge on Wellington the following week in a tight finish. Wins against Northland and Southland saw us well placed to qualify for the semi-finals, but a win against North Harbour was needed to make sure. The 9–14 victory in North Harbour Stadium was a desperately close affair but it allowed us to scramble into third place on the final points table.

Our reward for getting to third was an away semi-final against title favourites Canterbury.

Some verbal jousting preceded the game. There was some pressure on Canterbury to allow the match to double as a Ranfurly Shield challenge, but the idea was quickly dismissed by the Canterbury CEO, who stated that 'There is simply no opportunity or mechanism for a challenge. I think the Bay should just concentrate on the NPC and get on with it.' So we got on with it.

We missed a couple of opportunities in the first half but weren't too far away. In the first few minutes of the second half, we scored a setpiece try off a scrum. VC and I had not even got back to our seats in the coaches' box. The try put us within reach and I clung to the hope that upsets happen, tempered by the reality that upsets of this magnitude don't tend to happen very often. And it wasn't to be, as Canterbury got away in the final quarter. They then won comfortably enough away to Wellington the following week, and were deserved champions.

There was still plenty of satisfaction for us at the end of the Championship. We'd broken new ground by winning the Ranfurly Shield and by qualifying for the play-offs. VC was announced as NZRU coach of the year, an accolade that I thought he thoroughly deserved. When I reflect on an incredible two years, I can't help feeling that I got more out of the experience than I added to it but that I'd worked hard and enjoyed the challenge.

Towards the end of the NPC, I fielded a few inquiries from Super Rugby franchises. I was flattered by their interest, while also being intimidated by the prospect of being involved in the fully professional realm of the game. It would mean that I would have to leave the Bay of Plenty unless I opted for a part-time role with the Chiefs. I decided it was better to be fully invested in one team, and David White, the Auckland and Blues CEO, was convincing, so I opted for the Blues.

6. The Blues

The excitement of getting started as assistant coach in Auckland was very much tempered by the fear of not measuring up. The Blues were littered with All Blacks and had a history of vying for honours at the top of the competition. They'd won the Super Rugby title in 1996 and 1997, with Graham Henry at the helm, and again in 2003 under Peter Sloane. David Nucifora, who coached the Brumbies to the Super Rugby title in 2004, had recently been appointed as Technical Advisor. When I heard David White say that 'it was felt Schmidt's technical knowledge, along with the innovative approach he has clearly brought to the Bay of Plenty backline over the past two seasons, best complemented Sloane and Nucifora's coaching attributes,' I shuddered. It was unsettling to hear somebody proclaim that you had something to offer when you weren't sure that you really did.

Shortly after my appointment, I met up with Peter Sloane and really enjoyed his company. He was understated and encouraging, which reassured me a bit because his playing and coaching CVs were daunting. He had played 147 times at hooker for the province of Northland and was capped against England at Twickenham in 1979. He had been assistant coach to Wayne Smith when the Crusaders toppled the Blues for their first Super Rugby title in 1998 and he had assisted John Hart with the All Blacks in 1998 and 1999 before becoming head coach of the Highlanders for the 2000 and 2001 seasons. In 2003, his second season as head coach of the Blues, they beat the Crusaders 21–17 in the Super Rugby final. Rupeni Caucaunibuca was phenomenal that season, scoring some freakish tries. He was in a back three with Joe Rokocoko and Doug Howlett, while Mils Muliaina and Sam Tuitupou had class and power in the midfield. Carlos Spencer had been mercurial at No. 10, directing a forward pack littered with All Blacks and complemented by half-backs Dave Gibson and Steve Devine who provided plenty of spark and sharp passing.

Peter quickly became 'Sloanie', and his wife Doreen also helped our transition. Sloanie offered some sage early advice: to avoid reading newspapers and listening to talkback radio shows. The newspapers would either be building you up beyond what you were capable of, or chopping you down to a level that was well below what you were capable of. Talkback radio preceded social media for some contributors, especially those with caustic opinions.

As backs coach I was replacing Bruce Robertson, who had been the player I'd wanted to be when I was growing up. His All Black career had spanned the best part of a decade, and I'd also watched him play many high-quality provincial matches for Counties. It was his ability to swerve and accelerate to get into space that I most admired, but he had all the skills and courage of an outstanding player. I had tried to play in a similar manner in the centre as a teenager but had been a very pale imitation. It was pretty incredible to chat with him. He conversed easily, which helped considering I'd idolized him as a youngster, and it was ideal to get his impressions about players and how they melded into a unit on and off the pitch.

The performance staff were a great group and I learned a lot from them. I still stay in touch with the strength and conditioning coaches, Mark Harvey and Byron Thomas, as well as the team manager, Ant 'Strawny' Strachan. Liam Barry came on board in the second year as the skills coach and we still stay in regular contact. David 'Nuci' Nucifora and I have crossed paths again on the other side of the world and he has been great to work with. We worked hard, while at the same time we would regularly catch up for lunch or a coffee, and many of us still meet up each year when I get back to NZ. They're great company and quality people. We reminisce and kick around ideas about current trends and the state of the game, but the conversation is just as often about families and various interests outside of rugby.

Before the season started we had to go through the selection and draft process. Players were centrally contracted by the NZRU and they were very keen that the top 150-odd players be spread across the five Super Rugby teams. It gave them the best value for money as well as allowing spectators – including the national coaches – the best opportunity to observe and compare the top players playing against each other. Each of the franchises chose a protected 'match-squad' of up to twenty-two players, with most of the franchises leaving some gaps in their squads so that they could draft in players from outside their region. The squads were then topped up to twenty-eight players. When the coaches assembled for the draft at the NZRU in Wellington, the protected squads were projected on to a wall so all the coaches could see who had been selected. We skimmed through the names, worked out who had not been protected and tried to anticipate how many of our players that we'd been unable to protect were likely to be drafted into other franchises.

It took a number of hours to work our way through the rotation to complete all five of the squads. The main stumbling block was that Brock James was declined as a selection option for the Hurricanes. He'd been playing well for Taranaki, but because he was an Australian he was not NZ-eligible. After being denied the opportunity to select James, the Hurricanes applied pressure to try to get Andrew Mehrtens because the Crusaders had protected Daniel Carter, Aaron Mauger and Leon MacDonald, all of whom could potentially play No. 10. A number of phone calls were made, but Mehrts could not be reached for some time, which stalled proceedings. When he was finally contacted, he decided that he'd rather stay with the Crusaders, leaving the Hurricanes with Jimmy Gopperth and Riki Flutey as their key options at No. 10.

We felt that we had a strong squad but that there was plenty of work to do. Nuci led the scheduling, making sure that we had a rationale for what we were covering and a methodology or progression that we were going to work through. He was incredibly organized and specific in his coaching. Sloanie was more relaxed and intuitive, and would vary the content based on how the training was going and what he felt needed to be done. For my part, I was flat out, learning about the people we had and the way that they wanted to play while trying to incorporate a few ideas that I felt might help.

During the pre-season, I travelled up to Auckland very early each Monday, then drove back to Tauranga on Friday evening. We wanted the kids to finish their year at school in St Mary's, and it gave us time to look for a house before moving up in the break over Christmas.

We managed to buy a house, thanks to Peter Thompson from the real estate firm Barfoot and Thompson along with a bit of financial help from my brother, Andrew. Peter

Thompson is a great supporter of Auckland and Blues rugby and, after I'd rushed in from training totally unprepared, he helped me work my way through the auction. My bid fell short of the reserve price, but I heard later that some prime seats at the Lions test match at Eden Park the following winter may have helped to bridge the gap.

While the family settled into life in Auckland, the Super Rugby season started. We began with an away win against the Highlanders in Dunedin but missed the winning bonus point. After scraping home 18–15 against the Queensland Reds and losing away to the Chiefs in Hamilton, questions were asked about our title prospects. But the real criticism came after our 41–19 humbling at the hands of the Crusaders. They bullied their way forward, scythed through us and outflanked us to have a bonus-point 31–0 lead at half-time. It's difficult to describe the sense of dread you feel, sitting in the coaches' box, when the opposing team shreds your defence and bullies you in the manner that the Crusaders did. You're desperately trying to engineer solutions in your mind but when the other team's superiority is so comprehensive it's difficult.

We won the second half, but things got worse rather than better. After some really good lead-up work, Daniel Braid was dragged down just metres from the Crusaders' line by Richie McCaw, who didn't release and fell forward over the ball, killing the opportunity to play quickly. Ali Williams stamped him on the left shoulder. It didn't look good and it was too close to the head. There was no TMO in Super Rugby in those days, so the assistant referee, Paul Honiss, flagged the incident from the far touchline and explained that it was 'over the top in terms of rucking'. He added that 'From where I was 50 or 60 metres away it looked like he got his head.' The referee, Paddy O'Brien, responded immediately, 'If he got his head, he's off,' and Ali was sent off.

On the TV3 *Sports News* the following evening, they showed a montage of shots where Richie McCaw had slowed the ball down in a similar manner during the game – but that's one of the many reasons he was so good: he played to the edge of what the referee would accept during the match.

It got even worse for us, because both Dave Gibson and Sam Tuitupou also got cited for stamping in the same incident and they both received two-week suspensions, while Ali got six weeks.

A report following the judicial hearing explained that 'Tuitupou and Gibson admitted going for the player and not the ball, but they received a lighter sentence as the judiciary found they rucked McCaw's lower back rather than near the head.' It was agreed that Ali didn't stamp directly on the head but because it was repeated and it was close to the head the six-week ban was imposed. We appealed the sentence but it was upheld. We had been humbled on the pitch and in the judiciary room.

With injuries mounting and the team not performing, we decided to freshen things up. A number of changes were forced through injury and the three suspensions, but we decided to give Tasesa Lavea a start at No. 10 and to give Carlos Spencer a rest. It was a difficult conversation to have with a legend of the game, but it was more about offering opportunity to the wider squad than anything else.

Carlos is one of the most talented players that I have ever worked with. His acceleration and power, combined with exceptional skills, meant that he could change a game at any moment. But at that point we were struggling for continuity against well-organized defences. Our ruck ball was often slowed or untidy, so Carlos wasn't getting a great platform to play from. He was struggling a bit to combine with the new players and combinations weren't gelling as well as we'd hoped. Realistically, every player would need a rest at some stage and Tasesa's enthusiasm had rippled through to the players around him at training, so we gave him an opportunity to bring that to a match day.

You try to ignore the external pressure when involved in competitive sport, but it seeps through. Family or friends will mention something, media requirements mean that questions have to be answered. I remember walking up the steps at Eden Park for the Brumbies match and my chest was so tight that I was struggling to breathe.

The Brumbies had been Super Rugby champions the previous season and were spearheaded by the likes of Stirling Mortlock, George Gregan and Stephen Larkham, along with the combative John Langford, Julian Salvi and George Smith, who had great success with the Brumbies and went on to have further success in the Northern Hemisphere. The 17–0 victory was a relief for everyone but particularly for Nuci, who had coached the Brumbies to the title the previous year. They were hampered by losing Stephen Larkham after just twenty-five minutes, but we showed some cohesion and enterprise in attack along with the sort of grit we needed in defence.

Wins over the Cats and the Sharks followed, but most supporters expected us to win those two matches, and we missed the bonus point in the Cats victory, where we struggled to get going on a wet evening. During training that week, Carlos fractured his cheekbone at training and missed the remainder of the season. Another injury, but at least we only had one player who was still suspended at that stage.

The following week we journeyed to Cape Town for our match versus the Stormers. For me, the travel is one of the biggest drawbacks in Super Rugby – the sheer distances that you cover, as well as the flight connections and the time zones crossed.

Keen to recover as much as we could and limited by the number of sore bodies in the group, we trained very lightly in the few days we had leading up to the match. One stark memory I have is of our arrival at Newlands Stadium for the captain's run. There was a good-sized crowd of people gathered, made up almost entirely of Black or Coloured fans, just to see the players walk from the bus to the entry of the famous old ground. They were *Blues* fans and their enthusiasm was impressive. They knew every player. When Nick Williams, in his first year of Super Rugby, stepped off the bus to hear his name called out with the same fervour as the others, the surprised expression on his face turned into a wide smile.

In the first twenty minutes of the match the following day, De Wet Barry cannonballed through a number of defenders to score, Jean de Villiers followed suit, and then the flying Tonderai Chavhanga raced in for a third try. We made an emphatic comeback, scoring three tries ourselves before the break. Confidence and a constant supply of possession kept the momentum with us and three further tries secured the 37–24 win, with the Stormers kept scoreless for the last hour of the match.

It was a great result but, unfortunately, we were about to lose another player to suspension. In the second half, when Luke McAlister slipped the tackle of De Wet Barry and accelerated into space, Rua Tipoki went to go with him. Jean de Villiers scragged Rua by the jersey, then fell off him. The ball went through another phase and, ironically, Rua arrived at just the right time to step the final defender and cross the try line.

As players were walking back after the try, Jean de Villiers was down injured, with a bloodied face. Replays showed that when his jersey was grabbed, Rua got rotated and Jean de Villiers was shrugged off as the result of a potent three-inch punch that is difficult to see, even in slow motion. When I chatted to Jean de Villiers after the match and expressed regret about the incident, he shrugged and said, 'No, man, I deserved it for pulling him back.' Lamentably, the judiciary were not as forgiving and Rua's three-week suspension ruled him out of the final three matches we had left to play.

We had lost Rua, but we had finally made it into the top four, and with spirits boosted we headed to Kruger National Park for an afternoon safari. We almost got to see the 'Big Five' but the leopard eluded us, despite reports of a sighting that we chased after for a fruitless hour or so.

Pretoria, where we played the Bulls, was as hostile as everyone had said it would be. The near-capacity Loftus Versfeld crowd were quietened by an early try from Isa Nacewa but came to life after the Bulls had scored and then followed up with an incredible solo try straight from our kick-off by their new winger, Bryan Habana. We trailed by just a point with ten minutes to go and had three tries so only needed one more for the bonus point. We had a couple of half-chances late on, but a potential bonus-point win became a body-blow loss as they got away to score two late tries.

As was the habit for many Super Rugby teams arriving back in New Zealand from South Africa, we lost our next game too. Playing the Hurricanes in front of 45,000 fans at Eden Park, the 3–3 half-time score belied the manic pace of the match; but two tries from turnovers in the second half were the difference. We still had a slender chance of qualifying if results fell our way and we could get a bonus-point win in Sydney, but we were glued together at that stage, with a number of players drafted in to cover for injuries. We got another great start, with Doug Howlett finishing off an early overlap, but despite frantically trying to find the fourth try and the win in the dying seconds, we came up short.

There was plenty of fallout, and Peter Sloane took it upon his shoulders to step away, leaving David Nucifora to assume the hot seat as head coach for the following season. There was plenty of dissatisfaction with the way the season had finished. I found it very tough, but it was going to get a whole lot tougher.

Before the 2006 season kicked off we headed for a training week in Australia, finishing with a match against the Queensland Reds. Nuci's training template and the set plays were put up at the start of the week and every box was ticked. But it's not about box ticking, it's about being better, and to do that the players needed to take ownership of their learning and commitment. Despite the analysis, organization and feedback, the players seemed to be going through the motions. In their feedback, they said that they felt they were learning; but they were passive, when they needed to lead, and I guess we needed to help them to take that ownership and adopt that leadership.

There was also a realization that the players weren't as collective as we'd have liked them to be. We went out for dinner after a few days of hard work during the training week. It was an enjoyable evening and it certainly didn't include excessive alcohol consumption, but a scuffle occurred on the bus on the way back to our training base. Nuci addressed the incident the following morning, emphasizing that if we are divided, then we will all suffer, so he flogged the whole squad during training to ensure that the message had landed.

The Super 12 had expanded to become the Super 14 and I was hopeful that the new season would start more positively. In Round 1, we played a very solid first half to lead the Hurricanes 16–3, but in the second half they scored a number of times on the break. In that second half I got that same helpless feeling that I'd had when we'd played the Crusaders the previous year. Jerry Collins and Chris Masoe attacked or disrupted our ball with bruising efficiency, while the flying Lome Fa'atau weaved his way to the try line. Trying to work out a strategy to get back into a game where momentum has shifted away was causing me considerable angst, because a strategic solution would never be enough. The more I thought about it the more I felt that we needed the players to have the mental resolve to stay task-focused instead of being distracted by the scoreboard or losing their confidence after errors had been made.

We followed up with another loss, this time against the Highlanders in Dunedin, then managed a very narrow but hard-earned victory over the Reds in Brisbane. Unfortunately, the glimmer of hope that we were starting to build some confidence was crushed by a dominant Crusaders pack in the next match. We were bullied comprehensively in the second half and it hurt.

We had started all four games positively, including the Crusaders game, where we scored the first try after Ants Tuitavake and Rua Tipoki broke the Crusaders' defence and Doug Howlett finished off. The curse of indiscipline continued to have an impact, and when Joe Rokocoko got yellow-carded just before half-time, Dan Carter kicked the goal to narrow the score to 9–10 at the break. Ali Williams got our second yellow card towards the end of the match, but the damage was done at that stage with the Crusaders well on top.

We had a meeting the following morning, enlisting the aid of the sports psychologist Gilbert Enoka to guide the responses and to challenge the honesty and commitment of the players. There were some pretty emotional reflections and promises of greater discipline and collaborative commitment, but the test would be to translate the commitment into consistent actions.

A bye and a good win back at Eden Park against the Brumbies was followed by another drubbing, this time at the hands of the Waratahs in Sydney. Despite lashing rain, a crowd of over 30,000 watched us concede four tries, making just 73 per cent of our tackles. Looking at the game, I was gutted. It was a record defeat but I was determined to find some positives. We were in a big enough hole without focusing on how deep and dark it was, so I looked hard for one or two positives to bring to the start of the following week.

Confidence and energy levels were down and we needed to be ready for the following week with the Bulls, fresh from a win over the Western Force in Perth. I remember how tough that Monday was. It didn't get any easier when I got home. My son Tim was upset after being teased at school because his dad was no good as a coach and should be fired. There were a few people in the media who were driving the narrative and at the time I honestly thought they might be right, but I was working as hard as I could to find solutions.

When work gets tough, the home can be a bit of a sanctuary; but when the negativity spills into the home, then it is time to reconsider. I talked to Kelly about finishing the season and going back to teaching. I had signed a three-year contract and felt that I had a responsibility to see it out, but not if my family were going to be unhappy. I still thought that the team could make progress and be competitive at the top end of the table, but I didn't need to be a rugby coach: I'd only fallen into coaching rugby after a series of conversations and coincidences in the first place.

A win and a solid performance against the Bulls were followed by good wins over the Stormers and the new Perth-based team, the Western Force. We were back within range of the play-off spots and the pressure eased a little, especially as we left the Auckland spotlight and flew to Durban. Unfortunately, a loss to the Sharks meant that qualifying was pretty much impossible. A narrow win the following week over the Cheetahs in Bloemfontein left us relieved but drained. There had been an armed hold-up in the shopping complex next to where we were staying on the Wednesday and later in the week almost all of the players had got a bug causing bad diarrhoea. Even Stuart Dickinson, the referee, had been affected by the bug. The following week we underperformed and lost 34–33 to the Cats in Johannesburg. We limped home to finish our season with a subdued loss against the Chiefs at Eden Park.

Nuci's response to the media after the game pretty much summed up our season: 'Until we learn as a group to be able to close out and be mentally strong enough to be able to work through situations like that, we're not going to be good enough to be at the right end of this competition.' The player reviews remained positive about the coaching, and it was enough for me to commit to finishing the final year of my contract. I didn't want to give up and not meet my three-year commitment. As well as that, I wanted to help prove that we could compete at the top end of the competition.

To strengthen our culture, Nuci brought in Leading Teams,

an Australian-based company founded by a former Royal Australian Air Force leadership and training officer, Ray McLean. The company focuses on leadership development and building team culture, and they did some great work helping players to define the best version of themselves while also clarifying and committing to the expectations of the group. Players got better at keeping themselves accountable but they also became more adept at identifying what they needed others to 'keep doing, start doing and stop doing'.

Alongside the work from Leading Teams, I presented a mental-skills introduction that we were keen to build into the daily preparation and match-day performance of players. There was definitely a need for players to keep their confidence and to stay task-focused in pressure situations. I didn't feel particularly confident in presenting a mental-skills programme, but it was important to embed some key techniques that might improve player concentration and decision-making in the pressure-cooker moments of a match.

I used our team manager, Strawny, and skills coach, Liam Barry, as sounding boards, along with our no-nonsense head of strength and conditioning, Mark Harvey. Dave Hadfield, whom I'd met when he was presenting the mental-skills modules during the Practicum at Massey University, did plenty of contract work for the NZRU and provided me with support. He had the experience that I lacked and a down-to-earth manner that inspired confidence.

The first challenge we faced was to get the genuine buy-in we needed from the players. We did a set of five formal sessions entitled 'The Top Two Inches'.

Mental skills can't be seen, but they're certainly visible in the actions of those who have them. We needed players who could stay focused in tough moments and who were capable

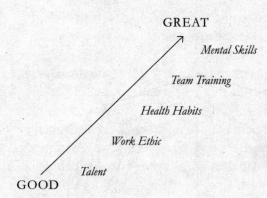

GREAT

Mental Skills

Team Training

Health Habits

Work Ethic

Talent

GOOD

Nothing in the world can take the place of persistence. Talent will not: nothing is more common than unsuccessful men with talent!
Calvin Coolidge

of delivering the actions required every time that they were required. A core of mentally tough players can help other players to keep their belief and focus, so the group can stay competitive even when fatigue and pressure dilute a player's ability to concentrate and compete.

We faced a few harsh realities first. The NZRU had commissioned some research, seeking the opinions of stakeholders, who were asked to rate the Super Rugby franchises in New Zealand alongside a number of metrics. The stakeholders included supporters, media and sponsors. I showed the results to the players. We had trained hard the previous season, and we'd tried hard, but we needed to add something to make a positive change.

It didn't make good viewing that, according to stakeholder perceptions, we had delivered the poorest quality of rugby, we had not demonstrated the traditional down-to-earth values that were so admired in rugby and we had not worked hard enough.

In my own presentation, to create a concrete image of what our perceptions were of the mental strength in each

SUPER RUGBY 2006

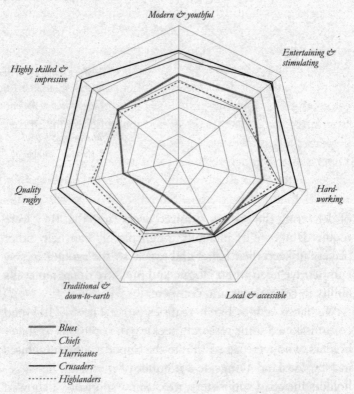

of the five NZ franchise teams, we used five different sets of Duplo blocks borrowed from my kids' toy box. Players were divided into five different groups, one for each franchise. Any player who had played for a different franchise the previous year, such as Dave Holwell and Isaia Toeava who had both played for the Hurricanes, was put into that group. That way, they could offer some genuine insights about the mental strength of that squad of players.

The players were first asked to consider the physical

capabilities of the franchise they were assessing. They were encouraged to scrutinize the quality of the athletes that were in the franchise and the strength, speed and skill they might have. They were to determine their assessment by using the All Blacks as the benchmark. If the All Blacks rate 10/10 for their physical capabilities, what number of blocks would you offer out of 10 for your franchise? The players were given five minutes to debate the physical capabilities and then they presented their tower of blocks.

Four of the franchises were rated as 8/10, with the Highlanders rated 7/10. Each group gave a brief summary explaining their ratings and brief discussions were had, but in general everyone agreed that the distribution of the blocks was about right.

Each group was then challenged to do the same thing for the mental capabilities in each of the five franchises: the ability to stay focused and competitive in the really tough moments. When the blocks came back from each group after five minutes, the group assessing the Blues rated us at 5/10.

The most striking of the block towers after the mental capabilities assessment was the Crusaders. The group assessing them had added one of their leftover blocks from the physical capabilities and had rated them as 11/10. The explanation and discussions that followed regarding the mental strength of the Crusaders – seen as superior even to that of the All Blacks – was really interesting. It allowed me to ask the question, 'Well, if you rate the Crusaders as more than twice as mentally tough as we are, then how do you expect to beat them?' We had to move the group from hoping to compete with the Crusaders to believing that we would compete. The group agreed and were keen to try to focus on improving their mental skills.

In pre-season we did plenty of physical sessions, but we also completed some interactive mental-skills sessions, along with some soul-searching directed by Leading Teams. We weren't going to have to wait very long to see how well we'd match up to the Crusaders because we had them in the first-round match at Eden Park. The NZRU withdrew a number of players from the first six rounds of Super Rugby to enable them to focus on getting themselves into the very best physical condition they could in advance of the 2007 Rugby World Cup, so both teams had personnel missing, but the Crusaders were disadvantaged more than we were. Despite that, winning 34 points to 25 was promising. It was close throughout, but when Troy Flavell, our skipper, was sin-binned for the last ten minutes, we stayed competitive and controlled play well to keep the Crusaders in their own half.

It was a relief, but no one was getting ahead of themselves because we had a trip to Canberra for our next match. Isa Nacewa demonstrated his ability to stay focused when converting an injury-time try to win the game against the Brumbies on a cold and wet evening. It left the Brumbies coach, Laurie Fisher, lamenting that the Blues 'probably weren't the better side' but that they 'were able to close out the game when it mattered'. That hadn't often been the case in the previous two years, when we'd start well then lose our way as pressure and fatigue accumulated.

Away to the Hurricanes, with Tana Umaga playing his 300th first-class game, we came agonizingly close to winning three in a row. The 23–22 loss, while frustrating, showed that we were still playing with plenty of positivity. The lead changed five times in the second half and we managed to score three tries to two, almost creating a fourth in the final quarter. Big wins followed against the Reds, the Highlanders and the Lions. It was particularly frustrating to miss the bonus point against the Highlanders as Rudi Wulf was forced out in the corner twice and Isaia Toeava was held up over the line by Jimmy Cowan. But we were on top of the table and in control of our own destiny.

Exacting some revenge over the Waratahs two weeks later helped us cement our lead. We'd had a bye in the lead-up and some positive preparation was borne out in one of our best performances. Waratahs coach Ewan McKenzie said of us after the game that 'they are on top of their game mentally, they have speed, they seem to find space and the interaction between the backs and forwards is good.'

Next up, we headed to Hamilton where, after a scratchy start, we managed the game well enough to deserve our seven-point victory over the Chiefs. Doug Howlett scored his fifty-eighth try in the match to set the all-time Super Rugby try-scoring record. Despite scoring some great tries the following week, we again missed the four-try bonus point at home to the Cheetahs.

During the week leading up to the visit of the Sharks, my brother Jamie and I flew down from Auckland to Danne-virke to visit our father. He was ailing and we were worried. I was keen to stay back from the upcoming South African tour because we were due to leave the day after the Sharks match in North Harbour Stadium. But Dad encouraged me to go on the tour. He said that he'd be watching the games and he promised me that we'd catch up when I got back from Africa.

The next few games were tough and we made them tougher. We had lost some of our rhythm and cohesion as we tried to integrate our returning All Blacks. In wet conditions against the Sharks in North Harbour Stadium, they kicked well and poor discipline cost us in an ill-tempered match. François Steyn's 55-metre angled penalty kick just before half-time afforded them a 19–6 lead at the break and while we got close at the end it was frustrating to leave for South Africa on the back of a loss.

We served up our worst performance of the season the following week in Cape Town. A quality first fifteen minutes gave us a 10–0 lead. The Stormers came back as we went into our shell, and after yet another yellow card the game swung in their favour. When we looked like getting back into the match, Jean de Villiers intercepted in front of his own posts and ran 90 metres to score just beyond the clutches of the chasing Joe Rokocoko. The 33–20 loss was described by Nuci as 'the worst possible performance in one of the most import-ant games of the season'.

We had put ourselves under pressure, and the confidence that we'd had earlier in the season had become frayed. We were back to where we'd been and it was incredibly frustrat-ing. Well able to start strongly, with a 9–0 lead over the Bulls, we again became vulnerable when the pressure came on. At Loftus Versfeld there is always plenty of pressure, and the 40–19 loss shows how poorly we coped with it. Our mental fragility seemed to be back.

I rang Dad after the game. My youngest sister, Helen, said he was short of breath and couldn't talk but was really pleased to hear from me. He had slept through the game but knew I'd be disappointed with the result. I was worried, but at least we'd be on our way back towards New Zealand the following day via Perth, where we would finish with what had now become a must-win game against the Western Force.

As soon as I arrived in Perth, I rang my brother to see

1. Mum and Dad on their wedding day, way back in 1963

2. My mum with a very fat-faced and grumpy-looking me along with my older twin siblings, Anna and Kieran

3. In my first year of primary school at St Joseph's in Te Aroha

4. With the Woodville School Midgets team and our school principal, Jack Salt, 1974. I'm second from left in the front row

5. As a scrawny Manawatu winger, weighing in at around about 70 kilograms, in 1989 [Maurice Costello]

6. Double jobbing as Napier BHS play their traditional fixture against Te Aute College, with Ella in my left arm and Tim alongside

7. With the family and the Ranfurly Shield at St Mary's Primary School. Kelly has Ella, I have Luke, and Abby and Tim have the Shield, which Bay of Plenty won for the first time in 2004

8. With Vern Cotter on the Clermont team coach after winning the Top 14 championship in 2010, at the end of my last season with the club [Vincent Duvivier, ASM Clermont Auvergne]

9. With Abby, Kelly, Tim, Ella, Luke, and the Bouclier de Brennus
[Vincent Duvivier, ASM Clermont Auvergne]

10. With Brian O'Driscoll after losing to Edinburgh in September 2010: our third
loss in four competitive games at the start of my first season with Leinster. With
good support from senior players we turned the bad start into a great finish,
winning the Heineken Cup [© INPHO/James Crombie]

11. Like father, like sons: me, Tim and Luke [Stephen McCarthy/SPORTSFILE; Stephen McCarthy/ SPORTSFILE; Pat Murphy/SPORTSFILE]

12. A joke in our house is that the two girls are regularly deleted from Wikipedia. Just to confirm that they are real, here are Abby (*left*), who is living back in New Zealand, and Ella, on a recent visit there

13. With my friend Jas Gillespie, in his kitchen in 2012, trying to repair the Heineken Cup after the base fell off at a function earlier in the evening

14. With Isa Nacewa at the start of a training session in 2013
[© INPHO/Donall Farmer]

15. With Jono Gibbes, Greg Feek and Richie Murphy and the 2013
Amlin Challenge Cup [© INPHO/Dan Sheridan]

16. With Isa Nacewa, Johnny Sexton and the last trophy we won
together at Leinster, after the Pro12 Grand Final against Ulster in 2013
[© INPHO/Dan Sheridan]

how Dad was. He said he wasn't good and that I needed to get home. Strawny booked the flight straight away, but I had to wait a few hours before it was due to leave, and in that time my brother called back to say that Dad had died. Strawny was in the room but I couldn't talk, it broke me. I had feared it would happen and I hadn't been there. I still have to take a deep breath when I'm involved with a team that wins a big game. My brother, Andrew, texts me and says that 'Dad would have been really proud' and I know he would have been. He used to love telling his buddies that I'd scored a try when I played or that I'd been picked for a team or that the team I was coaching had won a big game.

It was a lonely flight back to Wellington and a pretty quiet trip back up to Dannevirke. We spent some time with family before attending the funeral the following day. I left straight after the funeral to fly back for the game the following evening, trying to escape the melancholy that I felt. It was a wet night but we managed, with a little bit of luck, to get the four-try bonus-point win that we needed to make the semi-finals.

I didn't notice until the end of the match that the players had worn black armbands. No one had said anything to me about doing it, but I really appreciated the gesture and I know my dad would have as well. I went for a walk, leaving the players to enjoy the relief of qualifying for the semi-finals.

We travelled to Perth for the last game of the regular season, with a home semi-final possible and a trip to Christchurch the most likely scenario. We beat the Western Force to secure a top-four spot, but the Reds conceded thirteen tries and ninety-two points against the Bulls, which allowed the Bulls to surpass both the Crusaders and us on points differential.

It meant that after having just flown in from South Africa, we were going to have to fly back there again.

I had not been in Perth when Ali Williams had gone out during the week for his birthday. He again went out until very late when we stayed overnight in Sydney. While it was a night off, there was an expectation that players would be recovering and have their feet up. It was not ideal, but the leadership group of players got together at the airport before our flight and decided that we should leave Ali out of the squad for the semi-final. It became complicated because Ali's bag was already on the aircraft; Qantas said they couldn't remove it and that Ali would have to fly to Johannesburg. Strawny was going to have to explain the decision to Ali but decided to wait until we arrived at Johannesburg so that the issue didn't cause any angst on the long flight back to Africa.

Once we arrived in Johannesburg, we trooped across the airport to connect to the flight to Durban, while Strawny explained the situation to Ali, organized him to stay over-night at the airport hotel and gave him his tickets for the flights home to Auckland. Ali was obviously unhappy but had no real choice. Many in the leadership group were his friends and felt awkward about the decision that had been made, but believed that it had been made in the best interest of protecting the team values, which all the players had committed to.

The whole furore was an unhelpful distraction in such a crucial week. I sympathized with the leaders and respected them for the difficult decision that they'd made. Really, I just wanted to get to Durban so that the players could rest and so that we could get a brief couple of windows to prepare for what was likely to be an incredibly combative and potentially fractious semi-final.

It was as physical as expected. The Sharks managed the only try of the first half to lead 14–6 at the break. We had plenty of excuses to fade in the second half but showed the resilience that we'd demonstrated earlier in the season to score two outstanding tries in the third quarter. Leading 18–14 approaching the final quarter of the game, I think we still hoped more than believed that we could win, especially as Isaia Toeava, instrumental in the build-up to both tries, was helped from the field with an injury.

Two late tries to the Sharks saw them through to the final and sent us limping back to Auckland. We had regrets, but we'd definitely made some progress. Wandering around the expanse of the Kings Park car park among the car-boot parties and braais, we were invited to watch the end of the Bulls v Crusaders semi-final match. A turning point in the Bulls' fifteen-point win was when Richie McCaw received a yellow card and the Bulls took their chances well. The following week the Bulls secured the title in Durban with an incredible injury-time try and conversion after the Sharks had appeared to have the game under control.

When I got back to Auckland, I took my two-year extension as Blues assistant coach home to sign. I felt that we were heading in the right direction, but Kelly was intrigued by one of the other expressions of interest that we'd had. A contract was sitting on the table from ASM Clermont Auvergne. We'd gone to a place in the middle of Ireland that we'd never heard of; why not do the same thing in France? And we had a link to Clermont, with VC being there as the head coach.

The thought that it would be great for the kids, learning a new language and experiencing a different culture, plus the opportunity to see the rest of Europe, held plenty of appeal.

The reality for me was that I didn't speak the language, so communicating with players was going to be challenging.

In the end, we decided to go. We thought that it would be a fantastic opportunity for the family to spend two years in Europe before we settled back into New Zealand life, richer for the experience.

PART TWO
Ball in Play

Some thoughts, reflections, experiences and learnings, based on thirty years of teaching and coaching.

7. Mindset

I am not what happened to me, I am what I choose to become.

Carl Jung

Viktor Frankl said that 'Between stimulus and response, there is a space'; and in that space, we have the power of choice. In other words, much of what happens in life might be beyond our control, but our reaction to it determines how it impacts upon us. A positive mindset is a good starting point when you're in that 'space' and about to respond to a difficult situation.

When Shakespeare's Hamlet laments 'there is nothing either good or bad, but thinking makes it so,' he shows a similar understanding. Hamlet is conscious of the need to control his thinking, but he is frustrated by his inability to do so and feels that he 'cannot reason'.

I think we all want to feel that we have a sense of control. Sometimes after a negative stimulus I've found that it helps to take a breath, to remind myself that my response is still my choice. I've tried to do this a few times after matches that we've lost, when I've felt frustrated or inadequate. I have tried to rationalize my thinking and attempted to focus my response on what the players might need to hear or what we can do to move forward.

Research shows that people who believe intelligence can be built incrementally are more resilient and better able to cope with setbacks or failures. The psychologist Carol Dweck has extensively researched and promoted the benefits of having a 'growth mindset'. If you find yourself thinking or saying something like 'I'm not good at mathematics' or 'I'm not good at catching high balls,' her simple piece of advice is to add 'yet' to the end of the statement. Having a growth mindset is as simple as believing that if you sustain your effort, then you can add to what you know or what you're capable of doing.

Deciding to leave the security of my job with the Bank of New Zealand and to go into teaching; and shifting our family from Palmerston North to Napier then on to Tauranga to take new teaching jobs – these were positive choices made with an open mind. There was always a fear that things might not turn out well, but the potential for growth and the reward of new experiences provided sufficient motivation to counter my apprehension.

While working at the butter factory in the very small village of Mangamutu during my university summer holidays, I got to know one of the forklift drivers. He really enjoyed his job. He would scoot around on his forklift, stacking butter-laden pallets into the cool store or retrieving them and loading them on to trucks. On fine days, his wife would bring along a picnic lunch and their little one, and they would sit outside at the picnic tables to enjoy a pleasant half-hour together.

I remember talking to the forklift driver about it. He was almost thirty, he had a home with a mortgage, a job he enjoyed, and he'd started a family. He didn't have an ambition to see the world or to do something different; he just wanted to enjoy the days and weeks as they went by. I envied his contentment and the simplicity of having what he wanted. In contrast, I wanted to see and do new things.

I wasn't sure what those new things were, and I didn't know how I was going to find out or how well I'd measure up, but teaching gave me the opportunity to work my way through a number of new challenges. Later, when stepping into coaching, it was good to do it with the security blanket of a career that I could go back to.

The challenge of coaching the Blues and being involved in Super Rugby was draining. It was frustrating to work so hard and to be judged so publicly by people who didn't care how hard I was working or even how well I might have been doing the job – not that I'm claiming to have been doing a good job, because I was learning a lot at the time. One thing I did learn about professional sport is that external perceptions are hugely influenced by scoreboard results, and in my first two years with the Blues ours weren't good enough.

The decision to go to France generated excitement mixed with fear and uncertainty. It wasn't just a new coaching challenge for me: the whole family was about to take on the challenges of integrating into a new and totally unfamiliar culture.

We arrived at Aéroport de Lyon-Saint-Exupéry with a bag each, plus one big rugby kit bag jammed tightly with shoes and sleeping bags, ready to last us for the two years we planned to spend in Europe. After working our way through security, we were met by the Clermont manager, Neil McIlroy, and the *préparateur physique*, Sébastien Bourdin. Neil and Seb were welcoming and highly organized. Driving a couple of spacious vehicles, they got us safely to Clermont-Ferrand and into our house on Avenue Marx Dormoy. The house was ideal for a family of six, with three storeys, five big bedrooms, a compact enclosed backyard and minimalist but functional furnishings. Neil showed us about and we had a snack, then sorted the youngsters into sleeping bags for their first night in France.

The challenge of learning a new language was both invigorating and exasperating. I would repeat the words exactly as I thought I'd heard them, and would get frustrated to be informed that I'd got it wrong. '*Non, non, c'est "beaucoup"*. You are saying "nice bum" instead of "a lot".' As a family, we tried to use French when we were at home, endeavouring to help each other, but the kids soon started to roll their eyes at Kelly and me as we butchered pronunciations.

Kelly, who had taught Māori in New Zealand, stuck French labels on doors, chairs, cupboards and their contents. Each noun was preceded by the appropriate masculine or feminine articles. As for the tenses and conjugation when starting to put sentences together, they were beyond difficult!

Driving on the right-hand side of the road, filling the car up with *gazole* (diesel) and not petrol, the complicated one-way system in Clermont-Ferrand, purchasing things at the supermarket – all of these basic things required new levels of concentration and preparation. Even getting a haircut was complicated. Trying to work out how I could say 'Just a trim, please,' I came up with '*une coupe, pas trop, s'il vous plaît*'. I practised it under my breath all the way down to the *salon de coiffure* on the corner. The hairdresser nodded slowly when I mumbled my request and duly clipped away for the next twenty minutes, chatting in stilted English between bouts of raspy coughing.

Gradually we settled into French life, utilizing a mix of minimalist French and basic body language. I tried to watch French television to improve my communication skills and to acquire a few of the common phrases useful in day-to-day greetings and conversation.

ASM Clermont-Auvergne was owned by Michelin, the famous French tyre company. They were global but very proudly French, and it was important to speak French when coaching. Vern Cotter had played in France for many years, so he was well able to express himself in French. I did my best and tried to build my stock of generic rugby phrases as quickly as possible. I wasn't good at speaking French . . . yet!

My first pitchside interview was a challenge. We were playing down in Perpignan, and I had been warned that the television presenter was going to ask me a few questions. Perpignan were literally a very big team at the time. They had the French tighthead prop Nicolas Mas and the former English loosehead Perry Freshwater, along with Marius Tincu, the powerful and aggressive Romanian hooker. Nathan Hines was in their second row, and big Gerrie Britz the South African was on the side of the scrum. And at the back of the scrum was the most imposing human I'd seen playing rugby: Henry Tuilagi. He was a colossus.

Naively, I'd prepared a few responses to the generic questions that I expected to be asked, and I rehearsed them during the warm-up on a breezy but mild and sunny day at Stade Aimé Giral. '*Oui, on a bien commencé ce match,*' was a good starting point . . . Followed by '*Notre mêlée est forte et notre touche est très efficace, jusqu'à maintenant.*'

The problem was that once the match started, we did not 'well start the match' – we were being beaten backwards – and our scrum and lineout were not 'strong' or 'efficient'. I couldn't think of how to say my rehearsed responses in the negative, so I uttered fillers '*ar, ah, ah*' desperately trying to work out what to say. It was embarrassing at the time – and very funny when it was played back to me three years later, at a farewell event when I left the club. Thankfully, they spliced a more recent interview to run straight after it, which showed that over the intervening period I'd learned to converse with some pretty good French, albeit with a pretty average accent.

There was a fair bit of satisfaction involved in getting good phrases out and in understanding what was being said in the team environment. The pressure was eased a bit by the fact that much of our game strategy was communicated by our Australian out-half, Brock James, formerly of Taranaki. The captain, Aurélien Rougerie, and, on the other wing, Julien Malzieu both spoke reasonable English, while the robust midfielder Kiki Chanel was always keen to translate things with his own particular flavour.

Keen to impress and to communicate, I started to incorporate more complex phrases into my coaching. On one occasion, I tried to modify the running lines of Thomas Combezou. A young ball of energy, Thomas was nicknamed *poulet sans tête* – headless chicken. He was great value but had a habit of drifting away from the ball when catching it, and I was keen to help him to straighten up at the defensive line when running on to the ball.

I asked Fabien, my French teacher, how I could best say it. Fabien, knowing my limitations, was keen to make it as simple as possible, so he suggested: '*Il faut rentrer bien droit, s'il te plaît,*' meaning 'It is necessary to go well straight, please.' It made sense, especially with a bit of arm thrusting to indicate the ideal angle of attack. I rehearsed it a number of times during the lunch break prior to training that afternoon.

After the warm-up, the backs unit session started with some phase plays. In a break after a few repetitions, I approached Thomas.

'*Thomas, il faut rentrer bien droit, s'il te plaît,*' thrusting my arm forward on the running angle that would square him up. Wow, I thought, that's so French.

Thomas looked at me, nodding, but politely asked, '*Oui, mais pourquoi?*' Yes, but why?

I understood his question but had no answer for it: I'd used up the limits of my vocabulary. At least there were a couple of good learnings for me: firstly, not to overreach and bluff your capabilities, but also to anticipate likely responses or reactions so you can be prepared for them.

Some of the challenges that life confronts you with are very difficult to respond to, regardless of how positive your mindset is.

In my first season at Clermont, we were on a training camp in Barcelona. It was a non-match week during the Six Nations and I got a phone call from Kelly to ask if I'd noticed anything strange with Luke. Had I noticed him 'phasing out'? I hadn't, but when I got home Kelly encouraged me to watch him more closely because she was pretty sure that there were times when he would glaze over and be unresponsive for a few seconds.

The following week, it didn't take long for us to confirm to each other that he was definitely phasing out at times. One instance was when I took him to the bathroom to wash his hands before dinner. He approached the sink as I turned on the tap, but instead of washing his hands he stood in front of the sink looking confused, wringing his hands together. When I quietly repeated the request, he looked at me and at the sink in confusion.

We were worried. Neil McIlroy helped us to arrange an appointment with a neurologist, and acted as interpreter. Luke was tested, and it was confirmed that he was having what they described as 'absence seizures'. He was prescribed sodium valproate, or Epilim as it is marketed in the UK, and we were reassured for a few months because his 'phase-outs' seemed to stop.

When the seizures came back, the neurologist decided that Luke should have an MRI, just to rule out the slim possibility that there might be something physical causing the seizures. I headed off with Luke so that he could have the scan in the early evening a few days later. Blithely confident that there would be nothing to worry about, I was also planning to pick up some beer and snacks, because we had the Saracens out-half Glen Jackson coming to visit, along with his wife, Fiona. I'd coached Glen at Bay of Plenty and we had gotten along well. He was a very down-to-earth 'Kiwi Bloke' as well as a very skilled and smart rugby player.

The hospital was just across the road from Stade Marcel Michelin, where we trained and played, and I knew the radiologist there, Pierre Cellerier, because he had been involved in organizing and reading scans done on players. After Luke's scan, we followed Pierre into his office and he looked disconcertingly serious. When he showed us the scan and the size of the tumour wedged between the two hemispheres of Luke's brain, I welled up and didn't really know what to do. Luke, just four years old, was sitting on my knee and Neil McIlroy was trying to get more detail from Pierre. I understood what was being said, and a number of scenarios went through my mind, including, 'How am I going to tell Kelly?'

I didn't have to tell her. By the time we arrived home, Luke had gone to sleep. I lifted him out of his car seat and had my arms full, so I rang the doorbell. Glen answered, with Fiona and Kelly standing just behind him. When Kelly saw my face she burst into tears.

We got Luke changed for bed. I hugged him and left Kelly to read him a story, then joined Glen and Fiona in the dining room. Glen suggested that they should head to a hotel and give us a bit of time and space, but I was keen for them to stay and I knew Kelly would be as well. Sometimes, maybe, you need to extend the space between stimulus and constructive response so that you can dull the initial shock? We stayed up late chatting. We drank quietly and spoke softly. We planned to tell the kids in the morning, but first we needed to decide what we were going to do. Awake again at 4 a.m., Kelly and I talked about going back to New Zealand. I guess it's a natural reaction, to think about scuttling back to the security of family and familiarity when the fear of the unknown leaves you feeling isolated.

We didn't really know what we were going to do, but we were going to make a plan over the next twenty-four to forty-eight hours, which at least gave us something we could constructively think about. We were going to need some help and advice about what was best for Luke, and we weren't sure where best to get it, being so far away from home.

I went to work the next day and distracted myself with training in the morning. I was about to head home at lunchtime when the club President, René Fontès, arrived in the coaches' office. He'd flown up from Aix-en-Provence as soon as he'd heard about Luke. He came in, embraced me and asked me what I needed. I thanked him and told him that it looked as though Luke would need surgery as soon as it could be arranged. René said that wherever we wanted to go for surgery, whether it be in the US, New Zealand or somewhere in Europe, the club would make it happen. I thanked him again and said that we really didn't know quite what we were going to do yet, but his effort in travelling up and the offer of support was hugely appreciated.

That afternoon we went to the Centre Hospitalier Universitaire de Clermont-Ferrand (CHU), another of the local hospitals, and met with the paediatric neurosurgeon Jean Chazal. I knew Jean – he was a keen supporter of the club and a gentleman – but I hadn't realized the esteem in which he was held in the medical world. He explained the likely type of tumour that Luke had and explained how surgery might be done to resect the tumour. It would be intricate, because of how deeply the tumour was lodged between the two hemispheres of the brain. Our confidence grew during the meeting, and we accepted his offer to do the surgery in a few days' time.

Between stimulus and response, we felt we had filled the space as best we could. It was a difficult time for the other kids, and we didn't share much of the information with Luke. We just explained that we were going to go to the hospital and that the bad bit in his brain was going to be removed while he had a sleep.

On the day of the surgery we got the kids off to school and headed to the CHU. We tried to normalize the day as best we could. After Luke had headed into surgery, I left Kelly with two of her good friends and went to training. I struggle with sitting still, and we'd been told that the surgery would take about six hours. A couple of hours later, I went back up to the hospital and into Luke's room on the ward, where we were to wait until the surgery was completed.

Soon after, the first pathology results came back: a nurse told us that the initial biopsies were benign. It was what Jean Chazal had said was most likely, but it was still a relief to hear that first result. Six long hours later, after eight hours of surgery, Jean came in and explained that he was confident that he had resected the tumour completely and that the surgery had gone as he'd hoped. The tumour had been difficult to access and was very close to some vital areas of the brain, so it had taken a little longer than first anticipated.

There were going to be many challenges ahead for Luke, and for us trying to help him along the way, but at that moment, watching him in the recovery room and waiting for him to stir, there was the potential that he would recover fully. We certainly felt blessed that we still had him and shared the hope that he would have a seizure-free future.

I was not at all confident about taking the head-coach role at Leinster. The possibility was first mentioned during a conversation with Isa Nacewa. I had called Isa hoping to convince him to come to Clermont, and I was disappointed when he said that he was just about to sign a new three-year contract with Leinster. He then added, almost as an afterthought, 'Why don't you come over here?'

I laughed it off, but a few weeks later I received a phone call from the Leinster CEO, Mick Dawson, asking me if I was interested in the head-coach position.

I had become comfortable with the French language and we were settled in Clermont. The team was playing well, we had developed a strong squad and we were well placed in both the Top 14 table and in our Heineken Cup pool. I was also very comfortable being an assistant coach, contributing to the strategy and the coaching without being particularly visible. I could enjoy the time working with players and identifying appropriate recruits without the pressure of the tough conversations around selection or dealing with contracts. My involvement with media and sponsors was minimal, which meant that I had more time to focus on reviewing footage, devising strategy and interacting with players.

I decided not to accept the position, but Mick Dawson didn't give up easily. He encouraged me to spend a couple of days in Dublin to have a look around and to meet a few people, including some of the players. He was also very keen that Kelly should come over to have a look at schools and a few of the areas where we might want to live. A couple of days in Dublin sounded harmless enough, and it would be nice for Kelly and me to get some time together. It wasn't as if we were making any commitment to Leinster by going over for a look . . .

Kelly was impressed with the schools she saw in Dublin, and she was excited by the prospect of the kids moving back into mainstream education, as opposed to the international school they attended in France. École Massillon was excellent in many ways, being bilingual and with small classes, but there was not the same co-curricular life connected with the school that exists in Irish and New Zealand schools.

Before the visit was over, Kelly had already pretty much made up her mind that we should shift to Dublin. I also felt much more positive about it after chatting to some of the players. I met Leo Cullen and Johnny Sexton and spoke on the phone with Brian O'Driscoll. When I first started coaching top players I felt I needed to have the right answers; but what I've learned over the years is that to lead others, it's probably just as important to have the right questions. I was not particularly confident about doing the job in Leinster and I asked the players what they thought I could bring to the environment.

The players had watched Clermont and felt that they

would like to play in a similarly expansive fashion, but with some good structure at the same time. I said that I could try to help them with that but I also said that I'd never led a big team before, and asked them what might happen if some of the players didn't commit to the way we wanted to play and did their own thing. A young and ambitious Johnny Sexton was quick to respond, saying, 'Don't worry about that, we'll take care of that . . .'

Wow, that was interesting, I thought. More than that, it was encouraging. The three players were convincing and were not fazed by my lack of experience as a head coach, or by the uncertainty that I'd expressed. The confidence I already had in Isa Nacewa as a person and as a player re-assured me about the authenticity of the group's commitment. Considering that Kelly had already decided that it was a good idea to take the role, I felt that it was worth at least trying to see if I could do the job.

I remember getting a phone call from the player agent who had tracked down my full contact details for Leinster. He said that his company would be delighted to represent me and that they knew the 'market', so would be well able to get the best deal. I thanked him but said that I'd be okay, that I hadn't decided to go because of the money but because of the schools and the new challenge that the head-coach role offered. His riposte was: 'What happens if you get fired?'

I was confused by that, and he explained that almost all the top coaches had been fired at some time in their careers, reeling off a list of high-profile coaches and then adding that his agency would get me a far better payout than I could negotiate myself.

My response was that I'd be gutted if I failed because I'm

competitive, but that I wasn't too worried about any payout. If I got fired, I'd just go back to teaching and chalk it up to experience.

The agent didn't really have any answer to that, and conceded that I probably didn't need to have his agency represent me, but he wished me well and said to let him know if they could ever do anything for me in the future.

The other thing we had to make sure of was that Luke would get the care he needed in Dublin. We met with Professor Arthur Tanner and were heartened by what he told us about the quality of the medical support we would have access to. The trio of doctors at Leinster – Arthur, who died in 2017, Professor John Ryan and Jim McShane – have offered great help to all the members of our growing family during our time in Ireland.

I still remember sitting in my office in my first week as Assistant Principal at Napier Boys' High School. I was trying to sort through a flood of different applications for students to sit external examinations and, at the same time, I was trying to sort through the first round of scaling for internal assessments.

Crunching the numbers, I didn't really know what I was doing. It was one of the many times that I took a breath and made a conscious decision to recalibrate my thinking. In that moment I was having doubts about the wisdom of taking on this new challenge, but I convinced myself that I could work hard enough to ensure that the decision I'd made was the right one.

I know that might sound like semantics – wrapping the same situation up in a different set of words – but shifting my mindset helped to get rid of the distraction of negative self-talk. I was where I was, and I needed to get on with making it as positive as I could.

It wasn't too different sitting in my office one late-September Sunday morning during my first season coaching Leinster. We'd lost to Edinburgh the previous evening in the Magners League. It was our third loss in four games and, worse still, Edinburgh had scored the four-try bonus point, while we'd failed to claim any points from the match, after missing a late conversion that could have at least scrambled a losing bonus point.

I was gutted, and I remember phoning Kelly after the match had finished. Standing in the tunnel at Murrayfield before going to the press conference to face the media, I asked her, 'Did it look as bad on TV as it did live?'

She answered, 'Um, well, did it look really bad live?'

Ouch!

Late the following morning, I was mulling over solutions, looking to simplify what we were doing in order to make things easier for the players to understand and execute. The post-match medical check-ups were close to finishing and a few players started drifting in and out of my office to chat. The mood was pretty glum but some of the players, including Johnny Sexton, Leo Cullen and Brian O'Driscoll, encouraged me. They felt that we were heading in the right direction but that the players hadn't quite put it together . . . *yet*. At the same time, they felt that the team wasn't far away from getting it right and when they did we would be very hard to beat.

Peter Breen, our media officer, later sent through some of the articles that had been written after the Edinburgh game. One pundit in particular claimed that 'this is a coach that has lost the dressing room'.

It was clear that, while I was keen to challenge myself,

others would also be challenging me and, with the results we'd had, they were likely to be outspoken and cranky. Regardless of your occupation, people are likely to question or provoke you at times; but in professional sport the provocation is likely to be more public.

Confidence can be fickle, but the positive urging from key players helped galvanize my resolve to make things work. The isolation of being a head coach, especially when things aren't going too well, can be uncomfortable. But to hear an expression of faith in what we were doing, particularly from Johnny, Leo and Drico, was a catalyst for me to have a positive conversation with myself. I started putting together some 'repair' footage – and we turned things around to become European Champions at the end of the season. To be fair, the pundit who slated me and claimed that I'd lost the dressing room has been behind me ever since . . . with a 12-inch blade! He's consistent, at least.

Having support can definitely help people to maintain their commitment to a challenge. In his book *The Power of Habit*, Charles Duhigg discusses replacing one 'habit loop' with another and then committing to it in order to make a permanent change. Ideally if you can do this with support from others, even if it's only one other person, it greatly increases your chances of making the change long-term.

Imagine that you're looking to make a lifestyle change and you plan to exercise more regularly. If you have a small group of like-minded people who are biking, jogging or walking a few times a week together, then it becomes a small support network and you encourage each other to commit to the exercise and even enjoy it. The reward can be the interaction as much as the benefits of the exercise.

For me, the support of my family has made a huge

difference. And I've got great support from mentors and colleagues – going right back to Jack Salt in primary school, or to Dave Syms when I first started at Palmerston North Boys' High School. Isa's encouragement to take the head-coach role at Leinster, and the senior players showing faith in the way we wanted to play the game when we got off to a tough start, reassured me that I could add something useful. Their confidence in me helped build the quiet determination that I have. I would definitely not have had the confidence to go to France without Kelly's urgings. Her belief that I'd learn the language quickly was greater than my own. It was the same when shifting to Leinster and then into the Ireland role: she was resolute. At the same time, we were both realistic. We knew that there were many variables that would be out of my control when coaching and that, no matter how hard I worked or how much I'd learned, things could still go awry.

One of the great things about having a positive mindset and challenging yourself is that it helps to prepare you for the challenges that others create for you. In professional sport, where accountability is visible and ruthless, it can be uncomfortable. At the start of each English Premier League season, bookies offer odds on which managers will be sacked before Christmas. During the All-Ireland football championship in 2018, the Kerry football manager, Éamonn Fitzmaurice, spoke out about a letter received by a player that told him to 'jump off a cliff and take three or four others with him', with the other players also named in the letter. A chorus of other managers spoke about their own boxes of hate mail, and that's without factoring in the growth of abusive online commentary.

One pitfall for managers and coaches is allowing their

self-worth to be too greatly influenced by the opinions of others. It's a difficult aspect of the job, especially because it impacts on families and is hard to escape from. Retaining the power of choice when facing these challenges is crucial. While others may be questioning your ability or, even more damagingly, your character, you can choose to stay focused on doing the job as well as you can and to trust those close to you and those you respect to help guide your thoughts and actions.

8. People

Talent sets the floor, character sets the ceiling.
Bill Belichick

It's not original, and I know that similar things have been said in other sports, but I think it's true to say that I don't coach rugby players, I coach people who happen to play rugby better than most. And getting the right people gives you the best opportunity to build the most competitive team of players.

Earlier I mentioned my Masters research, poring through numerous journals and research papers learning about what companies did to recruit young people. The theory at the time was that an organization's 'competitive advantage is driven off their human resource base – the excellence of the people recruited and retained' (Lewent, 2002). I think this is even more relevant today, as is the consequence of not getting the right people and the adverse impact that this can have on an organization. Put simply by the famous firefighter Red Adair: 'If you think it's expensive to hire a professional, wait until you hire an amateur.'

In a sporting context, I remember attending a presentation delivered by Bill Beswick in 2006. I was coaching with the Blues at the time but was in Europe during the off-season. Bill has a high-performance coaching background in basketball but has become recognized as a leader in the field of applied sports psychology as well as being a quality mentor for coaches. At the top of his list of reasons why coaches fail was that their recruitment and selection weren't as good as they needed to be.

Getting good people and retaining them is a common-sense starting point to create a consistently high-performing team. Unfortunately, most coaches or managers are under time pressure from the weekly demands of preparation and coaching. This stress can contribute to hurried decisions based on insufficient research. I have made this mistake on a few occasions and have tried to become better at being more thorough when recruiting people. Another pitfall for coaches is that they can become too focused on the visible onfield ability of an individual player at the expense of truly considering the player's character and their 'fit' in the team.

When first arriving at a new place of work, you tend to inherit a team put together by others, as was the case when I joined Leinster. Guy Easterby was the team manager, and he dealt with player agents and contracts, while Jono Gibbes was going to be taking on more responsibility as the forwards coach, after having done the role in tandem with Michael Cheika for the previous two seasons. I accepted the job at the start of January 2010, but with me being busy coaching in Clermont, and Jono and Guy being busy with Leinster, it was difficult to meet up to get started on player recruitment.

The situation became more complicated in late January, when Clermont was drawn to play Leinster in the quarter-final of the Heineken Cup. In light of the draw, Michael Cheika was not keen that I have contact with any of the Leinster players, or meet up with Jono or Guy in Dublin, until after the quarter-final was played in early April. We knew that we would need to have our recruitment well underway before then, so we met in February, at a hotel adjoining Charles de Gaulle airport.

When I'd accepted the role at the start of the year, the IRFU were considering a request to increase the number of non-Irish qualified (NIQ) players in each provincial squad from six to seven, because two Italian teams were joining an expanded twelve-team Magners League for the following season. But by the time we met in Paris the limit on NIQ players had actually been reduced, from six to five, which put a further squeeze on our recruitment options. At the time I was irked by the decision but, in retrospect, I think the outcome has been positive for both the provinces and the national team with the emergence of so many talented home-grown players.

Under pressure to have sufficient players in one particular position, we signed an Irish-qualified player. We were under time pressure and there was a scarcity of options, but committing to a three-year contract in haste was a mistake. After one inauspicious season, we released the player. We'd seen footage of the skills that he had and were too easily convinced about what he could add on the pitch without sufficiently investigating his drive and commitment. It meant that we had a less than effective player during the season and a costly payout at the end of it.

Even when we felt that we'd worked hard in the process of recruiting a player, the result wasn't always as we'd hoped. In one particular case, I phoned the player's coach and a player who'd played with him, whom I knew and trusted. The feedback was that the player added good value, was durable, trained hard and slotted in well with the group. The coach lamented that not having the player would be a big loss for them. With hindsight, I think the culture of that club was different from ours. We thought that the player was the sort of dogged competitor that we needed, but when he arrived we saw that he lacked the keen edge required and defaulted to shortcuts in the gym and on the pitch. We had invested substantially in the player both financially and strategically, but decided that it was better to cut our losses than to allow his apathy to fester in the group.

A person's character, commitment and willingness to help others are very difficult to instil or transform. The subtle slackers or disrupters can be just as damaging as more obviously undisciplined individuals. Players who undermine others or who selfishly look to promote themselves at the expense of teammates can cause ill feeling and derail team cohesion. As tempting as it can be to allow them to see out their contracts, I've learned that it is usually better to accept the financial penalty and preserve the positive standards and culture in the group.

Equally, getting the *right* person can send a positive ripple through a team and promote greater cohesion. In January 2012, when injuries depleted our second-row stocks in Leinster, we made a call to Brad Thorn. Thorny was well known in rugby circles for his character and competitive drive along with his professionalism. He was good friends with our scrum coach, Greg Feek, and we were fortunate to get a three-month release from his Japanese club. Some media grossly overstated the very modest salary that we paid to Brad; in reality, his motivation was that he wanted to win a Heineken Cup. He'd won pretty much everything else he could in Rugby Union as well as in Rugby League, and straight after arriving he made a positive impression.

At the end of the captain's run at the RDS the day before

Thorny was due to come off the bench for his first Leinster appearance, he ambled down to the corner closest to the changing rooms and started doing 'down and ups' and shuttle runs out to the 22-metre line and back. Shane Jennings, another quality character, eased alongside and also did a few repetitions. The ripple had started: when other players saw a Rugby World Cup winner doing extra work, they were more inclined to do the same thing. Seven years later, in a post-match interview after Leinster had beaten Toulouse in the 2019 European Cup semi-final, Devin Toner commented that 'people still talk about the impact [Thorn] had. Just his work ethic and the way he speaks his mind really well, the way he plays, the way he eats, looks after his body so well.'

Thorny was a big man with a big engine, and when he did things, other players tended to follow his lead. The best people tend to model positive behaviours and others are likely to follow suit.

In pursuit of good people who are good players, it doesn't mean that you recruit people with the same temperament, just as you don't recruit players with the same playing strengths. The diversity in the group is important. Mike Ross worked away quietly, but he was a rock-solid character who could be relied upon. On the other side of the scrum, Cian Healy was more of a maverick as a youngster, with an explosive ability to influence the game. At scrum half, Eoin Reddan would exhort constant effort from those around him with a positive volatility. He could run the game at a tempo that would stress opponents. In the same position, Isaac Boss was the ideal foil, being more measured but with a skill set and sheer physical commitment and consistency that made him effective.

The commonly held belief in rugby is that the forwards do all the heavy lifting and work harder than the backs, who do the flashy stuff, drinking lattes in between times. As I mentioned earlier, I don't like to draw divisions between forwards and backs. They do operate as independent units at times, but they very much share the responsibility for working hard and contributing physically. The high-speed collisions in the backline and backs scrambling to get their ruck entry takes a physical toll, while more often than ever there is an expectation that forwards have the ability to do the 'flashy stuff'.

Wingers Keith Earls and Fergus McFadden are very tough and their clean-out technique and commitment at ruck time are formidable. Keith is quiet and utterly professional in the hard work that he does, while Fergus is a prankster but every bit as professional when getting the hard work done. It's important to have this diversity. Ferg threw maximum energy into whatever he was doing, whether that be combating opponents or catching teammates unawares.

I remember getting caught out by some Fairy Liquid-flavoured sweets that Ferg had bought from the joke shop and placed in a small bowl on the snack table at the Shelbourne Hotel. I was in the team room making a cup of tea when Rob Kearney, Sean O'Brien and Ferg came in and Rob and Seanie asked me if I'd like to try one of the sweets. Ferg slipped out of the room as he realized that I was just about to be duped. When the awful flavour became apparent I saw that Rob and Seanie were almost in tears watching my face crease and brow furrow, trying to work out the flavour, then trying to find somewhere to spit the 'sweet' out. Of course the two lads immediately blamed Ferg.

*

Along with having quality players, it's essential to have the right people working with them. Jono Gibbes did a great job, and grew in confidence, during the three years we worked together in Leinster. He went on to add value in Clermont and Ulster before guiding Waikato to win promotion into the top division of the NPC. He is currently getting strong performances and some impressive results from his team at La Rochelle, both in the Top 14 and in Europe. Jono is good company and works well with people. He has presence and encourages players to contribute and to enjoy their work, but he doesn't tolerate 'effort errors' and will be candid when delivering feedback, whether it's positive or negative.

Just like players, coaches have different personal styles and different ways of getting things done. During my first year as Ireland coach, John Plumtree helped to instil an abrasive edge in the forward pack, especially in the lineout maul; but he had a laid-back coaching manner. Similarly, Greg Feek is quietly spoken when delivering his detail on the scrum but does a great job of guiding and adding confidence to the forward pack. Richie Murphy, our highly effective skills coach, has an engaging and encouraging style. I think it was ideal that the personal styles of those coaches differed from the intense demand for precision that Les Kiss and I brought to the coaching mix. When Simon Easterby replaced John Plumtree, he brought a lineout acumen and thoughtful approach, while Andy Farrell's clarity and conviction immediately resonated with both the coaching and the playing group when he joined us in 2016.

Our two analysts work long hours to aid the coaching staff. They are continually scrutinizing opposition performances and building profiles on key players as well as collecting data on what we do. In the role for fifteen years, Merv

Murphy is methodical and meticulous, and this is complemented by Vinny Hammond's ability to problem-solve and
think laterally.

I've spent nine years working with Jason Cowman, a superb
strength and conditioning coach who consistently challenges
himself to stay at the top of his profession. 'Jayo' has the confidence of the players, and works with them to individualize
their programmes to suit their needs as much as he can. He is
constantly reading the latest literature to stay current with
what is considered to be best practice, not just for physical
conditioning and recovery but also for mindfulness, sleep
hygiene, coping with jet lag and various other factors that
contribute to players' performance and well-being.

Our medical team is led by Dr Ciarán Cosgrove, or 'Dr
Rock', as we call him, because of the superb physical condition he's in. Dr Éanna Falvey was his predecessor and, as a
former heavyweight boxer, he was well able to understand
the needs of athletes involved in contact sports. The head
physiotherapist was James Allen, who shifted across to the
incredibly successful Dublin Gaelic football camp a few seasons ago. Colm Fuller has come in to replace him and, along
with Keith 'Foxy' Fox, all three have added tremendous
expertise, to aid player robustness and rehabilitation. They're
ably supported by two of the most positive characters I've
met, in 'Willie B' Bennett and Dave 'Revs' Revins. Willie B
and Revs are the team masseurs and, with some part-time
help from Michael 'Thomo' Thompson, another quality
individual, they help the medical team to ensure that the
physical needs of the players are well catered for.

As a group, the medical team are incredibly professional
but personable at the same time. They're also good fun
and Colm Fuller's uncanny ability to impersonate people is

hilarious. His impersonation of the legendary GAA commentator Mícheál Ó Muircheartaigh, when doing a mock interview with former GAA and AFL star Tadhg Kennelly while we were on tour in Australia last year, was brilliant! Rounding out the support for the physical well-being of the players is Ruth Wood-Martin. Her nutritional expertise is matched by her caring and no-nonsense approach with both staff and players.

Enda McNulty brings a contagious positivity to the players' mental preparation and mental skills development. Our media liaison, David Ó Síocháin, doubles up as the 'Minister of Fun', and does a superb job of encouraging and facilitating the players' community service and staff social catch-ups.

John Moran, our genial baggage man, has inherited Patrick 'Rala' O'Reilly's 'ready for anything' mindset. The logistics are organized by Ger Carmody and Sinéad Bennett who, between them, ensure that the smallest details are taken care of and the stress of travel and daily life is minimized for the players. Former logistics manager Nicola Lyons was equally proficient. After we won our first ever test in South Africa, our seats on the flight to Johannesburg the next day were cancelled at the last minute; Nicola had to rebook tickets on a later flight and to organize food in the interim, and did it with aplomb.

Paul Dean, the former Ireland and Lions out-half, stepped into the manager's role in recent years and has worked away behind the scenes to assist in the smooth running of the team. His predecessor, Mick Kearney, was the person who convinced me to take the role as Irish coach. A casual 'catch-up' for coffee became a much more concerted discussion, with Mick outlining the reasons why I should consider the role. We've laughed about it since, because Mick managed to convince me that I would have more free time, but that has been far from the case! Mick has a tremendous ability to engage with people and a brilliant network of contacts to help him access all manner of resources. He also became a good friend and a valuable sounding board.

Through many years involved in coaching team sports, prioritizing the character of an individual and their commitment to team values has been fundamental. Good people will work hard to maximize their potential and will help contribute to the progress of others. Ideally they're also talented, but talent is never enough by itself. I think Calvin Coolidge exaggerated when he said that 'nothing is more common than unsuccessful men with talent,' but in a team sport where preparation and performance are dependent upon collective, coordinated effort, talent needs to be underpinned by the right personal qualities.

Believing that people need to keep developing their character just as they need to keep developing their talent, we have tried to orchestrate growth opportunities away from rugby from time to time. During my first Christmas camp as Ireland coach, at the end of 2013, we spent two days in Carton House reviewing the Guinness Series from the autumn and getting a bit of organization and training done in preparation for the Six Nations. We had a Christmas dinner, with a Kris Kindle involving all the players. The evening went on somewhat longer than planned because Rala, who distributed the gifts after dinner, had a story to tell about each player or staff member as they came up to collect their present. There were some funny stories, and time spent connecting socially is important. However, the following year, I was keen to do something different.

I spoke to Mick Kearney and we settled on the idea of visiting a shelter for homeless people. I rang Paul O'Connell, who was captain, to get his thoughts and we formulated a plan. We would usher the squad on to the bus under the guise of going for Christmas dinner in Dublin, but instead we would pull up at the Capuchin Day Centre. Mick organized the visit with Brother Kevin, and made a donation to the Centre at the same time. What impressed me when we arrived was that the players, though surprised, didn't hesitate, but immediately started mingling with volunteer staff and packaging food parcels. In some ways the squad were probably not as useful as they might have been, because most of the volunteer staff made full use of the opportunities to get selfies and to chat to the players; but it was a positive experience, and Brother Kevin voiced his thanks and delight at the end of the evening.

Last Christmas, after doing an organizational walk-through at the Leixlip gymnasium, the players were divided up to travel with volunteers from the charity ALONE. They visited elderly folk who were lonely, to have a cup of tea and a chat. Sinéad Bennett did a super job liaising with the charity to get it organized and, while it wasn't a huge time commitment, it was gratifying to see the way the players responded. The feedback from the people who were visited and from the volunteers was a credit to the players.

Many of the players volunteer independently to help charities, or to visit schools or hospitals. On tour we also try to help contribute locally. In South Africa, we assisted with a 'tag rugby' tournament at one of the schools in a township near Cape Town. It was on the down day so players voluntarily gave up their time, just as they did in Port Elizabeth when visiting the Missionvale Care Centre, a small oasis in the very grim Shackland township. The coaches felt it was important to contribute alongside the players, so we joined in for both the school and Missionvale visits, and also did a coaching session at Rondebosch Boys' High School.

There are other examples of community engagement, and I've mentioned a few here not to boost the image of the players, but to explain one of the ways in which we have tried to develop their individual character. If people have a wider understanding of the world and empathy for others, especially those who are struggling, then we'd hope that they will be better for it. The players also gained the opportunity to see the positive impact they can have on the community and they hopefully got a boost from being involved, which will encourage them to continue to contribute. Abraham Lincoln once explained his own personal code by reference to a man he'd met who said, 'When I do good, I feel good.' There's a contagious element to that feelgood factor in a group.

Within the team environment we try to encourage and reward positive behaviours, but there is very little tolerance for 'effort errors'. Effort doesn't require talent. The English scrum half Ben Youngs once said of playing against Ireland that 'they just love the fight . . . when I say the fight, I am talking about the breakdown, the aerial stuff, the bits of the game that are no-talent-required, niggly stuff.' I'm not sure I'd agree that these areas don't require talent, and they certainly require technique, but a big part of the formula to be successful in these areas of the game is full-blooded commitment. That's an attitude, a willingness to get beyond fatigue or fear to win the contest. The best people deliver on this consistently, and when the best people combine this attitude with the talent they have, then they become formidable.

When considering recruitment or selection, we always

want the best of both worlds, that combination of character and talent. But if we have to choose, then more often than not we will err on the side of character. We will look for those unselfish involvements on and off the pitch. If players show the motivation to recover well, prepare well and work hard during the game to deliver the less visible, unselfish behaviours and the repeated high-intensity efforts, then they're likely to play at their best, while allowing others the same opportunity.

Beyond the team for any given match, there is the wider squad of players, who are crucial to drive internal competition and to help prepare those who have been selected to play. Good people will get past their own frustrations if they're not selected and will be as positive as they can be in preparing the players who have been selected. One of the things I most love about rugby is the interdependence it demands. To be successful, no one player can individually play the game by himself, or for himself. It has to be about the team. It's a relatively simple formula, but a complicated recipe to get right if some of the ingredients are tainted.

9. Leaders

Let him that would move the world first move himself.

Socrates

The best people lead themselves well as individuals. It's also likely that there will be a number of good leaders in a squad of good people, making the job easier for those with designated leadership roles. I have benefited enormously from having good people working with me. In turn, I have tried to acknowledge their efforts and expertise and tried to be inclusive when decisions are made. Whether it's logistics, timetabling, medical, training content or team selection, I'd like to think that staff know that their efforts and their ideas are valued.

Sometimes I struggle when there's a battery of questions to be answered or decisions to be made, or I'm facing a series of tough conversations with non-selected players. I try to take a breath and be positive, or at least measured, when responding. It might be that a player is a late withdrawal from training and I'm frustrated that we don't have the correct training numbers. It might be that I'm acutely aware of how hard a player is working and how much he has improved – but he has missed selection and I know how disappointed he's going to be. It is crucial to effectively communicate the reasons for our decisions.

As a national coaching group, we have always tried to put

our thoughts together and write up a few key areas of positive feedback for a player who has not been chosen for a squad, but also a few reasons why the player has missed out, so that there is a consistency to the conversations we have. It's time-consuming, and selection is not always clear-cut. There are times in conversations with non-selected players when I say that I'm not totally sure that we've made the right call, but we believe the player we have selected has demonstrated enough of what we need and there is very little to separate the selected player from the disappointed player. It's probably scant consolation, but hopefully they will continue to trust that I am being as honest and transparent as I can be. I try to work out how best to convey the message as positively as I can, but the result is the same for the player: he hasn't been selected and won't get the opportunity to be involved in a match or a series that he's desperately keen to play in.

I try to bounce back quickly after defeats, but it's not easy. I'm emotionally attached to the job and to the challenge of meeting the high expectations we set for ourselves. I'm also aware of the tremendous support we have and feel pretty wretched when we don't win. In 2015, as defending Six Nations Champions, we lost a close game in Cardiff. We had our chances during the game, but Leigh Halfpenny kicked four early penalties and when we got on to the front foot, the Welsh defence scrambled and spoiled well to keep us out. It was a one-score game when, with a minute to play, our line-out drive was collapsed just two metres from the Welsh line. The final play of the game was a Welsh scrum which capitulated under pressure, but the assistant referee decided that our dominance wasn't legal and we were beaten. It had been a big effort from both teams. Frustration morphed into melancholy as the squad shuffled on to the bus after the post-match dinner.

Daniel Goleman, in *Primal Leadership: Realizing the Power of Emotional Intelligence*, states that roughly 50–70 per cent of how employees perceive their organization's climate is attributable to the actions and behaviours of their leader. I was conscious of this, but when we flew back to Dublin and headed to our training base at Carton House the following day, I didn't bounce back as well as I needed to. I hadn't slept, so I'd had plenty of time to review the match and to put together the strategy for the coming week. I felt that my energy levels were pretty good but I was distracted by discussions with the referee boss, Joël Jutge, over the inconsistency of the refereeing in the match. I was still embittered when I should have been focused on lifting the mood and urging the players to make the most of their bid to retain the Six Nations title. The squad trained as poorly as we've ever trained on the Tuesday morning and I knew that we'd have to rebound with plenty of zest for Thursday's training, which would be our last opportunity to prepare for our final match of the Championship, away to Scotland.

Paul O'Connell was also worried, and he suggested that I text each of the players and encourage them to forget about rugby for twenty-four hours, telling them to come back into camp refreshed and ready to train well on Thursday. I spoke to the coaches and we agreed it was a good idea so I texted each player and encouraged them to relax for the evening and the following day. I tried to personalize each message to include things like spending time with their partner or their kids or taking the dog for a walk, depending on their individual circumstances. I tried to do the same thing that evening myself and, after spending the afternoon doing some planning for Thursday, I spent the evening watching a movie with my two youngest kids.

When we reassembled on Wednesday evening, the mood was different. Players and management were rejuvenated, and we enjoyed the opportunity to reconnect. There was a very finite period of time left in the week to get prepared, and the group had a clarity of purpose that sharpened their focus. For training the following day, we'd planned for the session to be about fifty minutes, but we were sharp and accurate and I called a halt to training while we were still on the upswing. We had trained for just thirty-seven minutes and players left the pitch with a fresh confidence, despite an injury scare when doing a few extra lineouts at the end.

It's nice to reflect on the 'Super Saturday' that followed. Ourselves, England and Wales had lost one game each, so the Championship was likely to come down to points difference. Wales got a sluggish start in Rome but amassed a forty-one-point differential in the second half. This meant that, playing in the day's second game, at Murrayfield, we would have to beat Scotland by at least twenty points to get our noses in front of Wales.

An early Paul O'Connell try was followed by an excellent setpiece finish from Sean O'Brien, but Finn Russell got one back for Scotland leaving us with a 20–10 lead at half-time: exactly halfway to the twenty-point margin we needed. In the second half, we scored twenty unanswered points thanks to tries from Jared Payne and Sean O'Brien and ten points from the boot of Johnny Sexton. Big results swing on small moments, and when Stuart Hogg crossed in the dying minutes it seemed that our margin would be squeezed – but a desperate Jamie Heaslip tackle dislodged the ball.

Jamie had worked hard to keep tracking across the pitch

as the Scots launched their attack from the lineout. We had a comfortable margin and he could have slackened but he's a competitor. He threw himself into what looked to be a lost cause, because he was never going to stop Stuart Hogg from getting across the line. Just as Hogg started to fall toward the ground to score the try, Jamie grasped him with an extended left arm and reached over with his right hand to dislodge the ball. It's leadership in action because he worked hard enough to be in the right place and then adapted well enough in the tackle to get a hand on to the top of the ball to stop the try being scored.

It was a bizarre feeling at the end of the match. Our thirty-point win meant that Wales were now out of the running, and England would have to beat France by at least twenty-five points to overtake us. The relief at having overtaken Wales (while setting a new record for points scored by an Ireland team in Murrayfield) was counterbalanced by the angst of the pending kick-off between England and France. The stadium was emptied out after the match, before supporters were encouraged to come back in again to watch the England–France match on the big screens. Getting changed and prepared for the post-match dinner, we could hear the roars and groans from about 10,000 supporters viewing the match in the stands. The roars were for some early French tries, but they were interspersed with groans, which increased in number. By the time we headed up the stairs to the post-match dinner, England had forged ahead, to lead 27–15 at the break. Like we had been, they were pretty much halfway to the margin they needed.

The final moments of the end-to-end contest were extraordinary. With time up on the clock and England leading 55–35 – and needing a try to overtake us – France won a penalty just metres from their own line. In the post-match dinner we roared with delight. What had started as a miserable week had ended in elation. Then, the French winger Yoann Huget tapped the ball and played it to Uini Atonio, the 150-kilo prop. Atonio is a formidable player but highly unlikely to race the length of the pitch to score at the other end. He was put to ground after a couple of metres and we watched aghast as the ball squirted sideways and it looked as if the English were going to win it back on the ground. A ruck formed and Rory Kockott, the French replacement scrum half, finally scrambled the ball into touch. Euphoric, we leaped back to our feet to celebrate back-to-back Championships.

It was a phenomenal finish to the Six Nations, and the players went back out on to the pitch in their suits to receive the Six Nations Trophy in front of the 10,000 delighted and vocal supporters who had stayed on. A crazy day and an uplifting experience.

I'm always learning. I know that I didn't lead as well as I should have during that week, but with good advice from the leaders around me we got to where we needed to be and the players delivered the performance and the result that was required. For me, it's about adding to the knowledge and skills that can help me coach and lead better.

One danger, as a leader, is that there is so much literature and advice available that you try to become all things to all people. There's a risk that your own identity and authenticity become blurred. I think it's important to be who you are – this forms the core of your leadership – but also to keep learning new skills and developing your self-awareness. I'm still very conscious of the feedback Mike Chu, the NZRU High Performance Coach Development Manager, gave me many years ago: that I'm intense when I'm coaching. I don't think it is necessarily a bad thing; but that intensity needs to be balanced by periods when players can unwind, so I try to leave them to have their own space during downtimes in camp.

As a head coach, I try to make sure that my energy levels are high and that I work hard enough behind the scenes to be as well prepared as possible. On top of the hectic week-to-week coaching existence, I also try to find time to read both recreationally and across a myriad of performance-related topics. To supplement the professional reading, I chat with other coaches both within rugby and from other sports. I also attempt to stay abreast of what is happening in the commercial world.

I remember being at a fundraising event with Michael O'Leary from Ryanair. When he was asked what one word he would use to sum up successful leadership, his response was 'Paranoia'. I thought, 'Wow, that's at the very end of the spectrum,' but it made sense when he explained that he wanted to be in a constant state of high alert to mitigate any threats as best he could and to make the most of any potential opportunities as well. I would probably use the word 'vigilance' to slightly soften the same message. I want to be constantly aware of what's being done well in our environment and, at the same time, be conscious of what needs to be done better. I need to be vigilant when recruiting or selecting, and about what our opponents are doing, what trends are occurring in the game and how we might counter any problems that are likely to arise.

Being aware of what is happening in the sporting world, particularly in rugby, and maintaining relationships within the game are part of that vigilance. As well as watching games across the competitions in Europe, I also watch Super Rugby and the New Zealand NPC as well as the occasional Currie Cup match. Staying in touch with a network of people is helpful, whether it's on a review group for TMO protocols or on a global working group for Player Load Management, or just having informal conversations with other coaches. These interactions are part of keeping the saw sharpened, as Stephen Covey puts it: I try to step back and take stock of what's happening in the game in order to hone my response to it.

As Ireland coach, a good relationship with provincial coaches is crucial. While there are always going to be occasions where we mightn't agree, in the vast majority of cases the conversations are positive. Ireland is well served by the way players are managed across their provincial and national team environments. The national team's strength and conditioning staff and medical staff stay in close contact with the provinces so that targets can be set and strived for, and injuries can be rehabbed in a way that fits the needs of the player. The player management document in Ireland is individualized and flexible, and I have found that the provincial coaches are proactive in planning the management of their players. We have become more aligned, to the extent that Leo Cullen and Charlie Higgins, Leinster's Head of Athletic Performance and a top-quality operator, formulated their own document for the Leinster players during a portion of last season. When we looked at their player management plan, it was very much in line with what we would have suggested from a national perspective.

Irish players believe that the system is a point of difference for them in prolonging their careers. Conversely, England's Billy Vunipola expressed his frustration in a *Times* interview in September 2017, saying, 'It comes down to how much we play. My body could not handle it. I might think I'm strong and tough but I'm not. I just got worn down.' In the same month, Ben Youngs explained that in England 'Guys have been outspoken because they care about the length of their career. They don't want it four years shorter.' There was talk at the time of extending the English Premiership season, and Joe Marler tweeted that the 'season extension idea is horse-shit'. The RFU claimed that 'player welfare is its No. 1 priority,' but then, despite opposition from the English players and concerns expressed by the English Rugby Players Association representative, Damian Hopley, they pressed ahead with a bid to squeeze the Six Nations into a six-week window instead of seven weeks – meaning players would have only one recovery weekend during the Championship.

It's not just about the physical management of players: it's also vital to manage their mental well-being. A 2017 survey carried out by Rugby Players Ireland showed that over 40 per cent of professional rugby players have reported symptoms of anxiety and/or depression, and 70 per cent worry about what the future holds once their rugby career ends. Four English Premiership rugby players tested positive for cocaine use in the 2017–18 season. RFU medical services director, Dr Simon Kemp, explained that 'these are players who are dislocated from their clubs through injury or non-selection.' Such setbacks, along with the short-term nature of contracts, can cause anxiety levels to rise for players. Many occupations have volatility, but professional sport carries an emotional attachment and visible scrutiny that can be stifling.

'Project Aristotle' was a study undertaken by Google to determine why some work teams in the company succeeded and others didn't. Google, with all their ability to make sense of huge amounts of data, found the task incredibly difficult. After two years studying 180 teams, they changed tack and focused on team behaviours that amplified the collective intelligence of the group. They came up with five key characteristics of high-performing teams, and summarized them with two words: 'feeling valued'. I'm sure that players would say that I'm demanding as a coach, but I'd hope that they would also say that I value them and I try to encourage them to value each other.

I wrote a paper on captaincy when undertaking my NZRU coaching practicum twenty years ago, and I quoted Bill Beaumont. When he was asked what makes a good captain, he replied, 'Having fourteen good players.' While the remark was light-hearted, I think Bill was very conscious of the underlying truth in the response. As Seamus Heaney says in his version of *Beowulf*:

> Behaviour that's admired
> is the path to power among people everywhere.

If those admirable behaviours can be shared by the entire group, then the power is magnified and the responsibility for leadership is shared.

I remember the captains that we had at Bay of Plenty during the two seasons I was there. Clayton McMillan was captain in the first year and is now coaching both the Bay of Plenty and NZ Māori teams. When I caught up with him in Chicago in November 2018 he spoke about wanting to learn more. In the second year, Wayne Ormond led the side. He didn't say a lot, but his physical commitment was charismatic. He's now coaching at Rotoiti, still leading and learning at his home club on the eastern edge of Lake Rotoiti in rural Bay of Plenty.

Both men led the team from the front and were big physical performers for us, but they had great support from others in the team. On the flank, Nili Latu was hard-nosed and relentless, while Glen Jackson's tactical leadership was ably supported by the likes of Kev Senio, Grant McQuoid, Rua Tipoki, Damon Kaui and Adrian Cashmore. Players led themselves, making sure that they delivered what was required of them, which allowed both Clayton and Wayne to get on with what they needed to deliver themselves. When breaks in play occurred, they could broaden their focus to help guide the team.

Leading by demonstrating positive behaviours was a constant theme during the time I spent with Leinster. I've already written about Brad Thorn, but Isa Nacewa was another very influential imported player. During the three years I was at Leinster, Isa never once took a game sheet with the strategy on it, and I never encouraged him to, because we both knew that he would always have his preparation done. In the team room, the strategy would be mapped out on flip charts and the whiteboard would have plenty of detail regarding the threats that the opposition that week posed. Isa absorbed the necessary detail, then he would go out and play with a clarity of thought and physical commitment that was inspiring, whether it be his full-speed tackle on a rampaging Sébastien Chabal or the incredible individual try he scored against Leicester in the 2011 Heineken Cup quarter-final.

Sometimes, individual courage and commitment are enough to make the difference. In 2012, Brian O'Driscoll, as talented as he was, returned from injury just in time to play the Heineken Cup semi-final against Clermont in Bordeaux. In the first few minutes of the game, he hit Aurélien Rougerie with everything he had. Rougerie was Clermont captain for the three years that I was there, and his talismanic influence strengthened the belief of the players around him, so when Brian smashed him and Gordon D'Arcy piled in to help out, it lifted the team and others gained in confidence.

Leo Cullen captained Leinster with a quiet assurance. He would very seldom shout or become overly animated – others in the team would be more likely to do that – but Leo was the voice of reason, and players responded incredibly positively to him. Leo was professional but had a great knack for being awkward on the pitch, which would often frustrate opponents. I remember at the Pro12 awards evening sitting next to Sean Lineen, the coach of the Glasgow Warriors at the time. Leinster were announced as the Specsavers Fair Play Award winners for having the fewest yellow cards, red cards or citings during the season. As Leo walked past us on his way up to collect the trophy, Sean whispered to me, 'There's a bit of irony with Leo collecting that award.' I chuckled because we'd received just six yellow cards during the season, but Leo had managed to get three of them all by himself!

Paul O'Connell led with a presence and passion that were energizing. His professionalism and drive to be better every time he trained or played were incredible. He was a lineout nerd and a keen strategist, but it was his physical intensity that inspired those playing alongside him. He would encourage others but, if necessary, he could also be fierce and direct when demanding better from a player. During the second test in Argentina in 2014, a player had been cutting across others in defence during the first half. I'm sure that player still remembers the sight of Paul, in a dimly lit half-time changing room in Tucumán, telling him that he needed to realign himself and 'get with the programme'.

One of our players, when asked about Rory Best's leadership, said that 'He gets the best out of himself and those around him.' Rory makes sure that his contribution is optimized by committing to all aspects of his preparation and then invests all that he can during the game, with the requisite courage and experience to be as competitive as possible. He is relentless with his lineout throwing drills, and his breakdown work either side of the ball is smart and combative. He popped a rib in a game during the summer of 2019 and, despite being depowered in the scrum, played on with no discernible drop-off in performance in general play.

When a band of leaders get together with a single-minded purpose and steadfast belief that they physically commit to, they can become a catalyst for remarkable feats on a rugby pitch. Making our way down to the changing room at half-time in the 2011 Heineken Cup final, with Leinster trailing Northampton by sixteen points, Jono Gibbes and I were somewhat shell-shocked, but thinking clearly. We were focused on two key messages that we were about to deliver:

- In the first half, we'd made three clean line breaks that came to nothing because we spilled the ball with loose passes or poor handling. In the second half we knew that we could make at least another three line breaks and all we would have to do was hold on to the ball and make sure that we finished the opportunities.
- We needed to get our feet moving to get in closer and be more decisive in the tackle.

Looking back, I still think those messages were useful, but they didn't make the difference. The mood in the dressing room rallied on the back of what was said by the leaders in the team. Leo said a few words, as did Jamie Heaslip. Johnny Sexton stood up and passionately expressed his belief that we could come back, referencing a Liverpool match that I didn't remember. I'm not sure how many of the players remembered it either, at that particular moment. But it wasn't what he said, or how convincingly he said it. It was what he did in delivering a masterclass performance in the second half. Shane Jennings chipped in with a few words at halftime, and then followed up with an all-action second half as well.

Greg Feek and his front-row players solved Northampton's 'arrow' scrum approach, and we reversed their first-half dominance to get on to the front foot at the scrum. Knee-deep in shit, facing humiliation on a huge stage, it was one of the most productive half-time breaks that I've witnessed.

I know that Northampton had accumulated a volume of work in the weeks leading up to the final and showed signs of fatigue in the second half, but the leadership from the players who'd spoken at half-time, along with those who'd listened and committed to the messages, was apparent in their superb second-half performance. The 33–22 victory in a packed stadium of over 70,000 people was incredible. It set the benchmark for collective leadership under pressure.

10. Catalyst

Instead of worrying about what you can't control, shift your energy to what you can create.

Roy T. Bennett

Energy is contagious. It sounds like common sense, but it's also supported by research; and if you're a leader, your energy is even more impactful.

When I was a teacher, I found it difficult to bring visible enthusiasm to the classroom late in the day, toward the end of the week, when the room was stuffy and I had been marking essays until very late the night before. I remember consciously willing myself to keep the animation in my voice and the enthusiasm in my body language so that students might manage to do the same.

I've seen classrooms where a teacher's fatigue or lack of vitality contributed to a slump in energy levels – or to students sparking their own enthusiasm, which tends to lead them off-task.

All teachers and coaches relish working with responsive students or athletes, but even then there can be challenges trying to maintain motivation and effort in the group. One common teaching technique that I still attempt to make best use of is positive reinforcement. Rather than reprimanding disruptive students, we were encouraged to 'catch them when they're good', to reinforce and reward positive behaviours.

Amy Cuddy, in a TED talk with over 54 million views, contends that you don't just influence others with your body language; you can also 'fake it until you become it', by speaking positively to yourself through your body language. We have thousands of internal conversations with ourselves every day: reminding ourselves of what we need to get done or who we might be meeting that afternoon or how we feel about a certain situation. Some of these affect our mood, and Amy Cuddy contends that our body language operates in a similar way. If our shoulders sag or our head becomes heavy, then our enthusiasm wanes and we are very unlikely to inspire ourselves, let alone anyone else.

Responding to a late call from the former Ireland hooker Frankie Sheahan, I was one of the supporting acts for the American 'life coach' Tony Robbins at the Pendulum Summit a few years ago. To ensure his heart rate was up and he was ready to go, Robbins physically bounced up and down on a mini trampoline to energize himself, before going on stage to energize others. His enthusiasm on stage, including his audience engagement, his intonation and delivery were certainly invigorating.

There have been times when I have looked out at the adverse weather, felt fatigued and thought that the upcoming training is going to be cold, long and miserable – but it never turns out like that. Once the training begins, I'm engrossed in what I'm doing and the time disappears. Any negative thoughts are quashed as my full concentration is zeroed in on what's happening and my body language follows suit. There is so much movement and detail to scan for and I'm constantly registering small bits of feedback that I might ask about the next time play stops, or I might just yap away delivering it while the ball's in play. I'm lucky to enjoy what I do when I'm coaching – to be absorbed by it, so I don't have to 'fake it' until I become energized, because the energy is already real.

As a national team, we limit the amount of time we spend on the pitch. Based on conversations with other coaches, I think we probably do less onfield training than most other teams, but we have managed to win three of the last six Six Nations Championships. Part of that success is the amount of work that's done off the pitch. Our meetings are longer than I'd like them to be, and I'm sure the players sometimes feel overloaded early in the week, but we keep each other motivated because we understand how important the information is and that if we can internalize it, we will be more productive on the pitch.

The clearer the messages, the more efficient we can be. When I read something that Samuel Beckett once said to a critic – 'James Joyce was a synthesizer, trying to bring in as much as he could. I am an analyser, trying to leave out as much as I can' – it struck a chord with me. I often have a lot of information that I'd like to convey, but a key skill in coaching is prioritizing what is most important.

I remember getting a visit from the Clare hurling legend Anthony Daly, along with Richie Stakelum, when they were working together with the Dublin hurling team. Anthony Daly's smouldering intensity when talking about his team was almost tangible. At one point, we were talking about pre-match meetings. Anthony had a clipboard with him. There were ten messages on it, which he said he might deliver before the team got on to the bus to go to the game. I skimmed the points and asked him how he expected the players to remember them if he had to write them down? Having a clear head is probably the most important thing for the players before a match. Hitting them with too much information might create more confusion than clarity.

Anthony asked me what I did. I explained that what I did wasn't necessarily the right thing to do, but that I usually went for a walk the morning of the game and tried to sift through the things that I thought would be most important. I would retain just two or three key messages in my head for the pre-match meeting, maybe even just one – perhaps a galvanizing phrase that has been a theme during the week. We had a good chat about alternative ways of delivering multiple messages. One possible solution was that Anthony should deliver the three most important messages himself, while asking a couple of key players to keep other points uppermost in the thinking of the players at the relevant times. There's no right or wrong amount of detail for a coach to convey to players, but we agreed that having clarity of thought and certainty of action in the high-speed environment of competitive sport will likely be most beneficial to performance.

One of the difficulties for coaches is trying to anticipate likely responses or reactions, both from your own players and from opponents. Watching footage of opposition players, particularly those in key positions, I try to decipher their habits, or their likely responses to different situations. Coaching, like any other leadership role, requires an ability to predict what might happen, so that you are as well prepared as possible to exploit a perceived opposition weakness or to minimize the damage threatened by an opponent with particular strengths.

It's time-consuming, but the strategic element is motivating, particularly when you close down an opponent or you exploit an opportunity just the way you'd hoped to. In the semi-final of the 2012 Heineken Cup, we scored just one try, and it came from a strike play we'd never attempted in a match before. Central to the play was a pass back inside to Rob Kearney running at pace close to the breakdown. We predicted that the Clermont defenders were likely to push up and away from the breakdown, as was their habit, especially if we made it look like the scrum half was going to get a short 'run-around' pass from the first receiver. Thankfully, the defenders moved as predicted and Rob Kearney timed his run perfectly to scythe through the defensive line. He linked with Cian Healy after drawing the last defender and the vital try was scored. It's moments like these, in crucial matches, that make the homework worthwhile. Even for Isaac Boss, who got levelled by Jamie Cudmore because he thought Isaac was going to get the ball back again, there was a degree of satisfaction, despite being left lying on the ground gasping for air as Cian crossed the try line.

Bringing energy isn't enough for a coach. If a coach is to be the catalyst – to help accelerate the right reaction – then the players have to trust the information as well as the enthusiasm that it's delivered with. I remember sitting with Andy Farrell, watching a coach give a presentation. He bristled with energy and captured the attention of the players from the moment he stood up, but after five or six minutes the substance of what he was delivering became diluted. The key roles became blurred and the process was hard to envisage.

While being a catalyst for contagious energy is fundamental when coaching, being open to ideas is equally important. Sitting in a coaches' meeting in Chicago, in early November 2016, Greg Feek suggested the idea of forming the figure 8 in memory of Anthony Foley, who had died suddenly three weeks earlier. We'd all known 'Axel' and I'd spent a fair bit of time working with him. Simon had played with him and Richie had played against him, as had Feeky, while Andy had also worked with him briefly at Munster. I wasn't sure that it was the appropriate thing to do, but we decided to bring the idea to the leadership group, and they believed that it was the best memorial that they could offer for Axel.

That whole week in Chicago was incredible. We assembled at Carton House on Sunday afternoon and got ourselves organized, then had a light training on Monday morning before flying to Chicago later that day. The players had just finished heavy playing programmes with their provinces in Europe, so on Tuesday we did a light walk-through in the very impressive indoor baseball training facility at the University of Illinois at Chicago. That evening we celebrated Joey Carbery's twenty-first birthday in Chicago Cut restaurant, where we were hosted by the owner, Matt Moore, an irrepressible and generous Irish expat.

Wednesday was a rest day, and in unseasonably bright and balmy weather most of the staff enjoyed the Chicago Architectural Cruise, while many of the players headed to the Chicago Bulls training complex for a look around and to shoot a few baskets. That evening was the Game 7 decider for baseball's World Series. When the Chicago Cubs prevailed 8–7 over the Cleveland Indians, they celebrated their first championship in 108 years, and the city was vibrant with revellers.

The one full training we had that week was at Hope Academy, on the edge of a notorious neighbourhood where gun crime was rife. It's hard to fathom the 762 shooting deaths in Chicago during 2016, but we felt safe enough and were hosted incredibly well at the venue. Unfortunately, the pitch was sodden despite the bright and warm weather, and we slogged our way through an error-ridden training.

The coaches chatted after the training, and based on what we'd just delivered on the training pitch we had an uneasy feeling that we weren't going to be ready. The All Blacks had compiled a record eighteen consecutive test match victories. They had just finished a dominant Rugby Championship, scoring bonus-point wins in both the home and away fixtures against Australia, South Africa and Argentina, amassing an incredible thirty-five tries and conceding just five. Their already indomitable aura would only be magnified in the eyes of our players. We were unsure whether to 'hit them between the eyes' with the feedback from the sloppy training or to reassure them by smoothing over the cracks in an attempt to build their confidence.

We decided that we needed to deliver a reality check. We delivered the feedback in direct terms, explaining that if we weren't accurate, the reality was that the All Blacks would likely humiliate us. We had lost to the All Blacks after going achingly close the last time that we'd played them, in 2013. We'd got a head start with a ferocious beginning and made the most of a loose pass from them to lead 19–0 after twenty minutes. We'd led 22–7 at half-time, and we had the ball and a five-point lead with less than thirty seconds to play. But when the All Blacks were offered a lifeline, we committed errors brought about by fear and fatigue. They managed to break our line, bust a number of tackles and, finally, exploit an overlap with an offload from Dane Coles to Ryan Crotty. Even then, we still had time for one more error, attempting to charge down the conversion too early, which allowed Aaron Cruden a second attempt from wide out. He added the two points that gave the All Blacks a 24–22 victory. We wanted to make sure that we'd learned from the lapses that occurred that day, and wouldn't repeat them.

With 5 million people gathering for the World Series victory celebrations in the middle of Chicago, our captain's run, originally scheduled for 11 a.m., was brought forward to 9 a.m. It was ideal for us, as we were up early each day because of the six-hour time difference. We had a police escort alongside a rail line underneath the city, which was a great way to get to Soldier Field in good time. Thankfully the captain's run was much better than the previous day's training. Richie Murphy had drawn up positions for each player in the figure 8 to honour Anthony Foley, and although one player got his positioning wrong when they rehearsed it, it looked impressive all the same.

As we headed back through the city, the crowds of baseball fans were already starting to swell. With a big bus and a police escort, we were cheered by some of those gathered on the bridges above the rail line. I think they mistakenly assumed that the bus contained some of the Chicago Cubs being ferried into town for the celebrations.

From the roof of our hotel, we had a phenomenal view of what was reported in the media as the seventh biggest human gathering of all time. Later in the afternoon, I met some Kiwi friends who were over for the game. We had a coffee and they assured me that they'd be supporting both teams. The time waiting for big games can be nerve-racking, so it was nice to have the distraction for an hour. The following day I had breakfast with two of my brothers, who were also over for the game, then caught up with the coaches before we departed for the stadium.

As much as I try to be a catalyst for positive energy when coaching, I make an effort not to heighten anxiety levels in the lead-up to a match. We had a few key messages to reinforce after a light training week, but the players coped well and some of the leaders spoke aptly about what would be required.

Before matches, as the players go through their individual warm-ups, I mostly leave them to get on with their well-rehearsed routines. I have often wondered what goes through some of their minds as the pressure builds and the kick-off gets close, but I've very seldom asked. I was enlightened somewhat when I watched *Four Days in November*, a documentary on the autumn series. Andrew Trimble spoke of the first thought he had when woken up by Jared Payne at 7 on the morning of the match: 'This is the day everyone's going to find out how rubbish I am . . . nothing's going to go right for me today . . .' He said that he battled with those thoughts right up until kick-off. Conor Murray talked about the 'buzz' of arriving at Soldier Field and, during the warm-up, 'chatting with Zeebs [Simon Zebo] and saying, "This is class, this is unreal, this is where you want to be."' He was nervous, too, but his mindset was very different from Andrew Trimble's.

A team is made up of a diverse group of characters, and what best prepares one player may not work for another. Some players feel a need to be nervous, while others need to feel confident or relaxed. Going right back to when I started coaching professionally, Adrian Cashmore in Bay of Plenty used to throw up just before leaving the dressing room for every big game, while Ants Tahana would often jog out with a cheeky smile on his face – but they'd both regularly deliver full-hearted, full-throttle performances.

Soldier Field was brimming and, as we came out of the changing rooms, the charged atmosphere permeated down into the concourse under the stands. We coaches were due to be shuttled around to the other side of the stadium in a golf buggy because the coaches' boxes were on the opposite side of the pitch from the changing rooms. We jumped into the buggy but went nowhere. I said to the driver that we were all set and he turned around and responded in a very slow drawl, 'Yaaawl heerre?' Yes, yes, we said, let's go! He turned around to drive off – and we promptly hurtled backwards into the railing. After extricating ourselves from the railing, we zoomed around to the lift, which we were supposed to share with the All Blacks' coaches; but just as we arrived, the door closed and we had to wait until the lift came back down again. I thought to myself, 'Well, I hope we start the game more successfully than we've managed to negotiate our way to the coaches' box . . .'

We caught the end of the National Anthem, played by New York-based but Dublin-born and -raised violinist Gregory Harrington. (Chatting to Greg after the match, he explained that he played fullback for St Conleth's in the 1991 Senior B Cup final at Donnybrook, when I was coaching Wilson's Hospital School with Joe Weafer.) As the All Blacks formed their phalanx to perform the haka, the Irish players moved into position to form the poignant but impressive and memorable figure 8.

We conceded an early try when the freakish running ability of Waisake Naholo saw him scythe through our first line of defence. But we recovered well, and scored three first-half tries of our own to lead 25–8 at half-time, reminiscent of what we'd managed to do the previous time we'd played the All Blacks. In the changing rooms during the break, the players were adamant that they would continue to play at the All Blacks and not become conservative like we had last time.

An early try after half-time gave us a remarkable lead of 30–8, but the All Blacks stormed back into the match, and by the time Joey Carbery came on to replace Johnny Sexton, who was struggling with cramp, the score was 33–29. Making his debut with fifteen minutes remaining, Joey's first involvement was a superb angled kick into the All Black 22.

A first-half injury to Ryan Crotty had seen him replaced by Malakai Fekitoa, and when Aaron Cruden came on and Beauden Barrett was shifted to fullback it worked well for the All Blacks. Unfortunately for them, George Moala got hurt in the seventy-first minute, which meant that the reserve hooker, Codie Taylor, had to go to the side of the scrum and a flanker, Ardie Savea, moved to the wing. I sent a message on to the pitch that we should play at Savea from the scrum because, although he's a phenomenal player, he was out of position. The message was passed on, but we attacked the short side – not at Ardie Savea but at his brother, Julian Savea, who was on the other wing! I was exasperated, but it was my fault and it was a lesson to be more specific with directions. I sent on the more specific *Ardie* Savea message at the next scrum, but this time the All Blacks shifted him into the defensive position of out-half. As it turned out, Ben Smith got narrow defensively and we still got the space for Simon Zebo to kick ahead down the touchline. Conor Murray's huge hit on Julian Savea in the in-goal forced the 5-metre scrum that is now part of history.

After Robbie Henshaw scored from the scrum and the conversion was slotted, there wasn't enough time for the All Blacks to come back at us. It was surreal in the coaches' box, watching as we controlled the last few minutes of the game before the celebrations started. We couldn't wait for the buggy to come around, so Andy Farrell and I sprinted off around the concourse; but in my excitement I went the wrong way at one of the pillars and ended up heading toward the stadium entrance instead of following the concourse around. It must have looked bizarre as I ran off in the wrong direction but Faz thought it was hilarious. At least by the time I realized that I had to go back around the concourse, I'd had time to take a breath and calm myself down a bit.

The after-match at Soldier Field was a casual get-together but included speeches from the Irish and New Zealand Rugby Union Presidents. During the after-match function, I was standing with former Auckland and All Blacks coach John Hart, along with former All Blacks captain Sean Fitzpatrick. I thought that the Presidents of the two unions both spoke impressively, but as Stephen Hilditch finished speaking and was applauded, one of the Kiwis behind us whispered, 'Gee, we even lost the after-match speeches!' The IRFU President had spoken glowingly about our respect for the All Blacks and had reflected on how fantastic their season had been.

I have since read Sean Fitzpatrick's book *Winning Matters*, in which he mentions that one of his sources of motivation was the fear of failure. He used to tell himself, 'I will *not* be in the first All Black team that ever loses to Ireland, or Scotland (or whoever), it just isn't going to happen.' He was such a belligerent and indomitable competitor, and I can imagine that he was just the sort of catalyst that the All Blacks needed during the ninety-two test matches that he played, to make sure they didn't lose to anyone too often.

The celebrations weren't outrageous, because there was still plenty of jet lag and the players faded quickly after attending a gala dinner. It's great to reflect on those moments. In scoring five tries, we'd equalled the number of tries that had been scored against the All Blacks during the entire 2016 Rugby Championship. We'd scored forty points against them and the demons of November 2013 had finally been buried. The score line the last time that Axel had played against the All Blacks had been 29–40, so we'd balanced the ledger on his behalf – maybe that's karma? The only other Irish team that had beaten the All Blacks was the 1978 Munster team in which Axel's father, Brendan, had locked the scrum with Moss Keane. It was a blessed week and I think that a number of colliding variables had helped to spark an unforgettable result.

11. Value

Try not to be a man of success but rather try to become a man of value.

Albert Einstein

I think it's fair to say that people get a sense of satisfaction from adding value, along with a sense of belonging when they feel valued. When the Principal at Tauranga Boys' College sent the flowers and the restaurant voucher after my tough first week, I felt valued. When René Fontès turned up at my office after hearing about Luke, I felt that my family was valued.

Adding value has a strength and consistency that chasing success doesn't. Success is not easily defined, because different people have very different ideas about what it means to them. As a youngster I thought success would be playing for the All Blacks, being wealthy and driving around in a flash car. Perceptions change as we mature and become less preoccupied with what we want and more conscious of the value we can add. I'd still have loved to play for the All Blacks, but prosperity and a pretentious car are no longer priorities.

I coached with Alex King in Clermont, and it meant a lot when he said in a 2015 interview that 'Joe's got good values, that's his greatest quality. He's constant, so you know exactly where you stand with him and what he expects of you.' Sometimes I think we need to reflect on who we are, rather than obsessing about what we can achieve.

A definition of success that does work for me comes from the legendary UCLA basketball coach John Wooden: 'Success is peace of mind . . . in knowing you made the effort to do your best to become the best that you are capable of becoming.' This definition focuses on self-actualization and the drive to make the best of yourself and to understand what is important to you and to others.

I was at the RDS watching Leinster versus Munster in the Pro14 semi-final at the end of May 2019. An advertisement was played on the big screen at half-time, featuring Johnny Sexton. Johnny said, 'When Joe Schmidt came to Leinster, he was the first person to speak about values; before that it was all about winning.' It was nice to see the message had stuck, because I think it's ideal when the one comes before the other, or, even better, the one contributes to the other.

Dr William Mace, an American clinical psychologist and medical sociologist, wrote that:

> Those who believe, 'It's not whether you win or lose; it's how you play the game,' if one can be found, are looked upon as losers. Whether it's in sports, politics or finance, the most cunning and nefarious are the winners. We admire and celebrate the winners, not the losers.

It's an uncomfortable reality that we so often admire people not for their character but for the results they achieve, regardless of how they got the result and who they may have trampled on along the way. There is no doubt that there are plenty of high-achieving sportspeople with integrity, but there have also been some very high-profile controversies where athletes have tried to circumvent the rules and have been found out. Mixing with coaches from many different codes and at many different levels, I think that the vast majority of them still attempt to play by the rules and treat opponents with respect, while trying to get the scoreboard result at the same time.

Sporting achievements generate a sense of reflective pride. Supporters are likely to identify positively with teams that show endeavour, that work hard and perform consistently well. In the pre-season with Leinster in 2010, we focused on the behaviours we thought would best ensure that we'd be both hard-working and enterprising. It was all about who we could become, not what we could achieve. Will Durant summarized the thoughts of Aristotle when he wrote, 'We are what we repeatedly do. Excellence, then, is not an act but a habit.' This idea underpinned what we aspired to create at Leinster.

When I was at Bay of Plenty, Vern Cotter insisted that each person in the squad greet the others with a handshake at the start of the day. It is a French custom, and VC had picked it up and formed the habit himself. It was the same in Clermont, and I had adopted the habit myself, so it was easy enough to encourage the Leinster squad to embrace it. The daily handshake and acknowledgement was an ideal way to create a closer connection between the fully professional players and the Academy lads. It must have been reassuring and motivating for the young players when the likes of Brian O'Driscoll, Nathan Hines or Jamie Heaslip greeted them by name.

At the end of that first season, I remember sifting through the review documents that came back from the players. We'd managed to get through an incredibly tough group in the Heineken Cup, which included Clermont, Saracens and Racing Metro, before accounting for Leicester in the quarter-final, then Toulouse in a see-saw battle in the semi-final before turning around that record half-time deficit in the final against Northampton. We'd played some really positive strike plays and multi-phase attacking rugby and we'd combined organization with admirable resilience in defence, so I thought that there would be plenty of positive feedback on the strategy or skills that we'd focused upon. The feedback was positive in these areas, but the most commonly referenced affirmative change we'd made was the handshake and greeting at the start of the day!

The professional players recognized that they relied upon the Academy players to challenge them during training sessions on the pitch. The more pressure the players could be put under during the week, then the better prepared they would be for matches at the weekend. Acknowledging the younger players and investing a few minutes each day to engage with them or even a few seconds to greet them helped the sense of belief that the Academy players felt, allowing them to grow in confidence. The other bonus was that when the international players were away, the Academy players felt a greater sense of belonging in the group when they were drafted into match-day squads.

The three qualities that the squad decided they most needed to demonstrate were to be:

- Humble
- Disciplined
- Relentless

Stressing the importance of being humble acknowledged the interdependence of individuals within the group. Players would commit to knowing their role and delivering it as best they could, knowing that they were a cog in a wheel and that everyone had to work together to get the wheel turning. It included some specific behaviours, such as not leaving through the side door of the changing room post-match to avoid the crowds, as had sometimes happened in the past. As tired as a player might be, he needed to be conscious of the support that the team received and to be humble enough to acknowledge it by engaging with the supporters.

Being disciplined was about maintaining positive performance behaviours, such as time-keeping, quality nutrition and hydration, committing to recovery protocols, wearing the correct kit and other daily responsibilities. It was also associated with players performing on the pitch, including knowing the laws and the strategy, to make sure that they didn't concede unnecessary penalties or fail to deliver what was required of them at training or during the match.

Being relentless was a mentality more than a value. The players wanted to make sure that their preparation was as relentless as they could make it: that they would keep encouraging themselves and each other to be up to date with whatever they needed to be doing, and to be proactive about fine-tuning their individual skills. Players needed to maintain their concentration in all facets of a match, including actions that didn't require talent, just effort, such as getting up off the ground as quickly as they could to get back into the game with the accuracy and ferocity required.

In review sessions, including what became the infamous Monday reviews, all three of these qualities would be referenced, but none more so than the need to be relentless: the attitude underpinned the high-tempo game that we wanted to play. I had challenged the players to be 'the best passing team in Europe' because they wanted to play with width and speed. They had to be relentless with their passing drills, putting pressure on themselves to make good passes despite limited time and space, while being able to stay balanced and accurate and to be 'big' for a few strides after passing to help hold the space for the player they'd passed to.

The exaggerated reputation for the cold-blooded Monday reviews arose from two meetings, early in that first season. The first was in a backs meeting after we had lost to Treviso in our third match of the season in September 2010. Many of the international players were just starting their season with us and, when Isa Nacewa scored out wide after just a few minutes, it looked promising. Unfortunately, the game – played in persistent rain – got away from us and we were forced to play catch-up in difficult conditions. Running from deep in our own territory, with about a quarter of the game remaining, Gordon D'Arcy made a pass to Brian O'Driscoll that was dipping just below his knees, making it difficult to catch, and Drico knocked it on.

In the meeting, I asked Darce about the pass and he quickly volunteered that it wasn't good enough and that he would make sure that he worked on some focused passing drills during the week to remedy things for the next match. Turning to Drico, I asked him what he thought. He agreed that the pass hadn't been as good as it needed to be but that Darce would get it right next time. When I pushed him a bit further, he looked confused, so I explained that I thought that 'good players take those passes'.

There was silence . . .

I hadn't quite meant to call Drico out the way that I did. I'd shrugged my shoulders when making the point, and I'd been more questioning than forceful. The silence would have been uncomfortable if Drico had allowed it to continue, but he responded, thankfully, and conceded that yes, he could have caught the pass. Phew!

The players haven't let me forget that particular conversation. A few months later, after the Ireland versus New Zealand test match during the November Internationals, I was at the post-match dinner with Kelly. We had caught up with some of the players that I'd coached at the Blues as well as some of the All Blacks' coaching and management staff. As Darce, Drico and Rob Kearney were leaving the dinner they came up to chat. Drico had scored a super try in the match and I mentioned to him how impressive it was that he'd scooped the ball up without breaking stride in the lead-up to scoring. Rob Kearney immediately chimed in with 'Good players scoop those up' – and the quips have continued ever since.

The other meeting was with the full squad, after the Edinburgh game I mentioned earlier, the third loss from our first four league matches. We had been very conscious of their counter-attack threat, especially with Chris Paterson at full-back and Tim Visser on the wing. During the week we worked hard on trying to make sure that our chase line was connected.

Early in the second half, Paterson fielded a clearing kick and launched a mazy 50-metre counter-attacking run which led to Mark Robertson scoring Edinburgh's third try. Paterson breezed past a number of defenders in our fractured chase line – exactly what we'd shown him doing to other teams in clips during the week. We'd committed to working hard, smart and early to make sure that there were no gaps or 'dog-legs' in the line, so I showed the clearing kick and Paterson catching it. The clearing kick was in the air for three or four seconds. I froze the video and highlighted where some of our players were when the kick was made, asking them to let me know where they'd be in five seconds' time. They explained that they should have connected with other players and formed a chase line and progressed up the pitch to close down the space, and they also pointed out where on the pitch they thought they would have got to.

When I froze the video again after three seconds, it showed that a couple of them hadn't even moved and the dog-leg was clearly visible. I might even have been sarcastic and said, 'Fair play, lads, you've been doing some serious speed work because in the next two seconds you're going to get to where we needed you to be?' It was obvious that they were not going to get there in time, and as I played it on in slow motion for the next two seconds, Paterson carved through the gap they'd left. The players cringed.

I explained that it was really up to them if they wanted to commit to what we needed to deliver. They had decided on the values that they were going to demonstrate, and they understood that the behaviours underpinning those values had to be what they 'repeatedly did', not just occasional acts. To be connected in the chase line, there had to be a trust that they were all going to work to get into the line, that we'd work hard enough to make sure that 'effort errors' like the one just shown didn't occur. I left them to ponder that, and we moved on quickly with a huge game against Munster coming up the following weekend. Against Munster, in the newly constructed Aviva Stadium, the players knew that there was some urgency to get things right and to ramp up their individual commitment, because we would be trounced if we didn't.

It may sound simple, but the three precepts allowed us to have a constant reference point. We could reference behaviours during the week and on match days. It formed the foundation for how we played but also for who we were. It ensured accountability, not to me and the other coaches but to a small set of values that they themselves had generated. The coaches became the custodians of the values but so too did the players; they kept each other accountable as much as the coaching staff did.

Ironically, the serious influence of the values also gave rise to some boisterous fun. Having fun adds value in almost any environment, but in the pressure-cooker of professional rugby, fun is particularly welcome. The 'Sheriff', Eoin Reddan, would record any misdemeanours in his notebook during the week. Each Thursday, before the afternoon gym session, the offending players would toss a big fluffy dice over a hurdle in the gym, to make sure that the player couldn't contrive the way that it landed. On each face of the dice there was a punishment, such as a fine (donated to charity), having to wear your formal suit to and from training for two weeks, having to provide toiletries for the squad for the week, and various other ideas that the players came up with to amuse themselves.

The whole ritual became a weekly highlight. I'd hear it from my office: the slow build-up of 'Roll the dice, roll the dice . . .' steadily getting louder as some poor transgressor was about to learn his punishment. I'd hear a whoop, then a momentary pause, then a roar of approval as the player was stung with a punishment or the occasional groan when 'Get out of jail free' came up. It provided a bit of respite from the training regime. Camaraderie is difficult to engineer and it's almost always better if it happens organically.

There is so much that New Zealand rugby do incredibly well, but the player review document that the NZRU used during my time involved with Super Rugby always felt to me like an opportunity for players to dodge some of the accountability for their preparation and performance. I'm pretty sure that the document is different now, but it used to start with an array of questions about various aspects of player support, such as logistics, coaching and medical. It was all about what was provided for them, rather than starting with what they had provided. Our reviews at Leinster and at Ireland have had a very simple format, but they have been unequivocal about where the responsibility for performance starts.

At the end of the summer tour, the November Series or the Six Nations Championship the review was often as simple as responding to the three questions below:

In what ways do you feel you added value to the squad
during the Six Nations?
What can you be working on to add further value?
What worked well in the environment and what do
you think could be changed or added to help us to
do things better?

The questions always start with what the player has contributed. If they can first reflect on what they did well and what they added, or what more they could have added, then that hopefully becomes their default mechanism: to first look at themselves and then at what others can do to help them. It's also important that information gathered can be acted on, and not just filed or forgotten. For me, review is continuous and should start informally with self-review and peer review. Among the coaches, we view each other's presentations or segments of training, sometimes contributing, and then chat about how clearly messages were delivered, how energized we were or how responsive the players were.

We have tried different methods of collecting players' thoughts. One of these was called the 'Quickfire Continuum':

Quickfire Continuum

Character (Self-absorbed, fragile)   (Honest, resilient, empathetic)

   0   1   2   3   4   5   6   7   8   9   10

Self-awareness (Unaware, unsure)   (Know yourself utterly)

   0   1   2   3   4   5   6   7   8   9   10

Purpose (Floating, uncertain)   (Clear, driven, resolute)

   0   1   2   3   4   5   6   7   8   9   10

Athletic profile (Substandard)   (Ideal body comp, core, power, speed, durability)

   0   1   2   3   4   5   6   7   8   9   10

Mental skills (Fragile, poor control)   (Mindful, tough, focused)

   0   1   2   3   4   5   6   7   8   9   10

Recovery/recuperation (Haphazard)   (Personalized, diligent)

   0   1   2   3   4   5   6   7   8   9   10

Preparation for training (Irregular, casual)   (Planned, targeted, habitual)

   0   1   2   3   4   5   6   7   8   9   10

Esprit de corps (Passive, individual, stale)   (Actively involved, united, loyal)

   0   1   2   3   4   5   6   7   8   9   10

Commitment to role (Automating role in team, setpiece, phase play, defence)

   0   1   2   3   4   5   6   7   8   9   10

Commitment to team (Preparing yourself/others, sharing solutions, trust, work rate)

0   1   2   3   4   5   6   7   8   9   10

Discipline (Sleep hygiene, punctual, kit, nutrition, hydration, planning, laws, detail)

0   1   2   3   4   5   6   7   8   9   10

Onfield performance (Walk-throughs, training, skills, provincial and test matches)

0   1   2   3   4   5   6   7   8   9   10

First, the players assessed themselves. Then they assessed the team. Next, each player was handed a new sheet with a different player's name on it, so he could offer some feedback to that player before, finally, choosing a player that they'd like to give some feedback to and repeating the exercise. Each player received a bar graph of his results, which clearly indicated any inconsistencies between their own perceptions and the perceptions others had of them.

These results and other feedback that we accumulated, such as video clips of positive actions as well as actions or inaction that could be improved upon, were ideal discussion-starters. One particular player, who had assessed his self-awareness to be very high, received quite different feedback from his team-mates. In discussion with the player, I broached the discrepancy. He replied, 'Hmm, I'm not sure why that is, maybe they just don't know me well enough?' I'm not sure we solved the dilemma, that perhaps he didn't know himself as well as he thought, but at least we got to start the conversation.

I don't set personal goals, not because I don't believe that they can be helpful but because I think adding value works better for me than chasing targets does. I meet many young coaches or ambitious players who state their goals and affirm their commitment to them, and I can see how that might help drive them. The risk for me is that if those goals become too much of a focus, they have the potential to compromise some of their values. There's also a risk that the coach or athlete becomes so focused on achieving their goal, it actually distracts them from getting the process right or narrows their focus too much toward what they want, excluding other people or other opportunities.

For example, I once met a young coach who had mapped out his pathway. At the time he was coaching an All Ireland League team in the second division, but he was also helping with a provincial age-grade team, and his plan was to lead the age-grade coaching team within the next two seasons and then to use that as a springboard to getting a job either with a national age-group team or to get a role in one of the provinces.

The problem with this formula is that the coach was looking to add value to himself, rather than focusing his energy on adding value to the people he was coaching. I'm sure that this coach was doing a good job but, in the end, a coach's progress is due to the performances and feedback from players.

In the words of Elvis Presley, 'Values are like fingerprints. Nobody's are the same, but you leave 'em all over everything you do.' Having good values provides a solid foundation upon which the team culture can be built. If I've managed to leave behind some positive values in the coaching roles that I've had, then at least I might be getting closer to the 'peace of mind' that John Wooden describes.

12. Identity

Who we are is how we play.
                                        Vodafone Ireland

Understanding who we are and what's important to us can help us to feel a sense of self-worth and belonging when we're part of a group. In every good team that I have been involved with, the team has had an identifiable culture and players have had a genuine understanding of who they are within the team, who the team represents and what they expect from themselves and others within the team.

Playing senior club rugby for High School Old Boys in the Manawatu, we were labelled the Toffs because there was a perception that we were a wealthy club and that we had a sense of entitlement about us. Part of that perception was that we would be a bit fragile if the opposition started getting stuck into us. When we travelled to country towns like Feilding, Rongotea or Kimbolton, where the rugged freezing workers or farmers dominated the team sheets, they would tear into us: stereotypical robust and confrontational country folk roughing up the softer, fancy-skilled city folk. There were no TMOs and the rucking was vigorous. Even mates who I played with in the provincial team at the time offered no quarter because that's who they believed they were and that was who we expected them to be.

In the city, College Old Boys were viewed as working men,

harder-edged and more able to cope with any ramped-up physical approach during the game. There were families with a history in the club who were uncompromising and incredibly good at the game. In the mid-1980s, they accumulated an almost inconceivable forty-nine consecutive senior club victories, but were narrowly toppled by a talented Marist side in their quest for a fiftieth. The Marist coach, Robin O'Neill, was a gentleman and a man-manager who made people feel good about themselves.

Each club side had an identity, and being the Toffs we needed to alter the expectations we had of ourselves by developing a harder edge. With the likes of Rolf Leonards, Braeden Whitelock, Glenn 'Griz' Manahi, Kerry Whale and a number of other hard-nosed players, astutely coached by Ian Colquhoun, we became more combative. We began to expect more from ourselves, and so did others, including our opponents.

People are influenced by the expectations placed upon them. Robert Rosenthal studied the influence that expectations have and defined the 'Pygmalion effect' as 'the phenomenon whereby one person's expectation for another person's behaviour comes to serve as a self-fulfilling prophecy'. Furthermore, 'when we expect certain behaviours of others, we are likely to act in ways that make the expected behaviour more likely to occur.' It's easy enough to think of examples of this. Obviously, if you expect to get beaten and your opponent expects to win, then they might play with greater confidence, which confirms your belief that they're superior, and this perception contributes to the self-fulfilling prophecy that Rosenthal describes. Sometimes, as was the case with High School Old Boys, it's necessary to make a conscious effort to overcome the Pygmalion effect.

In Bay of Plenty, the team are known as the Steamers because of the geothermal wonders that exist within the region: bubbling mud pools and naturally coloured springs, with water that is famed for the benefits of its mineral content. The province has a high Māori population and the team were well able to create their own 'steam', with a mix of speed, skill and physical aggression.

For players, identifying with their region and the people they represent is often a good starting place for developing a shared identity. In Māori, the concept of *Tūrangawaewae* is a powerful part of a person's identity. It translates as 'standing place for the feet' and it is the solid piece of earth upon which an individual can feel empowered and connected. I think there is a depth to the strength of purpose that can be established when starting from a strong, tangible base.

Steamers midfielder Grant McQuoid, speaking in an interview ten years after the Ranfurly Shield success of 2004, talked about the camaraderie among players, emphasizing 'how close we became as a team, as mates. We just started playing really well for each other.' He spoke also of the team's 'chemistry' – 'if they could bottle what we had, they would' – and he mentioned that VC and I 'got the very best out of guys that maybe weren't superstars'. For me, though, it was the players' shared understanding of who they were and who they were representing which crystallized their purpose and consolidated the trust and commitment among them. From the first team meeting that I attended, when Paul Tupai welcomed me as I entered the room, I sensed a collective purpose that I'm sure others felt, and I think it formed the foundation for the competitive unit we became.

All three of the secondary schools that I taught in stressed the importance of their history and culture, and they continue to do so today. The young men involved in the elite sporting teams understand the school traditions and are conscious of the community that they are representing. The students also build close-knit friendships, so representing their school team means something to them as a group, which helps them to stick together and to strive with a collective purpose.

The difficulty for some teams is that they are not as connected. The catchment area for the Blues encompasses the sprawl of Auckland City and continues all the way up to the northern tip of the country. When I was involved in the coaching team there, the diversity of backgrounds in the group meant that it was more challenging to develop a shared identity and, while the players committed to each other and to the tasks required during training and matches, they weren't as connected socially or emotionally. At least the Blues now have a permanent training base, but players are domiciled in different communities within the city and, looking on from a distance, it still seems to be a challenge for them to develop the sort of tight-knit culture that other teams profit from.

When it comes to the All Blacks, there is such a tradition of success and support that the identity remains strong. Simon Poidevin, who played twenty-one test matches for Australia against the All Blacks during the 1980s and 1990s, felt that 'in New Zealand it is not just their national sport, it's part of their national identity.' In the age of professionalism, the All Blacks have worked very hard not to dilute that identity. The understanding of who they are and who they represent seems to have deepened, if anything. The All Blacks' dominance and the aura that surrounds them continues to galvanize their players, while intimidating their opponents.

New Zealanders feel a collective pride in the resilience,

skill and commitment of their national rugby representatives. It's a symbiotic Pygmalion effect: the players raise their expectations based on the high expectations of their support base, and the supporters are inspired and motivated by what the All Blacks achieve. Beauden Barrett said in an interview that 'From the very first game I watched the All Blacks and saw the haka, I knew straight away that was part of who I am.' The words in the modern All Black haka *Kapo o Pango* (Team in Black) stress the link between the players and the land. After beginning with *Kia rite, Kia rite, Kia mau*, meaning 'Get ready, get ready, hold fast,' the next line is *Ki-a-whaka-whenua au i a hau!*, which is 'Let me be one with the land.' A veteran of fifty test matches, Aaron Cruden, explains that the haka offers the opportunity to gain 'strength from the guys beside us, from the ground that we stand on'. Those connections – to the land, to their ancestors and to each other – are a key part of what the All Black identity is built upon, and it remains strong and relevant to the current crop of players.

In his book *The Culture Code*, Daniel Coyle discusses work from a research team led by Peter Fischer which found that 'Thinking about your ancestors makes you smarter … spending a few minutes contemplating your family tree (as opposed to contemplating a friend, or a shopping list, or nothing at all) significantly boosted performance on tests of cognitive intelligence. Their hypothesis is that thinking about our connections to the group increases our feelings of autonomy and control.' This probably needs further testing, but it's an interesting concept when considering the resilience required to sustain performance throughout the season and from season to season. It certainly suggests that having players define and grow their understanding of what is really important to them and the connections that they share, both past and present, can be beneficial.

When I arrived in Clermont-Ferrand, VC was searching for something tangible to bring the squad together in pursuit of the Bouclier de Brennus. The squad included players from twelve different nationalities, and some of the players were new to the team and to France, just as I was.

With some local guidance, VC focused on an historic battle in which Vercingétorix, chieftain of the Arverni tribe, united the Gauls to defeat Julius Caesar in the Battle of Gergovia, fought on the Gergovie Plateau 15 kilometres south of Clermont-Ferrand.

Looking to unite the team, just as Vercingétorix had united the Gallic tribes, VC retold the history, including the inspiring inscription on a monument erected by Napoleon III, which quotes Caesar:

> *La Gaule unie*
> *Formant une seule nation*
> *Animée d'un même esprit,*
> *Peut défier l'Univers.*

Translated, it reads: 'Gaul united, forming a single nation, animated by a common spirit, can challenge the Universe.' VC urged the diverse group of players to unite, with a common spirit and a shared purpose. It helped sustain their commitment to working hard for themselves and for others in the team in the quest to be crowned French champions and to claim the Bouclier de Brennus.

Arriving at Leinster, I felt that there was already a strong sense of identity. They had conquered Europe and, internally, there was a strong core of players who knew what they wanted to achieve.

Many strong friendships ensured that there were solid connections between players, although the really strong connections tended to be in pockets or smaller groups. I was told that some of these cliques had been detrimental to the group in the past, but by the time that I arrived, through the efforts of Michael Cheika and some positive player leadership, they were much less visible.

A shared identity doesn't mean that you have to share the same interests or undertake the same activities. The players were from different generations and were at different stages of their careers, but I think that the shared purpose was embedded more deeply due to the collective awareness of who they were as a group and what it meant to them to represent their team and their province.

The authenticity of purpose that exists in Leinster is one of the key factors in their sustained success. They have been European Champions four times over the past eleven seasons. And yet, after the hostile takeover and revamp of the European Rugby Cup (ERC) by European Professional Club Rugby (EPCR), there were a number of doomsday articles written, one of which claimed that 'it is nearly impossible to get out of your group now.' A lack of top-class foreign talent was regularly cited as the key reason why Irish provincial teams were no longer going to be competitive. There was little discussion of the need to grow local talent to make sure that the provinces stayed competitive.

Despite these exaggerated fears, the following season Munster and Leinster topped their pools and Connacht finished equal with French powerhouse Toulouse on 18 points, missing qualification narrowly on points differential. Leinster and Munster were toppled by two very good teams in Saracens and Clermont respectively. Even better, Leinster went on to win the title the following year. All four Irish provinces got out of their groups in 2019, with two making it to the Champions Cup semi-finals and Leinster being beaten in the final. Leinster had two foreign players in their match-day squad for each of the last two European finals. Both players were very good contributors, but that means that the other twenty-one players in the match-day squads were more locally sourced.

In an interview prior to the Rugby World Cup in 2015, England head coach Stuart Lancaster said that 'To create a team identity, you've got to understand it first of all. The history of it, the motivators, the drivers, the key anchors and that will drive your behaviour.' While a few variables conspired against England in 2015, Stuart Lancaster's understanding of team identity and culture, along with his coaching abilities, have obviously helped add positive value to Leinster over the past few years.

In his book *The Score Takes Care of Itself*, Bill Walsh, the legendary former coach of the San Francisco 49ers, emphasizes the need for coaches to create a team culture richer and more prosperous than that of the opposition. Knowing who you are and what's important to you will help consolidate the team values, the way that players interact and the shared purpose which drives them. Players have to contribute to defining who they are as a group and what is important to them. There have to be concrete reference points or behaviours; gimmicks or empty phrases will become 'white noise' and essentially meaningless. The reference points and behaviours have to be adopted by the whole group and reinforced regularly.

Coming into the Irish national team after an injury-ravaged season and a fifth placing in the Six Nations, I felt that there was a sense of frustration among the players that they weren't as unified as they needed to be. I had read quite a lot of the history of Ireland, and it seemed to me that if the Irish people had been more united, they could have had greater control of their own destiny. I expressed this idea to Professor Diarmaid Ferriter at University College Dublin. I think my naivety sparked his interest, and he agreed to address the squad.

Diarmaid began his address with a story of his very early days as a student at UCD. In his first history lecture, the lecturer walked into the theatre and posed the question: 'What is an Irishman?' The lecturer left then, without saying anything more. Diarmaid told us, 'You know . . . I've been trying to answer that question ever since.' He was the ideal catalyst to encourage the players to reflect on what characteristics made them Irish and how they might define themselves.

Through the first autumn series with the Irish squad in 2013, we only really had time to get ourselves organized, so that the players had a pretty good idea of what their roles and responsibilities were on the pitch; but during the Six Nations we pushed a bit harder for the players to demonstrate what it meant to be 'Irish'. Winning the Six Nations in the Stade de France was incredible, especially as the game ended on a knife edge, with us clinging to a two-point lead; but what followed was memorable as well.

After the celebrations and trophy presentation, Paul O'Connell got up to speak at the post-match dinner. He completed the standard pleasantries and then paused. He stated that at the start of the season the team had been challenged to define what an Irishman was, and he referenced a number of very positive traits that, ideally, would identify someone as an Irishman. I cannot remember them all, but courage and resilience were two of them. Then he added, 'And today, we say farewell to an Irishman,' with 'Irishman' emphasized to suggest that this individual was quintessentially Irish and representative of all the positive traits that Paul had listed. Brian O'Driscoll had just played his final test match. Drico was seated at the next table and I saw that his eyes had moistened. It was a special moment and tremendously well delivered by Paul.

Beyond that first season, we were keen to anchor ourselves to something solid. We decided that Newgrange would be an ideal 'standing place for the feet' or symbol for what we could aspire to create. We introduced the idea by doing a 'Big Picture' activity. A stylized image of Newgrange with the sunlight hitting the back of the chamber was chopped into twenty pieces and the players were asked to follow instructions to draw and paint each large segment in isolation. At the same time, they needed to make sure each piece connected up with the others. It's a little bit similar to what has to happen on the pitch, where different components of the performance need to be connected as seamlessly as possible. Not knowing what the overall picture looked like, players had to communicate with other groups to try to ensure that lines connected and the paint colours that they were mixing were similar. It was an entertaining activity, and the 'Big Picture' has hung in our gym since, with a copy being made for the team room when we are in camp.

Newgrange was constructed over 5,000 years ago, making it older than Stonehenge and the Great Pyramids of Giza. It is an incredible feat of engineering, which would have required meticulous planning and cohesive teamwork, in transporting and manoeuvring the huge kerbstones that form the base of the structure, and in aligning it so that the sun extends to the back of the 19-metre chamber at the winter solstice. It's almost impossible to understand how a Neolithic farming community could have coordinated their manpower and successfully undertaken such a feat of engineering. Newgrange endures as a testament to the ingenuity and collective effort of those who built it, and the challenge to our players was to build something equally well engineered.

To help engineer the alignment and accuracy of our performances for every test match, the players from the Irish squad do their Mind Gym workout. Similar to the physical workouts, the players are encouraged and, if needed, guided through mental workouts, to build confidence, to repair errors and to hone their speed of thought and action.

Each match week, there is a new Mind Gym posted on the team laptops. There are relaxation cues and examples of how to plan their Mind Gym slots during the week. There may be some examples of positive self-talk or cues to help players to stay moment-focused and not be distracted by an error. Players are encouraged to rehearse their key roles in the Mind Gym before delivering their roles in training, so that accuracy can be the best we can make it and we don't waste time having to repeat plays.

Using the Mind Gym, a player will first get themselves as relaxed as possible, using whatever relaxation techniques they find most effective. It may be as simple as focusing on their breath and calming their mind. Then they might look to start with a few mental 'reps' to boost their confidence, visualizing a few of their best involvements in recent games, slowing them down and 'reliving' them through the imagery they construct. It's a great way to do some extra contact work, stimulating the same neural pathways but without the punishing physical toll of the contact. This ability to mentally prepare has become part of the identity of the group: players expect each other to be mentally prepared, in order to enhance their physical performance.

Maintaining a group's identity is a shared responsibility. If team members contribute and commit to a set of positive behaviours that best represent who they are, it strengthens their sense of belonging and the collective purpose is driven from within.

13. The Game

Rugby is a game for barbarians played by gentlemen.
Football is a game for gentlemen played by barbarians.
Attributed to Oscar Wilde

Growing up through New Zealand winters, waiting for the weekend and the opportunity to play rugby, I revelled in the freedom of getting hold of the ball and running, the challenge of physically pitting myself against others and the exhilaration of scoring tries. As we got a bit older, we progressed from being self-invested to being more team oriented. Structure and specialization were gradually incorporated so that we could make the best use of the land available to us, and those best suited to different roles could become more proficient at them.

The appeal of the game was partly due to the heroes we had, from club and provincial rugby stars through to the All Blacks at the summit of world rugby. It was also the people that we played with, the friends we grew up with and the experiences that we shared: training, travelling and playing together. The friendships were strengthened by the physical commitment that we made. From a young age, knowing that others were relying on you to make your tackles or to make good decisions, whether you had the ball or were running a support line or making a pass, all contributed to an interdependence and sense of collective endeavour.

As youngsters we weren't really coached too much, we just played the game and received a bit of advice afterwards, which most often included a bit of praise and an ice-cream on the way home. We learned the game through playing. Skills were honed during lunchtime games of touch rugby, 'Bullrush' or 'Force back', which was a kicking game where you would force opponents back by kicking into space. The opposition would have to return the kick from where they fielded it, unless they caught it on the full, in which case they could take three steps (or giant leaps) forward before launching their kick. To score, you had to kick the ball between the posts. Often the rule would be that you had to use a drop goal to score. Hence, skill development was incorporated into informal but competitive games which we enjoyed playing.

In my second year at Tararua College, my English teacher was an American, Karl Wieneke. We enjoyed his quick wit, and he had an anecdote or maxim for most occasions. He enjoyed American sports but had grown fond of rugby and we would sometimes have conversations during class after big matches. When someone brought up soccer in an attempt to include it in the discussion one day, he was quickly silenced by Mr Wieneke's succinct remark that '"Soccer is a game played with the outside of the head, rugby is played with the inside of the head," so let's stick to a game based on strategy and intellect to stimulate the mind!' The riposte was well received in the rugby-dominated classroom, but both games require plenty of thinking and I've spent countless hours contemplating strategy on the sports field, over many years.

I've got to admit that I didn't think too much about what I was doing when I played, or what most of my teammates were doing for that matter, but since I first got involved with coaching, strategy and tactics have whirred around in my head. I enjoy the challenge of trying to construct plays or systems in an attempt to get the right people into the right positions to best create opportunities or exert pressure. There is always a danger of being too structured, where a team can lapse into 'PlayStation rugby', which is too predictable and doesn't encourage individual players to seize opportunities that may arise. It's a balance: to coordinate the fifteen players on the pitch, so that they have some awareness of where others are likely to be and what they will be trying to do, mixed with an ability to adapt, react and play on instinct.

I think that doing the basics better than others is a good starting point. At a conference I attended a few years ago, a battalion chief in the New York Fire Department, Chris Eysser, was talking about fatality reports and reflected on a couple of examples where the basics were overlooked and tragedy occurred. 'Fatality reports – it's always basics! So, basics are the priority, the base for minimizing risk,' he emphasized. On the rugby pitch, doing the basics well doesn't just minimize risk, it can also maximize opportunity. Strong body positions and connections in the scrum, timing and elevation of the lift in the lineout, and the execution of the right pass at the right moment can all offer the opportunity to attack with the ball on the front foot.

Prioritizing a key skill helps to provide a collective focus, which can offer a competitive advantage. I watched plenty of footage of the Leinster players before starting our pre-season training in 2010. The key players had said to me that they were keen to play with more width, referencing the way that Clermont moved the ball wide. In Clermont, a number of the players in the backline were accomplished passers of the ball, especially Brock James and Marius Joubert: transferring the ball wide, with flat and accurate passes, was something that they were very good at. I felt that some of the Leinster players were very capable but didn't have the same width to their passing game, and that was where the challenge for them to become the 'best passing team in Europe' came from.

The players committed to the task with some good pressured repetition, and while their technique varied – from the long-armed, lower loading of the ball by Johnny Sexton to the exaggerated elevation of the elbow by Ian Madigan – it was fine-tuning rather than the revolutionizing of their passing technique that we focused upon. We used basic drills and cues to get players to stay balanced and to get their top hand through to the target, while minimizing their upper-body rotation. The players were encouraged to reshape the ball in their hands to allow them to rotate their wrists and 'rip' their fingers across the ball to spiral it with enough torque and momentum to flatten the flight of the pass, rather than lobbing or heaving wide passes.

Without doubt, getting the basics right is important, but I think there's a risk of getting mired in the specifics of 'correct' technique. People move differently, and it is often more about getting the job done effectively rather than getting it done correctly. Sometimes you have to go back and try to reconstruct technique that is inherently flawed, but other times, when coaches break skills down and insist on technical adjustments, they can distract players. In fast-moving traffic, or when being manhandled, players are often not in total control of their movements. Rather than search for what's perfect, it might be better to aim for what's 'practical'.

During the twenty-five years that I've been coaching, rugby has changed a lot, as have my ideas about the game. The more I've watched, learned and experienced, the more I've tried to simplify things. I've watched players get bored

with skill repetitions that are slowed down or done in isolation and I've questioned how effective these drills are
when applied to the chaos of the game at full speed and full
impact. There are windows prior to training for individual
skill work, but once we start a session we try to keep the
pressure on players, squeezing their time and space. We
minimize contact but keep the threat of it uppermost in the
minds of the players so that they can be realistic about timing and momentum, encouraging them to visualize or
imagine the full impact when a defender gets well set to
stop them.

Rory Best recently described what I'm like during the
training sessions that we have with Ireland. 'He is probably
the first coach I have worked with that has been able to
get . . . look, you can never get the same level of pressure that
you get on a Saturday afternoon, at training. But he gets very
close to it. And he gets very close to it by the way he is, the
way he shouts, the way he moves around.' I explain to players
that we are trying to replicate match situations and that we
are going to put them under pressure so that they're better
able to cope in the furnace that test rugby can be.

The Tackle

Having players, especially young players, tackle as safely as
possible was a priority. I tried to connect up some of the
cues that had worked best for me when I was playing. Ian
Colquhoun had drilled into us that the tackle was about
keeping our heads up and our eyes open, and being quick on
our feet to get good shoulder contact and a tight grip on the
ball carrier. The formula was simple, and certainly helped a

scrawny player like me to compete with some combative opponents.

In contrast, the more I saw coaches slowing the tackle down and encouraging players to get 'cheek to cheek' contact, the less convinced I was of its efficacy. Encouraging the tackler to get their cheek on to the 'butt cheek' of the ball carrier often resulted in them turning their head away or putting their head down too early, and in the micro-seconds before contact a butt cheek could too easily become a hip or other hard point of the body. It's natural for us to turn our head away and close our eyes when contact near the head is imminent and it's important to reprogramme that reaction as best we can, so that we can see any late movement and make the adjustments required.

Using the 'eyes and feet' helps to get positive tackle entry, and I still drive this mantra with players. Even when first arriving in Leinster and seeing us slip off tackles early on, I asked the players for their thoughts on what was uppermost in their minds when loading into the tackle. The first response was to get good shoulder contact and the next was to drive their legs in the tackle. These are positive *outcomes*, but players need to get into good positions to deliver these. I explained to them the 'eyes and feet' rationale, and then the need to get the shoulder into the impact and 'bite' with the arms immediately on contact.

I'm sure there are other formulae that work for people but, realistically, no technique is foolproof when players are moving at speed. There are plenty of variables that can destabilize the tackler, but if these four cues – eyes, feet, shoulder, bite – can be programmed with some positive repetition and encouragement, they can help a player who's struggling with their tackle entry. Building their confidence to be decisive and to keep their eyes open is important, so that they don't drop or reach too early and offer the ball carrier a target.

One fear that I have about the game is that well-intentioned rule adjustments might potentially create further risk for players. The current focus on high tackles is understandable, but its application and some of the demands being placed on the tackler are concerning.

World Rugby has constructed a framework for determining the sanctions for any tackle that makes contact with the head or neck, including those tackles which slip up off a lower part of the body or slip up off the ball. The framework is an attempt to help referees make more consistent decisions and to help keep players safer.

When HIA (Head Injury Assessment) events were retrospectively classified, based on video evidence from 2013 to 2015 across the major competitions played at club and international level, 611 HIAs were recorded. Of those, 464 of the suspected head injuries came in the tackle. It was understandable that World Rugby's focus area became the tackle, but I think it's equally relevant that three quarters of head-injury assessments are performed on the *tackler*. There's a danger of becoming overly focused on high tackles at the cost of missing other examples of dangerous play. Increasing sanctions in an attempt to solve one problem can often contribute to other problems. In this case, creating a fear of making any high contact will inevitably cause tacklers to go lower in the tackle, even when it's not the right type of tackle to execute.

The England second-row Maro Itoje expressed his frustration in an interview in January 2019, saying that rugby administrators 'are not using rugby intelligence'. He explained further: 'I think more of the concussions . . . come from when players go too low. That is the irony. You go low and you have the full force of elbows and knees, you have your forearm to attack someone's head, so maybe it is being looked at from the wrong angle.' For me, Maro's point is valid and, while World Rugby are under pressure to make the game safer, I think their first consideration needs to be *primum non nocere*, 'first do no harm'.

I've spoken to a number of other coaches who share similar concerns with the framework, especially after seeing the way it was applied in the Junior World Cup in Argentina earlier this year. In just thirty matches at the tournament, twenty-six cards were handed out for dangerous tackles: five red cards and twenty-one yellow cards. Of these, four of the red cards and sixteen of the yellow cards were for high tackles. These interventions were heralded by World Rugby as an affirmative course of action in the interests of player welfare, but of the twenty-six heavily sanctioned tackles, none of the ball carriers required an HIA or suffered any injury.

More recently, there were three concussions in the 2019 Rugby Championship, all in the tackle and all by low tacklers. The heads of James Slipper, Jordan Uelese and Faf de Klerk collided with knees or hips as they attempted low tackles.

The RFU, despite reservations expressed by players and coaches, lowered the legal tackle height for matches in the Championship Cup, part of the second-tier competition in England. It was a hastily put-together trial, with tackles having to be below the level of the armpits. But the data showed that concussion rates were increasing, and the trial was abandoned in the interest of player safety. The RFU's acting Chief Executive Officer, Nigel Melville, explained the realization that they needed to 'be careful we don't have unintended consequences: you lower the tackle to solve one problem and you create another'.

If the tackler is allowed to choose how he enters the tackle, without unreasonable fear of sanction for accidental high contact, the ball carrier is kept guessing. But if the ball carrier knows that the tackler must go low, he can target the collision with a significant advantage. Despite the Championship Cup study being described as an 'extremely valuable exercise', I'm not so sure that the players who suffered concussions would agree.

In recent years we have played in matches where shoulder charges, late tackles and high swinging-arm tackles have failed to be appropriately sanctioned. Two games in particular stand out, in which we had players injured and out of the game for a number of weeks along with some pretty sickening concussions. I'm very conscious of how difficult it is for referees, their assistant referees and the TMO to see everything that happens on the pitch, and the targeting of foul play is a positive step by World Rugby, but they have to be constantly alert for any unintended consequences when focusing on one particular aspect of the game.

Sanctioning high tackles is important to modify tackler behaviour and to protect players, but it can't become such a driving force that it makes players more vulnerable and increases their risk of injury. Coaching players to be in control during the micro-seconds prior to contact will help, but I think that, like the tackler, World Rugby need to keep their 'eyes open'.

Big Rocks

It wasn't until I shifted to Leinster that I really took responsibility for setting up the full attacking and defensive structure for a professional team. It was an intimidating venture, but I had a clear idea about prioritizing the breakdown. I first heard Graham Henry describe the breakdown as the 'heart' of the game at a Super Rugby conference, and it made good sense to me. With the ruck being the most common source of possession in the game, it pumps the lifeblood into your attack. The more efficiently the heart functions, the greater the capacity for the ball to be circulated to different parts of the pitch.

Coaching at Top 14 level in France, it was compulsory to complete the Diplôme de l'Éducation Populaire et du Sport (DEPS). It included a number of three-day courses at the Fédération Française de Rugby training base in Marcoussis, Paris, as well as a major project detailing the planning, preparation and performance for an elite team for the entire season. It was a big assignment, especially when I was already so busy with the weekly coaching commitments of the Top 14. Much of the focus was on systems, such as defensive placement, alignment and movement and, on the other side of the ball, the *circulation offensive des jouers*, which focused on where players went in the attacking framework.

One presentation that had a telling impact for me was a statistical and technical study that had been done on ball retention. The focus had been on the ball carrier and the arriving players, and the results were prescient. Retaining the ball relied upon what the ball carrier did 60 per cent of the time, the next arriving player had a 20 per cent influence, and others who arrived or were involved after that had a 20 per cent influence.

The attacking kerbstones or 'Big Rocks' in the teams I've coached since I saw that presentation have been the ball carrier, followed by the two closest players. The ball carrier's ability to be dynamic on his feet as well as on the ground has been crucial, while the next two players, whose job it is to clean out any threats or to brace themselves over the ball carrier to ensure that the ball is secure, have allowed us to be highly successful in keeping the ball and processing it effectively. The 60/20/20 statistics gave me something tangible to sell the message to the players with.

When starting as the Ireland coach, I presented my ideas to the 'rugby sub-committee' of the IRFU. For my predecessors, it had been a requirement to present the strategy for test matches the evening prior to the test, so that the rugby sub-committee could assess the effectiveness of the strategy the following day. My presentation was a 'one-off' compromise to avoid the regular pre-test meetings, and I explained the very simple approach that I was looking to implement. The focus for the team would not be on any framework or systems for playing the game, but on the 'Big Rocks' that we'd build our game upon. That we would be focused on the security and speed of our ruck ball, based on the quality of the work done by the ball carrier and the players who clean out the ruck. If we could get the collision area sorted, then we could grow our game from there.

I explained to the rugby sub-committee that we were going to try to be better than anyone else in the contact area. I emphasized that it had been the key priority in our attack at Leinster and it had allowed us to get better-quality possession, which then gave us better opportunities to attack on the front foot. We would rely on our ball carrier keeping his ball focus from the start to the end of the carry. That they would commit to being square and strong into the contact, then fight their way through the contact, before being dynamic on the ground to offer the best-quality ball that they could. That their 'Body/Ball' would make them the most effective '60 per cent men' in the game.

When I was coaching with Bay of Plenty, we had Lipi Sinnott come in for our first pre-season training week and I remember him drilling the players on 'body first, ball last'. He was a rugby jack-of-all-trades, who had been masseur for the All Blacks as well as masseur and assistant manager of the Hurricanes Super Rugby team. He'd worked alongside some very good coaches, and I picked up the phrase from him before truncating it to 'Body/Ball'.

When Paul O'Connell's book *The Battle* was published, he rang me to apologize for being too specific about the detail he'd included on 'Body/Ball'. I wasn't too concerned, because the concept had leaked out over the years and it wasn't a groundbreaking revelation. But he summarized it well:

> When we were on our backs with the ball after carrying, he wanted us to contort, rotate, swivel – it was about stopping a poacher from getting on us. Great coaching is often about imagery and cues. Joe told us that he wanted us to be like the mackerel that had just been pulled in and was jumping around on the boat. It was the first part of what he called 'Body Ball'. The second part was about making sure your ball placement was good. It was so effective that I used to find myself commenting in my head a split second before I hit the ground. 'Body Ball!'

Aligned with the 'Body/Ball' were the 'barrels': the first two men arriving at the attacking breakdown. Again, the imagery and cues were an important way to help embed the concept. We associated the actions with having both barrels loaded, and the targeting was crucial. We wanted to fire in at point-blank range but with our eyes open, aware of our ball carrier but focused on any threat that an opponent might present. The barrels trusted the ball carrier to look after the ball, and their job was to look after the ball carrier. Ideally, with good anticipation and targeting, we could fire through lower and quicker than the nearest opponent or, if necessary, we could get the strong 'bite' needed to hit, grip and roll the threat out of the breakdown, or at least to wrench them off their feet so that they could not play the ball.

At meetings we showed footage of tries that we scored, where a few rucks before the try a ball carrier had done some great work on the ground or where the impact of the barrels had helped to create quick ball, which caused stress for the defence. I remember showing some tremendous barrels from the lead-up to the drop goal in Paris that started our march to the Grand Slam, including one from Fergus McFadden where his body position was spot on and his hostility visible. Building our attack on actions like these allowed us not just to retain the ball but to accelerate the play. Then, if we did break the line, as we did in the second test against Australia in Melbourne later that year, we had to make sure that brilliance didn't get let down by a failure to do the basics. Tadhg Furlong's barrel on David Pocock was impressive, with his chest slamming through the point of impact to jar Pocock out of the contest. The constant selling point was that you didn't apply pressure by *keeping* the ball, you applied pressure by creating *quick* ball.

Statistics never tell the full story, but I know that we have regularly topped the ball-retention numbers in international rugby. Some would say that it's because we tend to offload less than other teams, but at the same time we make more passes than any other team. We prioritized personal responsibility for looking after the ball and for looking after the ball carrier. We played well against England in 2014, losing by just three points in a high-quality game of rugby at Twickenham. In that game we retained possession in 93.5 per cent of the 108 rucks that we had. The following year, we retained possession in over 98 per cent of the 118 rucks that we had, and won by seven points. There is no way that I'd claim a direct cause and effect, but ruck efficiency certainly contributes to the cause. We have the ball more often and offer them fewer chances with turnover ball.

Going back to our 'identity', having the 'Big Rocks' gave us some anchor points in the game that we could 'stand for', that we judged ourselves upon and committed to. We connected them to the kerbstones of Newgrange because we had visited the site and had seen how impressive the boulders were, how solid the construction was and how precisely it had been put together. The challenge to the players was to make sure that their ball carry and their barrels could be every bit as solid, so that they could engineer the same degree of precision on the pitch.

Strike Plays

Strike plays directly from a scrum or lineout, where players knew where they were going and could predict where opposition players were likely to be, have often been a point of difference for us in tight games. It had worked so well for Bay of Plenty against big teams that I brought the same emphasis to the Blues when I started there in 2004. In our first game away to the Highlanders, we scored a superb try out wide by creating an overlap directly from setpiece. It encouraged me to keep pushing for the accuracy required; but Super Rugby is loose and fast, with numerous turnovers, and the teams that played best from broken play tended to get the best results.

I felt that I adapted during the three years that I spent at the Blues, helping players to sharpen their reactions after turnovers, whether it be connecting more quickly on defence to minimize damage if we turned the ball over, or seizing opportunities and reacting from depth on turnovers from the opposition. At the end of my three-year involvement with the Blues, we finished with a semi-final loss to the Sharks in Durban. But the two tries we scored – one from broken play by Rudi Wulf after a scything run from Isaia Toeava, and the other by Isa Nacewa after a phase play was executed with the right timing and running lines – demonstrated that both broken play and structured play could be used to destabilize opponents. One thing that I became increasingly convinced about was that it wasn't which play you opted to play but rather how well you played it that made it count.

I have sat next to players at press conferences and heard them talk about the importance of knowing their role, and I've read many articles on the subject, but I think coaching is really about helping players to understand the 'why' and 'how', which can potentially elevate them beyond the 'what' and 'when'. Strike plays involve a number of set roles, but it's mostly about players having a shared understanding about what they're trying to achieve, then honing the skills and timing required, along with reinforcing the trust that they have in each other that each will play their part.

The greater the understanding, the more empowered players are to adapt. I remember once defending our structure in an RTÉ interview by comparing it to poetry:

> You know, people presume there's a lot of structure and there is, just as there is when people are writing, so that others can understand what's written. I think some of the best poetry I have read, it goes beyond the bounds of standard grammar. When you know the grammar really well, you can utilize whatever you need to get the message across. It's similar when players have a structure that they know and are comfortable with, they can go beyond that and play whatever they see in front of them.

Key players will deviate from the planned strike play if they sense an opportunity or if they can see that it's not going to work. It's this understanding, at high speed with so much happening, that separates the ball players from the ball runners. It's this *sens de jeu*, along with a polished skill set and competitive nature, that allows Johnny Sexton to make so many good decisions when running the game. Despite years of honing his ability to read the game, even Johnny can become hesitant when he hasn't played for a while and is out of rhythm. Joey Carbery, Jack Carty and Ross Byrne are all building their understanding and experience to develop their ability to run the right play at the right time and then to make the best decision partway through, if they sense that they need to change tack.

On some big days, set plays have helped decide results. C. J. Stander's try in the Grand Slam clincher at Twickenham was part of a set play that we had worked on during the week. The vital late try to seal the victory against the All Blacks in Chicago in 2016 was a play that we had planned to use against South Africa on the tour during the summer, but the opportunity hadn't arisen; so when Jamie Heaslip got away from the scrum so quickly, the All Blacks were taken by surprise and Robbie Henshaw's line and timing gave him enough space to get over the line, reaching out in the tackle of T. J. Perenara to score.

Again against the All Blacks in 2018, in a game separated by just one score, the crucial try came from a play that we had done many times before but not executed quite as well as we'd have liked. The margins in the game are fine, and for set plays to work, especially when they might be across three or four phases, every player has to be across their detail but also coiled ready to adapt at any moment. Jacob Stockdale got the time and space to use the deft left-footed chip kick that he is so good at to get behind the All Black defensive line and to win the race to the ball, before reaching out in the tackle of Aaron Smith.

Playing a strong Springbok team in 2014, we were clear underdogs, with the South Africans coming off an impressive 27–25 win over the All Blacks in a fantastic game of rugby in Johannesburg. Chris Henry had been taken ill the morning of the match and Rhys Ruddock had come into the team late. Typically, Rhys played a stormer despite being out of position on the openside flank, but the crucial try from Tommy Bowe eight minutes from the finish was from a set play that we'd worked hard on. It's a good example of a set play where the strengths of players are utilized in an attempt to exploit a particular space that an opponent tends to leave on the pitch.

Conor Murray's kicking accuracy and Tommy Bowe's aerial prowess were definite strengths for us. Bryan Habana was an incredibly hard-working defender, but in his eagerness to cover across the pitch he had a tendency to leave his wing early, tracking the ball across the pitch. We didn't get the first part of the play right, but it's a great example of what I mentioned earlier about players like Johnny Sexton being able to adapt on the run. Johnny carried the ball, making a half-break from a scrum on the right-hand side of the pitch, on the 10-metre line in the South African half. The plan was for us to set up a quick ruck, in line with or just inside the near post, and that Conor would kick the ball back to Tommy, who would sneak out to the right-hand edge of the pitch. Conor was quick to the ruck and got the kick back across to the right, but dragged it a bit so that it was too far forward for Tommy to take on the full. Luckily, it bounced well for us and Tommy grabbed it to score, with Habana too late to get back to stop him.

Some set plays are not so visible, because they are played much tighter to the setpiece. In the run-up to Super Saturday in 2015, when we knew we'd be chasing the best margin that we could against Scotland in Murrayfield, Simon Easterby had done superb analysis as always and had identified an opportunity for the ball to be smuggled to the back lifter at the tail end of the lineout. The Scottish player at the tail was primed to get off the lineout or to get around on to our side before we could set the maul, so when Devin Toner caught the ball and immediately smuggled it to Sean O'Brien, Sean slipped off the tail of the lineout almost unseen by the Scottish forwards and stepped inside the final defender to score.

Even on the other side of the ball, we have tried to 'attack' with defensive set plays. In the run-up to our match against Italy in 2016, Andy Farrell showed some footage of how flat the Italian out-half, Edoardo Padovani, was taking the ball off their scrum attack, as he looked to get on to the front foot and to be aggressive with their passing options into the midfield. Andy decided that we should risk Jared Payne shooting out of our defensive line to look for the intercept or to try to get a man-and-ball tackle that might force a turnover. In the forty-second minute, when Jared cleanly intercepted Padovani's pass and coasted between the posts, it was satisfying to watch.

As much as the homework gets done – hours looking at footage and trying to match our strengths with perceived weaknesses in the opposition – there are many times when set plays don't come off, because there are so many variables that can cause them to come unstuck. The quality of the ball from the setpiece, the transfers and timing of the attacking players, or the opposition doing something different from what we'd observed or expected based on their habits from previous games – any of these things can ruin a set play. At the same time, when the margins are so fine and defences are so well drilled, a well-rehearsed strike play can potentially be the difference in a match.

Rugby has been a constant for most of my life. It's dominated my working hours for the past two decades, and many hours beyond. I'm either reviewing footage, ruminating on what didn't work, devising tactics that I hope will work, listening to others in coaching and leadership, working with people to help them become the player they hope to be, out on the pitch coaching or helping others to coach, watching games live or supporting those who run the game and help to keep clubs and youths enthused. I'm still just as motivated as I've ever been by the challenge it presents, but I'm also looking forward to the near future, when I'll be watching from a distance rather than being in the midst of it.

14. Coaching

Do what matters, now.

Leo Babauta

I don't mean for this to be an instructional chapter or an attempt to provide a definitive guide to coaching. I read a lot about coaching and leadership, but there still seems to be so much more to know or to understand. This chapter outlines a few thoughts on coaching, combined with a few experiences. Inevitably, things change on a regular basis and I think that's a key challenge for coaches: to keep questioning themselves, striving to stay current, while retaining the best of themselves and their ideas.

During the 2016 Six Nations, we were still reeling from our World Cup exit. We drew with Wales, lost by one point in Paris and played pretty well at Twickenham, with four debutants, but were beaten 21–10. I was being questioned about my approach. My response in an interview at the time was the same as my response when we're winning: 'I don't know if my approach is working but I work hard at it. I know people question the decisions I might make and the way we might play but I guarantee you that I question it more.'

I don't subscribe to the old adage that you learn more from your losses, because the result includes so many variables that you can't control. All you can try to do is keep learning from each experience – win or lose – so that you can help your players to get better and to combine as effectively as possible. It's that simple, and incredibly complex at the same time.

I'm not sure how best to achieve the simple task of helping a group of people to get better, but I think the following short list is not too bad a place to start:

- Be passionate and positive
- Have a growth mindset
- Be self-aware
- Have a deep understanding of the game
- Be organized
- Be a good communicator

Above all else, I think a coach needs to genuinely care about the people that they're working with.

As I've already discussed, it's hard to enthuse others if you don't have sufficient enthusiasm yourself. From what I've observed, it's important for coaches to be passionate, to have a strong connection to the game. Part of that emotional connection means that you show disappointment if things don't go well because, like the players, you're competitive and desperate to make things work. At the same time, it's important to move forward, to invest in positive solutions and to bring the players with you.

There was a great advertisement on television recently, in which a coach comes into a changing room full of downcast youngsters. The coach takes stock quickly, and then he says, 'Twelve goals . . . well done!' There's a pause, with the kids still looking disappointed, and then he adds with an enthusiastic smile, 'They'd have scored fifteen goals against any other team!' The kids cheer and are immediately buoyed by the encouragement. Being realistic and keeping things positive can often be a challenge, but it's worth working toward.

The worst time for me is when we lose our last game in a season. It tends to linger and cause frustration because we can't do anything about it until the next time we're together. Two seasons in a row at Clermont, that empty feeling after losing the Top 14 final was hard to shake, but it was also a reminder that it means something. The reality is that you know how hard it is to make the final in the first place and that it is going to be arduous getting back to the play-offs, let alone the final. But by the start of the following season I was always ready to go again, motivated by what we hadn't quite managed to finish off and more capable with the language. I also knew the players better and had a couple of new ideas about what might work, especially if we got all the way to the final again.

Being self-aware helps coaches to better understand the impact they have on others within the group, and for me it helps to balance the drive for high-performance behaviours with the need to gather input from players and allow time for regeneration. I am aware that I have an intensity when coaching. I think I get so immersed in what's happening that I am sometimes too reactive and don't deliver feedback in the best way.

No doubt Johnny Sexton was right when he said that 'Joe's got more of an edge to him than his smile suggests.' If that edge isn't there, then I think it's difficult to build the habits required to deliver consistently positive performances. I remember one ex-player publicly criticizing me a year or two after the 2015 World Cup for having been too harsh on him at a training with Harlequins during the lead-up to our pool game with Italy. I was sent the article, in which the player was quoted as saying that I'd 'absolutely rinsed' him 'in front of both teams'.

I was disappointed with myself when I read that, and saw it as a good opportunity to improve my self-awareness about how I'd made the player feel. I spoke to Richie Murphy and went back and looked at the video of the training, straining to hear the audio. The player's recall of the lead-up to the 'rinsing' wasn't accurate, but I still needed to be conscious of how I had delivered the feedback. He had dropped the ball four times during the training. The first few times I encouraged him to keep his 'ball focus'. The final time, he took an inside line on a pre-planned strike play, straight into open space, but dropped the ball from the inside pass. I rebuked him and my frustration was very evident. I often explain to players before we train that I am going to try to exert as much pressure as possible on them during the training to best prepare them for the stresses of the test-match arena. To be fair to the player, he bounced back and performed well later in the tournament.

It's hard to instil a growth mindset in others if you don't have it yourself. In my first meeting with Mike Ross after I'd arrived at Leinster, he said that he felt he was the best tight-head scrummaging option in the club and that he'd hit rucks. He was taken aback somewhat when my response was: 'And?' He'd pigeonholed himself and decided what he was capable of doing, and then set out his stall to offer those things within his comfort zone. I chuckled when I read about that meeting in Rossy's book, how he was made immediately uncomfortable because he would be expected to perform beyond his own expectations. He became the cornerstone of the Leinster scrum, delivering on his word, but he also grew his game to deliver more than he had previously demanded of himself.

Ambitious and highly competitive people are very keen to win things. They want to get to the top and to stay there, but they're also motivated to keep moving forward. When Brian O'Driscoll said that 'Joe has been fantastic for us these last few years and really rejuvenated me as a player. I learned an awful lot under his tutelage,' it was flattering. But it's also a reminder that the best at anything want to keep getting better. They're conscious that, in the words of Will Rogers, 'Even if you're on the right track, you'll get run over if you just sit there.'

Even if your tactics or techniques are on the right track, I think it's underestimated how important it is to sell them to players. If players are not fully convinced and they hesitate, even the best-laid tracks can be the cause of derailments. Trust is key, between coaches and players, and among the players themselves. Knowing that a lifter is going to get his job right allows the jumper to focus on his role. Getting the right technical direction on the entry into a tackle and being fully convinced by it will add decisiveness to a player's action. If the same advice is given to a different player but they are less convinced about it, their hesitation in the split seconds before impact can cause problems.

A deep understanding of the game is fundamental. Having observed the energy of Pep Guardiola during a Manchester City training session, I'm not surprised that he energizes his players. But to be the productive catalyst that he is, he also has to have a deep understanding of the game so that the ideas and advice he delivers are productive and that they're taken on board by the superstars he coaches.

During my first pre-season at Leinster, the squad began training at the start of July but the international players, who had been on tour to New Zealand and Australia, came back into pre-season training a few weeks later than the others. There was some lingering disappointment from the tour, mainly due to the heavy loss against the All Blacks in which Jamie Heaslip had been red-carded after just sixteen minutes. Richie McCaw had spreadeagled himself over Gordon D'Arcy just in front of the All Blacks' try line. Jamie had launched his knee forward in a frustrated attempt to shift the resolute McCaw, and he was duly sent off.

With the international players coming in late, they trained independently for the first few weeks before integrating fully with the rest of the squad. Toward the end of their first week back, I was casually watching them do a training drill being run by Richie Murphy, in which the forwards were defending against the backs. The defenders were eager and well connected, and they shut down the attack each time.

When the attacking players walked back into position to launch another attack they expressed a bit of frustration and asked me what I thought. I had been more focused on watching the forwards, to see how hard and smart they were working, but I encouraged the backs to launch their next attack and I'd have a look at them. Johnny Sexton, Gordon D'Arcy, Brian O'Driscoll, Rob Kearney and Shane Horgan launched their attack off a pass from Eoin Reddan and were again shut down as the defenders had good numbers and were well spaced to get off the line effectively.

I felt that I was under the microscope as the players walked back to me. When watching the defenders, I'd noticed that they were very zonal and square getting off the line. I suggested that if the attackers could swap zones at the last moment, without telegraphing any of their angle changes, then there might be space between the defenders. I was non-committal about the potential success my advice might bring, but I was prescriptive about Johnny playing flat and square, with Darce maintaining his spacing but staying very flat so that he was on the same plane as Johnny. Drico was to hold his run perched a metre or two from the outside shoulder of Darce. Just as they saw the pass released from Johnny's hands, aimed at Darce's back shoulder, Darce would step sideways, moving laterally away with the pass, while Drico would step in on a sharp arc to hit the 'inside drift' line. It's a common enough play, but they executed it precisely and Drico plucked the ball as he accelerated into space, scything straight through the line of defenders without being touched.

The players were pleased that I'd been able to interpret a defensive pattern and to have an idea of what might work to unlock it. I was relieved to have made a good first impression but, at the same time, realistic. If one of the defenders had chosen to do something different or had anticipated Drico's running line, then the play would have been unsuccessful. The margins are fine and confidence can be fickle, but I think that first bit of successful advice gave the players some belief that I could help them. Without that belief, half-hearted commitment to a set play or strategy would never be sufficient in the constant battery of fine margins that rugby players are confronted with.

Despite advancements in technology and the feedback it offers, live coaching remains incredibly important for me. Coaching on the run, staying conscious of the big picture, while also trying to be attentive to the most relevant small details, can benefit the players. If the coach's feedback can be delivered appropriately in the moment, it allows timely adjustments to be made. Shane Jennings explained that 'there's no doubt, he'll bark at you, but instant feedback is a good thing and being ruthless is a good thing. You have to have that accountability. A fella might be nice and get on with you and leave things off but you might not win a lot with him. There's a reason behind Joe shouting at you.'

Players can distract themselves with internal conversations during live training or in matches. Thoughts like 'If we don't score soon, I don't think we're going to be able to win this match.' Or 'I got knocked over there – was my body height the problem or was I not positioned squarely enough at the ruck?' Or 'Shall I run a line off the scrum half here or take a wider arc to offer a line off the out-half?' You want players who are as instinctive as possible and who don't distract themselves with variables that they can't control but are able to problem-solve in the right moments. The more unconscious or decisive these conversations become – adapting on the run, having a feel for the right body position or the right body height, knowing the running line – the more able the player is to win the split seconds that make it possible to take decisive and accurate action.

Being a teacher has provided plenty of opportunities to plan a programme and to try to plot a logical progression. Harking back to the Sunday evenings that I would spend in the editing suite at school, I still do the analysis in a similar way. There might be a theme to the week, and we'll work to get better at a specific aspect of the game. At the same time, there will be a rhythm to the week, where we will periodize work and recovery commitments. Being organized takes effort, and I try to make the effort wholehearted. I review every provincial game, taking notes on players of interest, including players who have never yet been in national camp. I do my own opposition analysis, watching games from start to finish so that the actions and decisions made by players have a context.

Something that I didn't anticipate before taking on the national-coach role was the number of events that I would attend for clubs or schools or businesses. These are all great opportunities to connect with people and promote the game. Sinéad Bennett and Carmel O'Dwyer have done a great job of helping me to keep my diary workable. One evening at home I was chiding Luke after he forgot to take his epilepsy medication. I said, 'Luke, you've got to take responsibility for yourself. Who would remind me if I forgot to do something that I needed to do?' He looked at me thoughtfully and answered, 'Sinéad?' Kelly and I laughed, because he wasn't trying to be cheeky – he was just answering the question, correctly!

Players want to feel that they're progressing, that they're understanding more about how best to prepare or how best to hone a particular skill or run a particular line. Mike Ross wrote that my 'advice was usually very precise, clear and actionable. It was never vague.' I work hard to make sure that I am thinking and communicating with clarity, and I try to pick holes in ideas or feedback to test their robustness. I know that I don't always get it right, but I know that I work hard to be honest and accurate with feedback, even when it's very difficult to explain the fine margin upon which a selection has been based. I didn't have too many discussions with Isa Nacewa regarding non-selection for big days, but he has seen me agonize over decisions and then try to communicate those to players. He emphasized to a journalist that 'It's not a text message, it's not an email, or a voicemail – it's a genuine conversation. If he wasn't picking you, and you wanted to know why, he would stay hours after training to explain.'

I was directed to a podcast by a friend in which the former athletics coach Frank Dick explained how important specific feedback is. When he was coaching the Scottish sprinter Cameron Sharp, he felt that Sharp's bend wasn't as strong as it needed to be in the 200 metres. The more he urged him to *drive* off the bend, the more it seemed that any improvement stagnated. When Don Quarrie, who had won gold in the Olympic 200 metres in 1976, observed a session, he interrupted to say that Dick shouldn't be telling Sharp to *drive* off the bend but to *lift* off the bend. Dick realized that he'd been using the wrong word, that *drive* suggests a lengthy foot contact with the ground, used to get purchase out of the starting blocks, but the light and quick contact of *lift* was the action he needed to be encouraging.

As a coach (or a teacher, or a parent), have you ever heard yourself say, 'Look, I keep telling you . . .'? Have you considered the possibility that you're not being accurate in how you're delivering the message? I'm lucky that I can often get feedback from other members of the coaching staff about what I've presented, and vice versa. Our coaching team help coach each other, with feedback on how clear or how inspiring a message might have been.

Most coaching environments have their own lexicon: particular words or phrases are used to create images or generate particular actions. Players are time-poor in the high-density traffic on the pitch, so the more refined the language can be, the more helpful the cue is likely to be.

Finally, I think players need to know that you care about them. Dave Hadfield, the New Zealand-based mental-skills coach, would often use the quote that 'Nobody cares how much you know, until they know how much you care.' I'm convinced that he's right, and while I know that I drive players hard sometimes, I'd hope they also know that I care about them.

15. Media

Harmony seldom makes a headline.

Silas Bent

There's often a bit of an uneasy truce between sports teams and some media. Plenty of journalists provide balance and build relationships, looking to offer genuine insights and taking the time to present a balanced critique. But there's always a sense that others are waiting in the long grass, just looking for the opportunity to pounce on a poor performance, or to create a furore if a player slips up, or to magnify any hint of discord within camps or between combatants.

When I started out in professional coaching with Bay of Plenty, we had a relaxed relationship with local media. Jamie Troughton, the sports journalist for the *Bay of Plenty Times*, even travelled on the team bus to some matches and on occasion spent time in the inner sanctum of the changing rooms after matches. He was local, trusted and positive by nature, and the access he had to the team and players was much greater than I've experienced since. I guess it was because Bay of Plenty was smaller and the competition for local readers was less intense. It didn't mean that his stories were always positive, but there was an opportunity to provide greater depth and a human element that's often missing from bigger teams, where the media competition is more intense and journalists report from a greater distance.

Anthony Foley was a realist. When he came under media pressure during his time coaching Munster, he returned to a maxim from his playing days: 'I was never as good as they said I was and I was never as bad as they said I was either.' It's a smart philosophy, because headlines and commentary tend to swing from one end of the spectrum to the other. I remember the first question at the press conference after we lost to Treviso early in my first season with Leinster: 'Joe, do you think that this might be the beginning of the end for Leinster Rugby?' One week during the 2019 Six Nations, a French newspaper called me a 'magician', and the next week I was sent an article with a headline referring to 'Schmidt's Shambolic Ireland'. I'm certainly no magician, but 'shambolic' at the other end of the spectrum seems a bit excessive as well.

Dealing with the media is part of a coach's job, but sometimes it goes a bit awry. Following a defeat in a Heineken Cup pool match a number of years ago, the then Saracens coach, Brendan Venter, gave an offbeat interview to Martin Gillingham of Sky Sports. Venter's wry response to a question about the genius of the Racing 92 try scorer Sireli Bobo was 'Bit of genius, bit of magic, Sireli Bobo, very interesting, very good, ya, very good, three cheers for Sireli Bobo.' His responses were a parody of the movie *Mike Bassett: England Manager*, and they were both awkward and amusing. VC and I had caught up for a beer, with our teams due to play each other the following day, and we were bemused but entertained by the offbeat responses.

I met an experienced Irish sports journalist for a coffee in New Zealand during the Irish tour in June 2011. He was perplexed that we had excluded a particular journalist from press conferences at Leinster toward the end of the season. He was conscious that the journalist had misquoted players and coaching staff and that he had been warned twice before being excluded. It was an amicable meeting and we chatted casually. He explained that the Irish Rugby Writers were a unified group and that, if one journalist was excluded, we risked a boycott from the group. He also conceded that quotations should be accurate and that there had been warnings, but we agreed that we'd start the new season off with a clean slate.

Coaches appreciate it when reporters make the effort to check facts. In 2012, a journalist phoned me and said that he knew Brad Thorn was coming to Leinster. The problem was that we were still trying to get confirmation of his release from his Japanese club. I was in hospital waiting for Luke to have more surgery, so I was already stressed. I asked for a few hours' reprieve, and promised that I would answer his questions if he held off reporting the story for a short while. As soon as I got confirmation of Brad's release, I phoned the journalist, which allowed him to expand on Brad Thorn's arrival with more detail.

Coaches don't particularly enjoy fielding media queries about things we can't really discuss, like detailed medical information or potential transfers. Understandably, the media are quick to look for medical updates on players because supporters want to know about player availability. When I first started as national coach, one journalist gave the following feedback to the IRFU: 'one personal bugbear is the transparency with regard to injuries and, having worked around Leinster in the past few years, I know what Joe can be like in being cagey in this regard.' The introduction of GDPR has made things a little easier, because people understand that individuals are entitled to keep personal information to themselves. It can still be a bit of a tightrope, balancing the right amount of injury information that is shared.

I was chided in a recent article for being unhappy that a team was leaked in the press the day before it was due to be named. The article suggested that I forget about the team being named early and turn my energies to getting the most out of the team. The journalist was probably right, because I can't control what gets released; I can only influence what we do to prepare. But I was frustrated, because knowing who they're going to be up against gives our opponents a competitive advantage. I know our players are always very keen to know who is playing in the opposition because it helps them better visualize who they might be duelling with in the match, and they can start preparing for the strengths or weaknesses they perceive the player to have.

In 2018, Ulster needed an out-half and targeted the South African international Elton Jantjies. We were concerned about this on two levels. Our World Cup draw meant that South Africa was a potential quarter-final opponent for us, and more importantly we were keen to develop our Irish out-halves to create depth in the position behind Johnny Sexton. It was far from ideal that David Nucifora and I approached Leo Cullen early on a Sunday afternoon at the beginning of a big European semi-final week, but Ulster had to make a decision on Jantjies by lunchtime the following day. We asked Leo if we could speak to Ross Byrne and Joey Carbery to see if either of them had any interest in transferring to Ulster.

Leo was understandably unhappy, because both players were under contract with Leinster and it was the start of a very big week. Our problem was that we were under pressure to have the national interest voiced and the time frame was incredibly tight. Our backup out-half at the 2015 World Cup,

Ian Madigan, had started just six games in the position during the twelve months before he started the quarter-final in Johnny's absence through injury. There was an onus on us to avoid a similar situation, and with three of the best Irish out-halves at Leinster (and Joey playing mostly at fullback), we were worried it could arise again.

Leo turned down the request, but late in the day he agreed to speak to the two players himself. At about 11 o'clock the following morning, he rang me to explain that neither player was keen to entertain the idea of going to Ulster. As it turned out, Ross didn't play in the semi-final and Joey came off the bench, so at least neither player was overly distracted by the question. Ross, who had already started over a dozen games at out-half for Leinster that season, wasn't distracted at all, because in a three-minute conversation he saw no reason to move anywhere else, which made sense. Joey, too, was keen to stay at Leinster, but he also wanted to meet up with me, along with his dad. When I met them, Joey was insistent that out-half was where he wanted to play, but that he was really enjoying the Leinster environment and that he preferred to stay.

Then came the article in the *Sunday Times*, in which it was claimed that:

> Schmidt and IRFU performance director David Nucifora visited Leinster's training centre last Sunday morning to inform head coach Leo Cullen that he needed to make a choice between the two youngsters – who was staying and who was leaving. Moreover, he needed to make his choice promptly.

It was not what had happened and when I spoke to Leo he apologized. Neither Leo nor I was sure where the journalist had got his information, but it was disappointing that he hadn't corroborated it with either David Nucifora or me. We had requested Leo's permission to ask the two players a question, not made a demand that one or the other had to go.

Ironically, the person who spoke with the journalist inadvertently contributed to Joey Carbery's departure from Leinster, because the *Sunday Times* story made Munster aware of the situation. When Joey wasn't selected at out-half against Connacht the following weekend, he asked if we could meet again, along with his dad. He still wasn't sure what he'd do, but asked if it was possible to shift to Munster. It was beyond my remit to say yes or no, but I agreed to pass on his question to David Nucifora. Joey, his dad and I met in a Milltown café, and a photo of us was circulated, with someone using their iPhone to send it on to Leinster. Joey was put on the spot when asked by Leinster whether he had met me again. He said that he had. Soon after, I received a copy of the photo from different sources – it was obviously doing the rounds – but all I could do was shrug my shoulders and continue to do my job.

Thankfully, as the saga dragged on, there was a very good piece from Gerry Thornley in the *Irish Times* that spelled out the conundrum facing Joey, the IRFU and Leinster. The piece was not emotive; it just highlighted the various aspects of the decision and the perspectives of those concerned.

We were in camp preparing to depart for the summer tour of Australia when Joey said to me that he'd decided to go to Munster. I had given him only one directive regarding where he would play the following season, and that was that he should make the decision before we departed, especially as he was going to start at out-half in the first test match in Brisbane. I said, 'I thought you were going to stay with Leinster?'

He replied, 'So did I.' We didn't discuss it further, because we were leaving for Australia the next day and had plenty to get done before we travelled.

I have written about leadership needing to be authentic: you cannot try to be all things to all people. It's hard to do some-times as a coach, when you see headlines or claims published in an apparent attempt to create friction. One annual frustra-tion is the interpro derbies. Some journalists have regularly made an issue of the fact that, under the IRFU's player man-agement rules, the provinces often rest some first-choice players for the derbies. One year, previewing a St Stephen's Day Munster–Leinster match, a journalist complained about 'the IRFU's frustrating festive rules'. The piece appeared at a time when Leinster had three games in eleven days, wedged between two sets of big European matches. The IRFU don't make the Pro14 draw, or put in the five-day turnarounds.

Journalists often wonder how the All Blacks have been able to stay at the top for so long. Among the reasons is the primacy of the national team. NZ Rugby make no bones about it. Prior to our match in Chicago in 2016, the All Blacks withdrew the Otago captain, Liam Coltman, from the final of the NPC Championship, because they thought he might be needed in the national squad. Otago were hot favourites for the final and were playing at home in Forsyth Barr Stadium, but they were beaten by North Harbour. Liam Coltman didn't play in Chicago or in any match on tour. He could have flown a day or two later and still played the final for Otago, but if the All Blacks had lost a hooker through injury during training they would have been compromised, so they needed Liam Coltman with them. The national team's needs trumped a provincial final.

Having the opportunity to be selected for the national

team is a huge reason why players stay in Ireland. By extension, provincial supporters get to see them play. Our supporters want good derby games and competitive teams in the Pro14, where Irish teams have dominated the play-off spots over the past ten years, but the players also need to be looked after. We cannot flog players, and that applies to the national team, too: no player started all four of the autumn 2018 tests. That's part of the deal for players who make the choice to remain here, often on lesser contracts.

At a Belvedere blitz towards the end of my first season with Leinster, a spectator came up to me and started chatting. He was delighted because he'd watched a Setanta Sports programme in which the host had done a great job of explaining the essence of how Leinster were trying to play. When I asked him what had been said, he said that the game plan was all about continuity and offloads. He looked confused when I said, 'No, it's all about the contact.' I explained that you can't get good continuity or effective offloads if you're not winning collisions. We chatted some more before I had to head off, and he thanked me for explaining the crux of what we were trying to do. I thought to myself that it was perhaps no harm if people thought that we were prioritizing offloads, because it wasn't what we were trying to do. Offloads were a positive outcome, if collisions could be won, but we didn't practise offloads at all.

The pundit who first claimed that I'd lost the dressing room four weeks into my time with Leinster took aim again during the 2016 Six Nations:

Thanks to a craven media, the Ireland coach had an uncritical assessment in power; his achievements were overblown and his failures ignored. Schmidt may well be the worst coach/selector in Irish rugby history.

Sometimes, when a pundit has made a prediction, they seize opportunities to back it up, so it wasn't too surprising that, when we finished only third in the 2016 Six Nations, this particular pundit reduced me to rock bottom as far as Irish rugby coaches are concerned.

This same pundit tried to sue Johnny Sexton during the same Six Nations, because Johnny dared to suggest that maybe the pundit was just saying things for effect and didn't really believe everything he said or wrote. Johnny approached Mick Kearney and me in camp one day with a solicitor's letter. Mick said to him, 'Don't worry about it, we'll sort it out.' Johnny was unsure, saying that he thought that he'd prefer to see the pundit in court, to show him how ridiculous his claim was. Of course it never came to anything, and the pundit later apologized, but it did present a distraction that we could have done without.

When listening to match predictions and then reviews of matches afterwards, it's worth considering some of the ideas put forward by Nassim Nicholas Taleb, the statistician-philosopher. In his book *Fooled by Randomness*, he notes how easily we are deluded by the narratives we impose retrospectively on complex events. Similarly, Matthew Syed's *Black Box Thinking* discusses the concept of 'narrative fallacy'. He describes the incongruous punditry of the English football media during Fabio Capello's tenure as England coach. Capello expected players to be early for meetings, clamped down on mobile-phone use and didn't allow family and friends into training camps. The results on the pitch were initially very good, and the journalists heralded his exacting standards. But at the FIFA World Cup the team emerged from a relatively weak pool as runners-up behind USA before suffering their biggest ever World Cup knockout-match defeat, by 4 goals to 1 against Germany. Some journalists now took the view that Capello's exacting standards made it too tough for the players, inhibiting their flair and taking the fun out of the game. An approach that had been heralded as being instrumental in improved performances was suddenly condemned as the reason why the team wasn't performing.

During my first season as Ireland coach, I was interviewed by a pundit who lamented that, while winning the Six Nations was a fine achievement, I must have been frustrated by that one poor performance against England. I responded by saying that I thought it was probably our best performance. The result wasn't what we wanted, but so many aspects of the performance had been first rate and the three-point loss at Twickenham to a very good England team had been a fantastic game of rugby. Pundits have a tendency to look at the result, then work back in an attempt to weave a narrative that explains why the result occurred. When analysing a sporting event that involves so many variables, the result is a very narrow starting point.

Following the 2015 Rugby World Cup, much was made of the gap between the southern and northern hemispheres. It is true that all four semi-finalists were from the southern hemisphere. But the reality was that Scotland were on the cusp of beating Australia in their quarter-final, when the referee made an incorrect decision very late in the game, allowing Bernard Foley to kick a penalty goal to win the match for the Australians. And Wales led South Africa with less than six minutes remaining when a behind-the-back pass from Duane Vermeulen gave sufficient space for Fourie du Preez to score in the corner to win their quarter-final. There was very little between any of those four teams. Admittedly, the All Blacks dominated the French, and Argentina deserved their victory over us.

Despite the supposed chasm between the hemispheres, by the end of the following year England had won all three tests away to Australia, and Ireland had won their first game on South African soil and broken a 111-year drought with a first-ever win over New Zealand. Argentina won just three of their thirteen test matches, including losses to France, Wales, Scotland and England. There are very fine margins between victory and defeat: a decision, a few injuries, an individual error or moment of individual brilliance can all determine a result without there being much at all between two teams.

In the words of Charles Leadbeater, 'You are what you share,' and there is more being shared than ever. I am not on any form of social media, but I remember one particular impersonator, calling himself 'The real Joe Schmidt', tweeting some pretty cynical and contentious things, especially about Munster. Peter Breen, the Media Officer at Leinster, finally convinced Twitter to close the account. The account didn't have Twitter's blue tick of authenticity, but it was still unpleasant seeing my name on it.

There are many things that players have to accept about being in the public eye. One very well-known Irish player was out with a group of about a dozen friends in London, the summer prior to the Rugby World Cup in 2015. He was photographed, and then the photo was cropped to show just him and a female walking along with a caption suggesting that the two were out in London together. It completely misrepresented the circumstances.

Social media is a great conduit for the transfer of information and can create a profitable platform for players. We continually remind players that they should only post what they would be prepared to say in a public forum. There is obviously the balance between saying what you believe and being conscious that you have a responsibility to the values of your employer, as the Israel Folau case recently highlighted.

There are some quality people working in sports teams and sports journalism. They are keen, in the words of Albert Einstein, to 'Be a voice, not an echo.' That will continue to be a worthy challenge for both sports teams and the media associated with them.

16. Community

Remember that the happiest people are not those getting more,
but those giving more.

H. Jackson Brown Jr

From the time we spent as kids playing rugby on Saturday mornings or running around the edges of the pitch while the senior team played, I have experienced the sense of community that is central to rugby. And ever since secondary school, whether travelling around New Zealand for matches or heading to Australia on tour, I've enjoyed the hospitality of families connected to the game.

The strength of the connections that rugby can create is really powerful. The High School Old Boys club that I played for in Palmerston North had a reunion in April 2019. It was thirty years since we'd won the Hankin Shield for club rugby supremacy in Manawatu, and players returned to New Zealand from the UK, Asia and South Africa. Only two members of that team didn't manage to get back for the reunion. The rest of us reconnected straight away and enjoyed a great weekend catching up on the intervening years and sharing a few old stories. It was very similar a few years ago when I attended the reunion of the Palmerston North Boys' High School First XV that I'd coached. They had played the national secondary school final twenty years earlier and they thoroughly enjoyed getting back together for the weekend.

I've already written about the fantastic support Kelly and I received from Mullingar RFC and those associated with the club during our first spell in Ireland. Knowing that we were far from home, a number of families invited us to share Christmas dinner or dropped gifts off to us. We felt included. Since moving back to Ireland in 2010, we've enjoyed brilliant hospitality from clubs all over the country – including the Terenure and St Mary's clubs, which are just down the road from our home in Dublin.

Having spent the past decade visiting clubs all over Ireland, I've been amazed by the volunteer work people do. Rugby blitzes, youth festivals, fundraisers and social events draw substantial crowds. I've been to a number of blitzes for youngsters, and it's fantastic to see literally hundreds and sometimes over a thousand of them swarming all over multiple pitches as they chase each other and the ball around. The black-tie fundraising dinner at Ballynahinch RFC in memory of Nevin Spence packed 750 people into a huge marquee. The Wooden Spoon charity, which helps disabled and disadvantaged children, benefited from a Ballymena RFC luncheon, with Syd Millar, Ian McIlrath and Willie John McBride all there to offer support. 'Dancing with the players' events in Tullow and Terenure were hilarious, while club luncheons and prize-giving events connect members and celebrate performances as well as helping clubs by raising essential funds.

Clubs survive thanks to the efforts of volunteers, organizing committees, local sponsorship and the enthusiasm of their members. The memberships are more diverse than ever, with the growth in women's rugby and the introduction of special-abilities teams. On the pitch, the special-abilities players can get distracted at times, but they're quickly guided back into the game, re-enthused by one of the coaches or support staff. I've spent a bit of time with the De La Salle Eagles as well as getting along to see the Terenure Tigers in action, and it's uplifting to see the commitment and enthusiasm of the coaching staff as well as the enjoyment that the players get. At an event in Portadown recently, it was great to hear about the popularity of their special-abilities team, the Portadown Panthers. The inclusivity of these teams is fantastic, and I've seen the work that goes on behind the scenes from so many people to keep teams like these up and running.

About six months after we moved to Dublin, Kelly and I were walking down to Dundrum shopping centre. After about three different people had greeted me with 'Hi, Joe' as they passed, Kelly said, 'Wow, you've met a lot of people already!' In fact I hadn't met any of the people who had greeted me, but that was how it was: we both felt that we had become 'part of the furniture' very quickly, and there was a warmth and familiarity from the people we encountered. It is no surprise that Ireland currently ranks second in the global Good Country Index, based on its contribution to 'the common good of humanity'.

Even when aspects of the community cause frustration, good people make a difference. Our home was burgled twice in the space of three years, both times when big matches were on, and there was a suspicion that the burglars had guessed that we'd be away. Both burglaries were reported in the media and they certainly caused some unease for our children. Despite this, Kelly laughed one afternoon when she left the house for a match at the Aviva and saw a van parked outside with a banner saying, 'Don't worry, Joe, we've got you covered'.

I think people make places, and in the small communities

that I grew up in, the rugby clubs that I've been part of, even if only visiting, as well as the neighbourhoods that Kelly and our kids have lived in, we have felt a sense of belonging. We have always felt that the wider Irish community have not just accepted us but truly adopted us. The support that Luke has received through his schooling at Stratford National School and currently in Terenure College has been a relief for us, especially for Kelly, who is constantly on call to support him if he has a bad day.

Our good friends the Tanners live close by, and we were very sad to lose Arthur a few years ago. He had been our first point of medical contact in Dublin when we were looking for reassurance regarding Luke. He was well summed up by Professor Freddie Wood as a 'living example of Ambroise Paré's dictum: "Duty of a doctor: To cure sometimes, to relieve often but to care always"'. I think communities work best when everyone tries to deliver the last part of Paré's dictum.

PART THREE
Slam Diary

Tuesday, 19 December 2017, Carton House

Rather than setting goals, we tend to build each campaign from the bottom up, committing to positive habits and the processes we build our game upon. At the same time, I've been thinking about the upcoming Six Nations being my penultimate Championship before finishing with the team at the end of RWC 2019. Time is running out for me to be involved with a Grand Slam team.

A number of the senior players have spoken of the same uneasiness, and a few of them talked to me about being forthright in targeting a Grand Slam, which was perfect, because the coaching group had already planned a similar approach for our 24-hour Christmas camp. We all feel the 2018 Championship is our best opportunity, based on a relatively favourable draw, the growing depth in the squad and the positive behaviours that we've managed to embrace over recent years. The confidence levels in the group are good and have been buoyed by the successful November test matches.

The customary glance back at the autumn test series focused on the positives from the record 38–3 win over South Africa and the solid, controlled performance against Argentina. 'Vicious accuracy' was the mantra leading into the game against the big South African side, and the first clip shown was of the Springboks attacking flat and hard just forty-five seconds into the match. Emphasizing that we didn't need to have the ball to attack, Johnny Sexton and Bundee Aki got off the line at speed and clattered into the 130-kilo South African prop Coenie Oosthuizen. Bundee hit the midriff, driving the big front-rower back, while Johnny ripped the ball loose. Dev Toner then threw his 6-foot 10-inch frame on to the ground to claim the loose ball. Watching it, I felt reassured by Bundee's first involvement in his test debut. He'd copped plenty of hostile media attention prior to the match due to being an overseas-qualified player, but he proved incredibly popular with the masses during the autumn series with his wholehearted, hard-working performances.

Sometimes set plays work exactly as planned, and Jacob Stockdale's try twenty minutes into the Argentinian match looked to have been perfectly executed. Chris Farrell squared up at the defender in front of him but, just prior to contact, he deftly pushed the ball into the space outside him. The ball was actually supposed to go to Jacob, but an Argentinian defender stumbled, so it worked even better that Johnny grabbed the ball on his left hip and accelerated through a gap because it meant that Jacob was left unmarked, running an inside support line. When Johnny drew the last defender and passed the ball back inside, Jacob had an unobstructed run to the try line. I showed the try to the players to emphasize the need for everyone to understand their role so that they can adapt if required. I know that showing the squad set plays like these, in which the many working parts function effectively to get a positive outcome, helps to breed confidence that what we work hard to get right in training can make a vital difference in tight matches.

The positives were counterbalanced by images from the disjointed win over Fiji and the two late tries scored by Argentina, both from grubber kicks into our in-goal area. In all three matches, there had been a third-quarter malaise of handling errors, discipline lapses and defensive slip-ups that we were very keen to highlight and problem-solve as the first steps to the Slam. I didn't want this to be cursory, but with just twenty-four hours in camp we had to move on quickly.

Mostly, the camp was about looking forward: an opportunity to plant a few seeds and to promote a few ideas for players to reflect upon. We had very seldom spoken about what we wanted to achieve, other than trying to be as effective as we could be from week to week in both our preparation and our match-day performances, but this time we wanted to let the idea of a focused tilt at a Grand Slam germinate.

We finished the camp with three minutes of video highlights, starting with documentary footage of the team arriving at Aviva Stadium to be greeted by drummers and an enthusiastic crowd massed at the entrance. A Tadhg Furlong voiceover described how 'the hairs stand up on the back of your neck' when you arrive to a scene like that on match day. We included some glimpses of the best training footage we could find, merging it into positive match-day moments. And we added the celebrations and euphoria of our first ever win in South Africa and the historic win over the All Blacks in Chicago, as well as the podium celebrations from the Six Nations successes in 2014 and 2015, before closing with snapshots from the trophy presentation to the 2009 Grand Slam-winning team. It stirred emotions and galvanized the feeling that we needed to win our own Grand Slam.

Sunday, 21 January 2018, Radisson Blu Hotel, Dublin Airport

It can be complicated to get a squad assembled quickly at the start of an international window. Ulster played away to Wasps in the Champions Cup in Coventry at 3.15 this afternoon. It means they got back to Belfast this evening, and the guys who are joining us for our training camp in Spain are driving down to Dublin tonight. We watched as much of the game as possible, while players from the other provinces filtered in, and we were concerned to see Jacob Stockdale limp off after seventeen minutes. A Sean Reidy try after Louis Ludik snatched up a loose pass from Christian Wade offered Ulster a bit of hope, but in slippery conditions on a mucky pitch they just couldn't get enough traction in the game and Wasps got away from them in the second half.

I felt for Ulster and especially Les Kiss, who was trying hard to get the best out of the squad in a tough pool, made even tougher by having to cope with injuries and the unavailability of some of his key players. Les worked with the national team for a number of years and did a superb job. As defence coach, he was a key contributor to the 2009 Grand Slam, during which Ireland conceded just three tries across the five matches. Les was also a friend and, on a personal level, I knew he would be gutted with the result. I texted Les but then had to shift my attention to a very full first-day itinerary.

Leinster and Munster, in the Champions Cup, and Connacht, in the Challenge Cup, had all qualified out of their respective pools, so there was plenty of positivity among the incoming players. We had twelve player meetings over a four-hour period following the conclusion of the Ulster match. Each meeting was scheduled to last fifteen minutes and included the player, the coaching staff and the head of strength and conditioning, Jason Cowman. We have further meetings planned with the rest of the players over the next two days. We'll follow pretty much the same format, referencing various benchmarks, from strength and speed to tackle statistics, ball-carry success, clean-outs and penalty infringements, helping players to formulate a plan for the coming week and beyond.

As part of the review meeting, three questions are asked of each player:

1. How are you travelling, both physically and mentally?
2. What are you going to do to add as much value as possible to the group over the next eight weeks?
3. What are the key things we need to do better than ever as a collective to get the performances we need to win the Grand Slam?

It was interesting and intense. We had between twelve and twenty video clips of each player from training and matches. We started with some of the things that they did well: the things that had contributed to them being selected. Following those, we had a few clips of parts of their game that we wanted them to focus on improving over the next five days, so that they were ready to start the week leading up to the French match as fresh, focused and up to speed as possible. Jason Cowman will factor in the player feedback, alongside medical and performance-based assessments, to determine how hard each player needs to work over the first three days of camp. For some of the players, the most important thing is to recover. Others, who haven't played so much in the European matches, can work harder in the gym and on the pitch. The aim is that, by Thursday morning, everyone will be ready to train at full intensity.

Monday, 22 January, Oliva Nova, Spain

The Ulster players didn't get to Dublin until after midnight, but everyone seemed reasonably fresh this morning. The players were looking forward to seeing the sun and to making a start on the work that needed to be done.

I checked in at home before going to the airport, and Kelly told me that Luke had not had a good night. He has recently begun a medically prescribed ketogenic diet, with food portions needing to be weighed and measured. It has been used for a long time to treat epilepsy and is very high in fat but includes almost no carbohydrates. Unfortunately, it can cause nausea, and Luke has been feeling unwell during the adjustment phase as his ketones increase. Kelly very seldom shares concerns when I'm away, but she told me that Luke had power-vomited all over the landing at about 11.30 last night. She was amazed at the coverage he managed: the carpet was pretty much totally covered, but he had still managed to get some of it on to the walls! He had been on his way from his bedroom to the bathroom but hadn't made it.

The risk when Luke vomits at that stage of the evening is that his medication does not get fully absorbed, which tends to impact on his seizure regulation. Kelly had cleaned up and settled him, but she needed to keep half an eye open all night, knowing that he would be more likely to seize. He'd slept restlessly until about 4.30 a.m. when he had a cluster of tonic seizures, culminating in a scary fifty-second tonic-clonic seizure. She administered a dose of midazolam, an anti-seizure medicine, to break the cycle, then managed to nurse him back off to sleep. I was keen to talk to Luke, but he was still sleeping so we left him to get the rest he needed. I empathized with Kelly and encouraged her to get some more sleep herself. Then I said goodbye and got myself organized to board the flight.

One of the downsides of Oliva Nova was the seventy-minute bus trip from Alicante airport, which meant that we didn't arrive until late afternoon. It was a balmy 19 degrees and the players were ushered straight off the bus and into the not so temperate waters of the Mediterranean. The team room was huge, light and airy, and the sunshine, quality food and comfortable beds fuelled good spirits and positive regeneration. The fellowship of card games, table tennis, the beach and the isolation encouraged players to reintegrate with their inter-provincial friends and foes.

Wednesday, 24 January, Heathrow Airport, London

The head coach and captain of each team are required to attend the Six Nations launch in London, so after training yesterday I had another seventy-minute ride back to the airport, then a flight to Stansted, and an hour's drive to the Syon Park Hotel, where the launch started at 7.30 this morning. We had decided that Rory Best would be better off not travelling to Oliva Nova for the first two days, as we knew that the match against Wasps would be attritional and the travel onerous, so he flew direct from Belfast to Heathrow yesterday evening and I met up with him at the Syon Park for an early breakfast.

I'm not a big fan of travelling and was pretty tired by the time I arrived at the hotel just after 1 a.m., but struggled to sleep. I'd received a phone call in transit to say that my elder brother, Kieran, had suffered a heart attack. I had rung him before taking off in Spain and he'd sounded okay, but he was obviously shaken and disorientated. Technology allows us to have long-distance 'close up' communication, but at difficult times, being on the other side of the globe still feels like a very long way away.

The Six Nations launch involves a battery of interviews and photographs. It is all part of the promotion for the Championship and, while it is laborious at times, I always try to treat it as a challenge. Rory and I worked our way through the day explaining, agreeing, contesting, swerving and repeating the same formulae, while at the same time trying to give fresh insights and impressions. Even the journalists start to struggle for credible questions, with one of them quizzing me about my recently devoured breakfast roll. I responded in full, describing the butter-smeared roll, with the salty bacon, the lettuce clinging to its last vestiges of crispness . . . delicious!

I'm always interested to hear what other coaches are saying about their teams and their upcoming opponents, including any injury updates. Coaches are generally guarded and determined not to reveal too much about likely selections or strategies, but there are always some interesting perspectives offered. Eddie Jones labelled Ireland and Scotland as the 'darlings of European rugby'. Despite his team being even-money favourites with the bookies, the England coach described us as favourites and said, 'If you go in as favourites it comes with massive expectations. Fans, supporters, media, sponsors . . .' It's a commonly held belief that Ireland are more comfortable being underdogs, and maybe this was Eddie's attempt to displace some of the pressure of favouritism from his players on to ours.

19. Ger Carmody, John Plumtree (*obscured*), Vinny Hammond and Les Kiss look worried as I deliver a message on our way to a narrow victory in Paris, to claim the 2014 Six Nations Championship [© INPHO/Dan Sheridan]

20. After a narrow victory in Paris, captain Paul O'Connell and the team got a warm welcome at Dublin Airport [© INPHO/Cathal Noonan]

17. With Mick Kearney, who convinced me to take on the role of Ireland head coach, in 2013 [© INPHO/Billy Stickland]

18. At training in 2014 with Andrew Trimble and Rob Kearney, trying to keep the pressure on Rob as he leaps for the high ball [© INPHO/James Crombie]

21. On 'Super Saturday' in 2015, four teams went into the final day of the Six Nations with a chance at the title. After we beat Scotland at Murrayfield, fans watched on the big screens as England narrowly failed to overhaul us and we retained the Championship [© INPHO/Cathal Noonan]

22. On tour in South Africa in 2016, we visited a township near Cape Town, where the Bhubesi Pride Foundation was doing good work with local children [© INPHO/Billy Stickland]

23. With skipper Rory Best in Cape Town in 2016, after Ireland won its first-ever Test in South Africa [© INPHO/Billy Stickland]

24. When we played New Zealand in Chicago in 2016, shortly after the death of Anthony Foley, the figure 8 facing the haka and the performance that followed made it a special memorial to Axel [© INPHO/Billy Stickland]

25. At the 'Purple Day' promotion for Epilepsy Ireland, an organization that we've tried to support as much as possible

26. With Simon Easterby, Andy Farrell, Richie Murphy, Greg Feek and the spoils of the 2018 Grand Slam. Faz and I are holding the Triple Crown trophy; Richie has the Millennium Trophy, for beating England; and the Six Nations trophy is out in front

27. Honing breakdown entry and body height in the warm-up before we played Argentina in November 2018 [© INPHO/Ryan Byrne]

28. A pre-match word with All Blacks coach Steve Hansen, November 2018. Our victory that night rounded off a brilliant year [© INPHO/Dan Sheridan]

29. At the draw for the 2019 World Cup, where our top-four world ranking had got us into Band 1 [© INPHO/Getty/Dave Rogers/World Rugby Pool Images]

30. The warm-up before our World Cup opener against Scotland in Yokohama. A bonus-point win put us in a strong position in the pool [© INPHO/Craig Mercer]

31. I'm still scratching my head at the error count and hesitancy we showed against the All Blacks in the quarter-final [© INPHO/Dan Sheridan]

32. On-field coaching is intense and often demanding but also highly motivating and good fun. I've loved that part of the job [© INPHO/Dan Sheridan]

While Eddie was talking down his team's chances, Warren Gatland described Wales as a 'great bet' despite them being quoted at the generous odds of 16/1. Gats seems to enjoy being provocative with the media. He uses them to encourage his players and to justify the strategies they employ, or to cast doubt on opponents by questioning the way they play or the personnel they have. He's had some really good success, so maybe it works, but I prefer to be deferential and save my thoughts and comments for when I'm interacting directly with the players.

After some staged photos and a quick 'huddle', where I was joined in a quiet corner by the Irish print journalists to answer any final questions they had, Rory and I staggered away from the launch event a bit dazed and weary. A twenty-minute bus trip brought us to Heathrow for a two-hour referee workshop. We discussed various priorities and were warned that there would be zero tolerance for foul play in the Championship.

Mostly we just nodded and took notes, but we got stuck on one of the clips that was shown, of Rory Best trying to win a turnover. He got called to release the ball by the referee, but it was explained to the group that, as the first arriving player, he should have been able to continue to contest the ball. Warren Gatland, wily as ever, questioned whether Rory's entry was legal, and after it was established that it was, he questioned whether or not Rory was in control of his own body weight. There was some brief discussion, but it was agreed that he was fine. Afterwards, the Scotland captain, John Barclay, said to me that if people were going to question the legality of that example, we might as well forget about trying to contest the ball at all.

Thursday, 25 January, Oliva Nova

Yesterday ended with a flight to Madrid, a dash through the airport just in time to connect to Valencia, and then the drive back to Oliva Nova, arriving just after midnight. I got a bit of planning done on the flights, and had a quick check-in with my brother in the car. He was still positive, despite feedback about the extent of the damage done by the heart attack, which limits his options for possible interventions. It played on my mind, but the fatigue from the last few days ensured that I slept soundly enough.

We had a squad briefing before starting today's work. After collating all the responses to the questions that we asked each player, I focused on the vital collective question of what we need to do better than ever to win the Grand Slam. There's nothing too earth-shattering about what we need to commit to, but at least it was written down and could be used as a consistent reference point when assessing our preparation and training performances.

I presented the six-point summary to the leaders, each of whom took responsibility for driving one of the messages during the squad briefing and for the remainder of the week.

- **DISCIPLINE** – Preparation and Performance
- **CLARITY EARLY, PHYSICAL END** – Detail by Wednesday evening, then 'Aggressive Edge'
- **COLLECTIVE** – Bibs better than ever!
- **BASICS** and **Phase Accuracy** – Positive Habits. Loading, Linking, Looking after the ball and each

other. Being early and smart defensively to be connected for sharp tackle entry

- **SETPIECE** – 8 Man Scrum, Lineout process, Maul and Kick-off – clear/quick
- **REGENERATION and READINESS** – Sleep, Recovery, Relaxation, Camaraderie, Mindfulness, Visualisation, Rehabilitation/ Prehabilitation

'Bibs better than ever' was particularly important. This meant that those players not selected in the starting XV – and who wore bibs in training – had to challenge the starters more than ever: put them under pressure and force them to work as hard as they could. Any flaws or weaknesses could be exposed and problem-solved during the week, rather than after the match when it would be too late. The players willingly committed to what they had themselves decreed necessary and we were set for the final two days of camp.

Training on Thursday morning had Andy Farrell to the fore, drilling in the defensive essentials and trying to fast-track a few very young players – some hesitant, others impulsive. The players worked hard and there was a competitive buzz among them, but in the coaches' meeting later we all agreed that there was plenty of work still to do.

Friday, 26 January, Dublin

This morning was overcast and very much cooler. A short and ideally sharp attacking session was planned, and it's what we attempted to do, but the heavy rain that swept in soon after training started made the session very challenging. As the bitterly cold wind cut through drenched clothing and numbed fingers, the players tried to maintain their accuracy as best they could. The conditions were at least good preparation for our return to Dublin this afternoon.

Saturday, 27 January, Churchtown, Dublin

The weekend offers a bit of breathing space after an intense week, but there is plenty to review and plenty of preparation to get done before opening the Championship against France in Paris. With Jacques Brunel having replaced Guy Novès as head coach just a few weeks ago, predicting their team and what they are likely to do is more difficult. Guy Novès was always good to chat with after matches, and his dismissal just two days after Christmas was another example of the ruthlessness that is now very much a part of professional rugby.

Jacques Brunel coached Perpignan when I was at Clermont, and I had a lot of respect for him. We played Perpignan in very tough Top 14 play-off matches three years in a row. We lost the 2009 Top 14 Final to them on a day when the Catalans had breathed fire. Jacques had coached Italy in the previous Six Nations, and he was head coach at Bordeaux just prior to being promoted to his new role. So, in addition to recent matches played by France, the coaches went through a number of Bordeaux games as well as a few Lyon games, because Julien Bonnaire was coaching there and he had been brought into Jacques's coaching team as a lineout specialist. I coached Julien in Clermont. He was a quality individual and a great loose forward, with a lineout acumen and athleticism that made him world class.

There has been a lot of hype around the two new

out-halves that the French have selected in their squad, Matthieu Jalibert and Anthony Belleau, and the French media are predicting that the nineteen-year-old Jalibert will start against us. We also know that our discipline will need to be spot on because the French scrum half, Maxime Machenaud, has been goal-kicking with 94 per cent accuracy during the season thus far.

The indifferent form that saw the French team fail to win any of their matches in the autumn, and the changes in the French management, means that we are favoured to win; but we know that counts for nothing. We know how hard they will contest the ruck and how physical they'll be. The athleticism and power of Yacouba Camara, Rémi Lamerat, Benjamin Fall and Teddy Thomas, among others, will stress our defence if we allow them any space to move.

We will need to play with tempo against the big French side. The Top 14 can be a bit of a slugfest, and we're keen to stretch their levels of fitness and discipline by keeping good speed in the game. At the same time, we need to get off our line defensively, because we can't afford to let their big ball carriers get momentum.

Friday, 2 February, Hôtel du Collectionneur, Paris

The pressure of a test against France in Paris has been heightened by the trial of Paddy Jackson and Stuart Olding, which started this week in Belfast. Most of the players in our squad have played or trained with one or both of them. Rory Best and Iain Henderson attended the trial on Wednesday, which is the players' down day. None of the management were aware that the two players were going to attend, and the outrage that followed was difficult for everyone in the group. Social media whipped themselves into a frenzy and there was a lot of coverage in the mainstream media. A number of people claimed it was inappropriate for the Irish captain to be released from national camp to attend the trial, but anyone who knows our weekly structure would have been aware that players return home on Tuesday afternoons for a break before reassembling on Wednesday evening.

We refused to comment on anything to do with the trial, and we didn't realize how hostile some of the commentary had become until today. It was uncomfortable for all of us, but it particularly magnified the stress Rory was already under, and he considered relinquishing the captaincy. He even thought about walking away from the game completely, such was the fallout for his family and those around him.

It has been an incredibly difficult time, and tension with the media was heightened when one journalist made the unacceptable error, in an online article, of mistakenly naming one of the players in the team to play against France as one of the defendants in the trial. The story was quickly taken down, but we decided to exclude the journalist from the 'huddle', where Irish print journalists for the dailies have a chat with me, after the main post-match press conference.

Sunday, 4 February, Carton House

The conditions at the Stade de France were greasy, and the play was frustratingly disjointed. We had positive control of the match but didn't make the most of our opportunities. We didn't play as well as we would have liked and it was probably similar for the referee, Nigel Owens, who struggled with the sort of scrum inconsistency that sometimes beleaguers matches. Elsewhere, we were sanctioned for having too many players in the lineout after the French cleverly called out '*Six*' when they actually had seven players, and duped Nigel. The number and nature of infringements from the colossal second-row Sébastien Vahaamahina could easily have earned him a yellow card. The frustration built as the infringements mounted, especially after a long kick was clearly knocked backwards by Keith Earls. Nigel ruled it as a knock-on, despite being a full 30 metres down the pitch on the same plane as Earlsy, meaning that it was impossible for him to see the direction that the ball had fallen.

When Teddy Thomas scorched up the right-hand touchline late in the game, then weaved infield to beat the cover defence, the dream of a Grand Slam was very close to being over before it started. With so little time left, I felt a sense of déjà vu. Two years earlier, in very similar circumstances, a late try had given the French a one-point victory.

With just two and a half minutes remaining, a superb 22-metre drop-out from Johnny Sexton, athletically gathered by Iain Henderson, gave us one last opportunity to get some reward from the control we'd had for the first seventy minutes of the match. In the stand, we took shallow breaths and watched the play unfold, willing the players to keep working. As the clock went into the red, we were still a bit shy of halfway. It was trench warfare in the middle of the pitch, and Keith Earls, arm elevated and waving, offered an option on the edge. Afterwards, Johnny told me he saw the opportunity but initially felt there was too much risk. But as our momentum stalled he backed his skill, and that of Earlsy, hitting a well-judged cross kick. Earlsy soared and his opposing winger, Vakatawa, backed off, knowing that he couldn't afford to concede a penalty. Momentum was re-ignited, and Henderson got us on to the front foot again with a powerful carry.

Johnny had missed an earlier penalty kick that would have put us 15–6 ahead, and he said later that he just wanted to get another chance. His assertiveness to take the drop goal as soon as he felt he was in range was crucial. He had been on the ground trying to stave off cramp in both calves just a few seconds before positioning himself in the pocket to receive Conor Murray's sharp pass. He had just enough time and space to send the ball on its way before any of the advancing French players could block it down.

It felt as though time slowed down as the kick arced towards the posts. We were side-on, so we couldn't see if it was straight, but we could tell it had been well struck. I looked back at Johnny, who was watching anxiously but with his arms half raised, which I took as a sign that it might be travelling straight enough. It looked like it had the distance – and then it seemed that gravity started to win the battle. It looked to us like it just sneaked over the bar. Nigel Owens, who had got into the ideal position to judge it, raised his arm and whistled to signal the goal. The coaches and our analyst, Vinny Hammond, grabbed each other in a collective hug, from which we quickly dusted ourselves off, acting as if we'd maintained our composure throughout.

Going down the stadium steps, I passed a group of French supporters, dismayed by the result but acknowledging the quality of the endgame: '*Bravo! Incroyable, le drop de Sexton était énorme!*' I stopped briefly to express my appreciation for their summary and sportsmanship: '*Merci, merci beaucoup, mais on a eu beaucoup la chance, je crois!*'

It was buzzing on the sideline, so I slipped down the tunnel toward the dressing room. Alan Quinlan shook my hand and said that he'd expressed a fair bit of frustration about the refereeing performance in his commentary, and that we'd done incredibly well to win it despite the conditions and the pressure. Shane Horgan was also perturbed by the refereeing and said that it had nearly cost us. The job referees do is incredibly difficult: they are human beings from whom machine-like accuracy is demanded. Nigel, at the top of his game, is the referee favoured by so many of us, with his feel for the game and clarity of thought, but no one is immune to having a difficult day at the office. That's what we felt as coaches after compiling our review.

The drop goal was a special sporting moment, with the build-up and final execution the focus of much attention in the days that followed the match. One amusing summary of the drop goal was provided on television by Matt Williams, who praised Johnny for the mastering of such a difficult task: 'To take the ball, to drop it, let it hit the ground on a wet day, bounce up [motioning with his hand the ball rebounding off the ground], and then kick it.' We chuckled watching this, because a kicker striking a long-range drop goal would never allow the ball to 'bounce up'. The foot strike is simultaneous with the ball hitting the ground. Ronan O'Gara was on the same panel and would have been far more able to explain the mechanics of the drop goal. Punditry sometimes seems to be more art than science!

Monday, 5 February, Carton House

Today's review of the France match was sombre enough, because we knew that we had made errors, and we didn't look to excuse them because of the weather conditions or any decisions that went against us. Vinny Hammond put together a great 'pile-ups' video, with examples from various sports, and then the footage of Bundee leaping on to Johnny and the two of them being buried beneath celebrating players at the end of the match. Even John Moran, the bagman, ran on to slap the backs of a few on top of the pile, though he showed sufficient restraint not to leap on top himself. We laughed at ourselves, wiped our brows, breathed a sigh of relief and turned our attention to the Italian game.

Thursday, 8 February, Carton House

Two head injury assessment (HIA) decisions made by the match-day doctor in the France game have been a lingering distraction this week.

In a test match, each team has its own medical personnel, but there is also a match-day doctor appointed by the home union. Matthieu Jalibert and Antoine Dupont were removed from the pitch for HIAs even though it appeared they both had leg injuries. When a player is taken off for an HIA or a blood injury, he may be replaced by a player who had been removed earlier as a tactical substitution; this is not the case for other injuries.

Jalibert plainly collided knee on knee with Bundee Aki. Jalibert held his knee and remained on the ground, but at no stage was he prone or did he appear dazed. The replays clearly showed the knee-to-knee impact being the cause of the injury.

The next knee injury in the match was to one of our players, Josh van der Flier. He fell into the tackle of Guilhem Guirado toward the end of the first half. His head made clear contact with the arm of the French captain. Guirado's arm was propelled forward into the contact and Josh's neck snapped back awkwardly. The referee blew his whistle in repeated short blasts to signal that play should stop immediately. The mechanism of injury was not immediately clear, but replays showed that Josh fell into the tackle and Nigel Owens described the head contact accurately: 'Pure accident, fell down.' When he saw Josh's positioning on the ground he said to Josh, 'I think it's a leg, yeah?' It was quickly established that it was not a head injury, and there was no HIA called for by the match-day doctor. Josh was replaced by Dan Leavy as a normal injury replacement.

The third knee injury, to the substitute scrum half, Antoine Dupont, just four minutes from the end of the match, was probably the reason why Six Nations Rugby decided to review the HIA decisions in the match. Dupont was tackled by Conor Murray, and there was no head contact. Nigel received an alert from his assistant referee and signalled a potential head injury, but it was quickly and clearly established that there was no head injury. The French medical staff on the pitch were beyond reproach, agreeing that there was no head injury. It was quite obviously a knee injury, but the match-day doctor sent on the fourth official to insist that an HIA must be undertaken, thereby allowing the starting scrum half, Maxime Machenaud, to come back on to the pitch as a substitute for Dupont.

As part of the review, we were required to have a number of players write responses to a list of questions regarding the replacement of Jalibert and Dupont. The players were asked to give their view of what had happened. We were asked to express any concerns we had regarding any laws or regulations that we felt had been breached. I was uncomfortable with the request, especially because we felt strongly that the medical staff from the French team had been totally professional and did not want to add to their angst, or to waste our time answering questions when the video evidence was so clear. Gathering players together to answer a questionnaire in a match week was a distraction that we could do without, so we declined to comment.

Roger Morris, who was leading the review, demanded that we answer the questions, citing the terms and conditions of the Six Nations agreement. We didn't have much choice, but tried to stay as impartial, factual and brief as possible so that the decision could be made based on the clear visual and audio evidence and not on the recollections of fatigued players.

Friday, 9 February, Shelbourne Hotel, Dublin

We believe that the Italians are going to cause plenty of stress for us. Conor O'Shea has been making a few tough decisions, bringing through a number of younger players. We've had a good look at them, and they managed to score some really good tries against England in their opening match. The England winger, Anthony Watson, had been razor sharp, scoring two excellent tries early in the first half. Italy, though, fought back and trailed by just ten points when the midfielder Tommaso Boni appeared to score, potentially bringing the score to 17–20 with thirty minutes remaining. But the try was disallowed due to an earlier infringement, and a few minutes later Sam Simmonds charged over from a lineout and the English started to draw away.

There were calls, as there sometimes are, to make whole-sale changes to our team for the Italian match, but the Six Nations Championship is our biggest annual event, and a number of the combinations hadn't meshed as well as we'd have liked them to against France. Speaking to the media, I tried to emphasize the threat that Italy posed and name-checked some of their dangerous players, such as the young fullback Matteo Minozzi. Most of our journalists were scep-tical, and insisted on a bonus-point win with greater attacking accuracy. It was hard to argue with them, because we were very keen to deliver exactly that.

After considerable deliberation in the selection meeting we made four changes to the starting line-up. Jack McGrath and Devin Toner will come in at prop and lock respectively, and Dan Leavy will start in place of the injured Josh van der Flier at openside flanker. Jack Conan, who was impressive on the summer tour, starts at No. 8, allowing C. J. Stander – who had forty-two clean-outs and twenty-three carries against the French – a bit of a rest. Andrew Porter, in for his first Six Nations match, has been added to the bench, along with Quinn Roux, Kieran Marmion and the exciting young-ster Jordan Larmour.

We had planned to bring Ultan Dillane into the match-day squad, but tragically his mum, Ellen, passed away early in the week. Ultan was shattered when the news came through late on the Monday evening, but despite his grief he was incredibly stoic. Ger Carmody and Sinéad Bennett, our logistics staff, were very conscious of the snowfall and icy conditions on the roads that night, so they drove him to Galway. Jimmy Duffy, the Connacht forwards coach and a top man, got him organized from there.

Everyone was shaken by Ultan's loss, and the euphoria of the win in Paris was replaced by a nervous melancholy. The camp was flat and the Connacht players were particularly quiet. After training on Tuesday I think everyone was thankful for a bit of breathing space and reflective time. The team manager, Paul Dean, and I decided to visit Ultan in Tralee, so after the team meeting this morning I excused myself from the captain's run. The players filed out to travel to the stadium, while Paul and I headed for the train station.

Monday, 12 February, Dublin

After a long day on Friday, there was an upswing on Saturday morning. The Shelbourne Hotel is always special on match days, with so many supporters crowding into the foyer and on to the steps, then spilling on to the street to wave flags and roar support as we weave through them on our way to the bus. Thankfully, we also managed to weave our way through the Italian defence early in the game and scored some very good tries. Jack Conan's sweetly timed pass to Conor Murray as they swapped attacking lanes and Bundee Aki scything through to set up Keith Earls were particularly memorable. The bonus-point fourth try was scored a few minutes before half-time.

A hamstring injury to Tadhg Furlong after just three minutes meant that Andrew Porter entered the fray very early for his Six Nations debut, and his 77-minute shift included plenty of positives. We also decided to withdraw Iain Henderson at half-time due to a tight hamstring. The third British and Irish Lions player to leave the pitch through injury was Robbie Henshaw. A few minutes after half-time he snaffled a loose pass from Sergio Parisse and sprinted 40 metres for the try line. Chased by the Italian winger Tommaso Benvenuti, Robbie held him at bay just long enough to make the try line. In the coaches' box I said quietly, 'Don't score it, Robbie.' I'd seen the same thing a number of times, where the chasing player lands on top of a player who has the ball tucked under his arm or who reaches out to score, causing the force to go through the shoulder and dislocate it. We needed Robbie more than we needed another score but, regrettably, he had to be helped from the pitch and will be sidelined for the remainder of the Championship.

As good as the 42–0 scoreline was after fifty-five minutes, it was the final twenty-five minutes and the injuries we sustained that captured most of the headlines. Three well-taken Italian tries followed some loose kicking, poor decision-making and passive tackling by us. Despite this, the highlight of the game was probably the angled 60-metre chasedown of the Italian winger Mattia Bellini by Keith Earls. It began after Jordan Larmour mesmerized the Italian defence with his footwork. When he was dragged down by the cover defence it looked like a four-on-two overlap would add to our try tally, but an intercept by Bellini saw him with clear space in front of him. Keith turned and chased from the middle of the pitch, mowing Bellini down impressively.

The squabble regarding the journalists' huddle had escalated since the Paris win. We were informed by Rugby Writers Ireland that we couldn't exclude an individual from the huddle. They said that they'd made a mistake in consenting to the exclusion of one of their people from the huddle in the Stade de France. We argued that it wasn't acceptable to defame the character of a player. They remained steadfast and decreed that it was to be all or nothing, so we decided it would be nothing.

It was awkward, because we wanted to engage positively with the journalists, but we had pleaded with the rugby writers prior to this incident to be more accurate and to corroborate details before printing them. In December, the Irish media had reported that C. J. Stander had been offered a contract of €840,000 per annum by Montpellier. Vern Cotter, now head coach at Montpellier, immediately contacted me to rubbish the claim. He explained that the pressure of the JIFF (Jeunes Issues de Formation Française), which limits the numbers of foreign players, meant that they were reducing their cohort of foreigners, not adding to it. I'm not sure where the journalists sourced their information, but I certainly trusted VC.

That same month, there was an almost identical situation when the *Irish Independent* reported that Gloucester were trying to sign Peter O'Mahony. I hadn't even seen the article before I was contacted by David Humphreys, the former Ulster and Ireland out-half, and now Director of Rugby at Gloucester. He explained that they had spent their player budget for the following year and had already recruited a top-level loose forward who they were very happy with and were not chasing Pete at all.

It was suggested to me that some player agents try to create pressure in the media to drive up players' value and accelerate negotiations. That may be the case, but wouldn't it make sense for journalists to corroborate these alleged offers before printing them as news?

There were a few barbed comments about the lack of a huddle after the Italy game, but we decided to hold our ground and move on. One bonus of not doing the huddle was that I got to spend a few minutes with the families of the players prior to the post-match dinner, and even caught up briefly with my wife and son.

Tuesday, 13 February, Athlone

The next job is preparing for Wales. At the same time, with two weeks until the match, we want to give the players an opportunity to regenerate, both mentally and physically.

We assembled for our Athlone mini-camp at midday and had a unit focus for the first afternoon. We primed the players to work hard and, while the backs did a strength session, the forwards went to work on the pitch at the Athlone Institute of Technology with Simon Easterby, getting some lineout fine-tuning done.

When we flipped it over, the backs went on to the pitch, which was pretty damp underfoot. We did a 'micro drill' focused on corner defence, with defenders trying to cover an overlap and the ball being put through behind them. Wales have caused us plenty of problems with these grubber kicks in recent years, so we tried to make sure that we could defend the front line, while also being able to get back and claim the loose ball. We'd then look to rebound and fight to our feet, before two players with shields would attack the player in possession and the two other defenders would have to get back and combat the attacking shields.

One of the keys to the exercise was to challenge the attackers to get through the line or 'soft-foot' the grubber kick through with as much control as possible, while the defenders were equally challenged. We created a few different scenarios. The idea is that there will be a moment in the match against Wales when they will put the ball through on the ground and we will offer them no access because we've anticipated them doing it and are committed to beating them to the ball and making sure that we can look after it.

In a meeting prior to the backs session, I showed some clips of grubber kicks used by the Welsh players in the Championship so far. We knew which Welsh players would be most likely to slide the ball through with their foot, and which foot each of them would prefer to use. We also noted that they were using wide passes to players running hard from deep, so we were preparing to defend the front line as well as any grubber kicks. In between the 'corner defence' drills, we made the players work hard with grapple drills, where they physically had to wrestle for possession. It heightened the challenge of defending the corner, staying sharp and being dynamic when retrieving any ball behind the line. The players put plenty of energy into it.

We split again into backs and forwards units. One group rotated through cryotherapy pods, while the other group focused on their mental skills. I felt that our focus on being mentally prepared was a positive point of difference for us. In the session, we reflected on some individual experiences, discussing how different players prepared themselves, what cue words they used and how they got the most out of their visualization. We went through some guided visualization of different moments in a match. The better the players were at immersing themselves in the action and increasing their sensory awareness, the more vivid and beneficial it could be for them.

It was great to hear Keith Earls explain to others how he had visualized himself running down Bellini after a line break before we'd played Italy. He'd visualized Bellini's left-arm fend coming out, and planned his response to knock it down or to fire in hard and fast below the fend. He was ready for either action and confident about what he could deliver, so that when it occurred he was decisive. Earlsy is so well respected in the group, and the example he gave added credibility to our focus on mental skills and the competitive edge they offer. It was great to share a few ideas and I think everyone felt encouraged at the end of the session.

A dinner out at a local gastropub, Grogan's, was well earned and it was great to see the Athlone local, Robbie Henshaw, despite his shoulder being immobilized in a sling. Robbie, positive as always, was philosophical about the injury but committed to getting back to full fitness as soon as possible.

Wednesday, 14 February, Athlone

Day two of the mini-camp was an attack-focused day but not physically demanding. With Johnny Sexton on light duties, Joey Carbery got a great opportunity to run the team. The training began with a walk-through focusing on our strike attack from lineout, then phase attack. We did plenty of repetition to automate as much of the 'loading' and timing of plays as we could. We used the interior of the indoor track at the AIT, which was perfect. Part way through the session, torrential rain pummelled the Perspex surrounds and ceiling panels. Thankfully, the rain had stopped by the time we went out on to the 3G pitch, where we could spread out and speed up.

Our head analyst, Mervyn Murphy, had braved the weather conditions in setting up to record the outdoor session, and was dripping and shivering by the time we got out to the pitch. He is, literally, a man for all seasons. He's meticulous, perceptive and absolutely committed. People like Merv are pivotal in a team. No ego, all effort and a thorough understanding of the game.

Despite having zero flexibility, I joined in with the players for the yoga session in the evening. The session encouraged us all to slow down and unwind a bit. We mixed the groups up with some mindfulness and a bit of relaxation using soundtracks players had put together for themselves. It was an important part of the camp: we wanted to expose the players to a few different ways to relax and recover.

Thursday, 15 February, Athlone

Andy Farrell primed the players with some no-nonsense feedback from the Italy game. The solutions to the defensive problems we'd had in the second half were tangible if we could get our hold/fold decisions right. Some players had stayed on the blind side and not bothered to go around the ruck to give us the right numbers on either side of the ruck. We also needed to get the spacing between defenders more consistent and connect up earlier to make collective decisions, not individual ones. The players committed to delivering an energetic and accurate training at the home of the Athlone Buccaneers, Dubarry Park.

It was an open session, and there was plenty of noise and enthusiasm from the spectators. The free tickets had been snaffled up within minutes of them being released, so the ground was packed. The U20s have become accustomed to joining us for these twice-annual trainings, and have become increasingly combative when challenged. The training is good fun. There is a buzz on the pitch and surrounding it as the players commit wholeheartedly to the fast-paced phase defence. There had been plenty of rain so the pitch was a bit gunky, further fatiguing tired legs, but the people at the club had done a superb job getting everything ready for us.

We combined the squads for lunch back at the Sheraton Hotel, where the staff have done an excellent job of looking after us. It was an opportunity for the two coaching teams to sit down and chat about what they were looking to improve upon, and we exchanged ideas about which players had done well and which parts of the training had most tested the teams.

I was pretty shattered by the time I got home for the brief hiatus of a couple of days off. There was still plenty of review work and preparatory work needed to set up the Wales week, but Kelly and I met Mick Kearney and his wife, Eugenie, for dinner on Thursday evening and they're always great company. It was refreshing and the sort of distraction that I needed, but we were home relatively early and I did a bit of review work before getting some overdue sleep.

Monday, 19 February, Carton House

Freshened, the players started the week with good energy in the morning gym session and were sharp on the pitch in the afternoon. We didn't do a lot, having banked some good work at the mini-camp, but it was good to reintegrate the players who had spent last week with their provinces. I chatted to each of the provincial coaches about who might go back to them again, as long as we didn't pick up any injuries during the training week. It's complicated in match weeks, because we try to let some players go back to their provinces after training on Tuesday, and this can compromise our own training resources a bit. Thankfully, the Academy Manager at Leinster, Peter Smyth, rounds up sub-Academy lads or U19 players so that we have sufficient training numbers. One really good by-product of this arrangement is that a few of the youngsters who came in to train with us in the past have now become part of the senior national squad.

We have some selection headaches. Luke McGrath, who'd gone back to play for Leinster, hurt his ankle and won't be available for the remainder of the Championship; Robbie Henshaw is out with his shoulder injury; and there is still doubt about Iain Henderson and Tadhg Furlong. We decided to leave the two talismanic big men out of the starting line-up and show confidence in two youngsters, James Ryan and Andrew Porter. We made the decision early in the week to allow the players more time to prepare themselves. It's one of the things I learned when coaching at Leinster: that it's often better to select a fully fit player, even if he's not normally first choice, rather than risk selecting a high-profile player who is only partially fit. That player may not make it on to the pitch on match day or, if he does, he's more likely to need to be replaced during the match, which can reduce our options for strategic substitutions. The other advantage is that the players who are selected gain confidence from the faith you show in them as well as gaining experience, which helps fuel the competition for places within the squad.

Andrew Porter has yet to make a start in the Champions Cup for Leinster, but we've selected him to start against a very awkward Welsh front row. His direct opponent in the scrum, Rob Evans, is a powerful scrummager and tricky customer at the best of times, so it's going to be a test match in every sense of the word for Ports. Chris Farrell, who did so well in the autumn against Argentina, will be teaming up with Bundee Aki for just the second time, but they did well on their first outing together in November and they've linked well in training.

The review of the HIA decisions in the France game, while not suggesting any 'impropriety', recommended that match-day doctors should be 'neutral of the two teams involved in the match', in the quest to avoid any 'perception' of impropriety. Roger Morris found on the balance of probabilities that the HIAs were 'unnecessary' but that no one was to blame.

Friday, 23 February, Shelbourne Hotel

Wales tend to squeeze the life out of teams and batter them into submission, so they're always difficult to play. This weekend Warren Gatland will be coaching his 100th test match, which is a really impressive milestone and it's likely to spice up what is already a keen rivalry. Also, because Gats has a reputation for making contentious remarks, journalists probe him for them. Earlier this week, in response to the question 'Looking at the first two games, Ireland have looked the strongest team in the tournament so far?', Gats answered bluntly, 'No.' There was a pause before the journalist pressed him for further comment and Gats added, 'I mean, England are a tough outfit . . .'

At the same time, I was probed about any frustration I

have with us being 'pigeonholed as blunt' by Gats. This is an ironic critique, considering the way Wales have used big midfielders and very direct 'around the corner' tactics in the past, but I didn't say that. Instead I observed that 'sometimes it is frustrating because one opposition coach has tried to create that story and people have picked it up without doing their own analysis'. I referenced Daniel Hourcade, the Argentinian coach, and Allister Coetzee, the former South African coach, and questioned why their rather different impression of the attacking threats we posed wasn't part of the narrative. I thought later that I should've referenced Conor O'Shea as well, and the legendary Italian captain, Sergio Parisse, who said after we'd played them in the previous round of the Championship that 'Ireland play much better rugby than England, for me . . . I like the way they play.'

Away from the pantomime of coaches' comments, the main media focus of the week has been the absence of three British and Irish Lions from our match-day squad, while Wales welcome back three influential Lions, in Leigh Halfpenny, Liam Williams and Dan Biggar. There's plenty of speculation regarding our vulnerability, but we've trained well this week. The scrum sessions have been really positive and Andrew Porter and James Ryan have slotted in with a quiet confidence. I feel we're ready to play well, and I'm just hoping that we start well to add a bit of belief to what we want to achieve.

Saturday, 24 February: Ireland v Wales

Dan Biggar kicks off and after just eleven seconds Chris Farrell makes a thumping tackle on Leigh Halfpenny, an ideal way to get straight into the game with confidence. Less than twenty seconds later, Wales receive a penalty for offside after we spill a high ball, and from a reasonably difficult angle Halfpenny strikes a superb kick that bisects the uprights. Farrell, continuing his positive start in the game, takes the kick-off, dominating the aerial contest with his 6-foot 4-inch frame. A phase later we have a penalty almost in front and just 28 metres out. Incredibly, Johnny Sexton's kick deflects off the right-hand post.

We get the ball back and Andrew Porter is solid in his first scrum. We play a couple of strong phases in their 22 and Johnny pivots to rifle one of the best passes I've seen, across the face of Bundee Aki to give Jacob Stockdale the space to score untouched in the corner. Johnny's sideline conversion attempt is well struck but slides just past the right-hand post.

Wales score a good try after some sluggish defence from us and despite looking dangerous and putting some really good play together we fail to add any further points on the scoreboard. Almost against the run of play, a super leap from Dan Biggar, to win an aerial battle with Rob Kearney, earns them another penalty. Halfpenny puts it over, and after half an hour we're trailing 5–13. I feel that it doesn't reflect the flow of the game. I have a sense of déjà vu: we had played so well in the early stages of the game against Wales last year, but failed to capitalize on the pressure we built and the line breaks we made.

We get back into the game after a set play sees Keith Earls scythe through the Welsh defence. At the end of the robust phases that follow, Cian Healy is held up on the try line but Johnny slots a penalty from in front and momentum shifts back to us, especially as the Welsh start to leak penalties.

After twenty pressurized phases, Bundee Aki bullies his way over the line and we finish the half with a two-point lead.

We start the second half well with Rob Kearney's offload to Keith Earls putting him into space, and when he passes infield to Conor Murray it looks as if he might score, but he bobbles the pass before regathering it. The forwards link up with dynamic carries and Dan Leavy gets over under the posts. We go straight back on to the attack but lose a lineout close to the Welsh line. In the defensive highlight of the match, Johnny's bone-jarring tackle on the powerful Welsh No. 8 Ross Moriarty traps the Welsh in their in-goal. We score from the ensuing scrum and have a 27–13 lead going into the last quarter.

With just four minutes left we appear to have repelled the Welsh fightback, leading 30–20. The quality from the Welsh bench is to the fore as Tipuric releases George North into some space. Then we get bunched and make some poor decisions as they move the ball back across the pitch. Scott Williams offloads to Josh Navidi, who links with the rapid Steff Evans. Suddenly, with just a few minutes left, our lead is down to a very narrow and nerve-racking three points.

We concede a penalty and Wales take the chance to attack from a lineout on the halfway. We seem nervous defensively, having made a few errors. This is a risk when new guys come into a side, and the pressure is visible in the players' body language. The lineout is untidy but Wales clear the ball, before attacking with good intent. They create an overlap on our left-hand side, but a lofted pass is picked off by Jacob Stockdale who accelerates away to score between the posts.

It's a huge relief to get the result, and Rory and I get through the press conference with plenty of positives, apart from the questions around letting Wales back into the game after having held a fourteen-point lead. Chris Farrell is a good-news story, as are the youngsters who did well replacing Tadhg Furlong and Iain Henderson. The standoff with the print media continues and the huddle doesn't happen, but at least it gives me time to catch up with the Welsh coaching staff.

Gats and I have a good chat and a chuckle about the media jousting. The other Welsh coaches are there and it's good to talk with Rob Howley, who explains that they're playing with more width and he's enjoying the challenge. We all keep a casual eye on the Scotland v England game. England, having lost just once in the last two seasons, are struggling with Scotland's intensity at the breakdown. Huw Jones scores an impressive try from the deep as we're watching and the unlikely begins to look possible. In the end, Scotland don't just win, they win with a margin to spare.

Friday, 2 March, Dublin

With another two-week gap before the Scotland game, we stayed in town for a 24-hour camp and an open session on Tuesday with the Under 20s at the Aviva Stadium. The forecast was for snow, with the arrival of the 'Beast from the East' imminent. We managed to get the training done as the first flakes fell. Conditions were cold but perfect for training, and the session in front of 5,000 rowdy fans had plenty of tempo and a freshness that belied the stress of Saturday's win. Chris Farrell twisted slightly when jogging and went down in pain. He recovered quite quickly and was keen to resume the training, but the medics, Colm Fuller and Ciarán Cosgrove, suggested that he sit out the remainder of the training and get a scan done.

I was gutted later in the day, as was Chris, when we discovered that he had ruptured his anterior cruciate ligament. It will need to be repaired and it's likely that it will be about nine months before he will be able to play again. The snow was falling heavily at that point and I lamented that if we'd scheduled our camp for later in the week, the training might have been cancelled and Chris would still have been fit. He had had big shoes to fill, replacing Robbie against Wales, but he'd slotted in seamlessly and turned in a man-of-the-match performance.

The rest of the week was compromised by the snow. I couldn't get into the office, where I had planned to catch up on a few things. We were going back and forth with the RWC people in Japan trying to confirm or adjust our accommodation, as well as trying to sort out our autumn match in Chicago with Italy. The Australian tour in June was coming together as well. The management staff posted photos of the snowmen they'd built. Vinny Hammond's robot snowman gained the most accolades, while Simon Easterby built his entire family in snow, including the dog, which was very impressive.

Friday, 9 March, Shelbourne Hotel

With the amount of snow that had fallen, we knew that our training pitches would be blanketed; but it wasn't until I arrived out at Carton House on Sunday afternoon that I realized how deep some of the drifts were. Thankfully, the drifts had gathered more at the edges, so it was still potentially an option to clear the snow. Ger Carmody, our logistics manager, had been working on getting it cleared earlier in the day with ground staff from Carton House and a crew of volunteers from the MU Barnhall Rugby Club. After a few hours, John Plummer, the head groundsman, was concerned that the pitch might be getting damaged by the scraping and the foot and barrow traffic transferring the snow beyond the edges of the pitch, so we decided to abandon the clearing and review the pitch the following day.

I met with John Plummer the next morning and we made a plan to have half a pitch cleared for Tuesday morning's training. In the meantime, our logistics people had sourced a pitch at the National Sports Campus in Abbotstown. It had only been dusted lightly with snow and the staff had cleared it during the morning, allowing us to train on it later that afternoon. I knew that the Scotland team would be training in the impressive Oriam facility, Scotland's Sports Performance Centre. I also knew that they'd be buoyed by their wins over France and England and that they would be well aware that if they could beat us, they would be in a strong position to challenge for the title, being away to Italy in the final round.

Garry Ringrose had been due to play for Leinster against Scarlets, but we withdrew him from the game because we couldn't afford to risk losing another centre. It became irrelevant anyway as the snow meant that all the games were postponed, apart from the two fixtures being played in South Africa. Garry had played just fifty-five minutes since returning from an ankle injury, while he'd also missed the autumn series due to a shoulder injury. It was a big ask for him to hit the ground running against an in-form and fast-paced Scottish side. Despite the magnitude of the challenge, there's a natural quiet and intelligent confidence around Garry that inspires confidence in others, including the coaching staff.

It was a muddled training week but an enjoyable one, with

the players fresh from a good break. There's always a bit of a feel-good factor when you've had a bit of success and when you've done something for others as well. Each of the players had been involved in doing some community service during the previous week: visits to schools, hospitals, hospices or shelters, organized by David Ó Síocháin, our media liaison.

Monday, 12 March, Carton House

On Friday evening I met with Gregor Townsend and two winners from an auction prize that Gregor and I put together for the Doddie Weir gala dinner to raise money for motor neurone disease last November. I don't know Doddie Weir personally, but he is good friends with Gregor and a number of other rugby people I know. The prize included flights to Dublin with the Scottish team, all transfers in Dublin, a tour of the Guinness Storehouse, an evening coffee with Gregor and myself where we presented the two winners with signed jerseys from the respective match-day 23s, dinner at the Michelin-starred Chapter One restaurant, a night in a deluxe room at the Shelbourne Hotel and brunch at the Shelbourne with Brian O'Driscoll and Keith Wood. The people at Guinness, Chapter One and the Shelbourne were incredibly generous donating their parts of the prize. An added bonus was that the All Black legend Sean Fitzpatrick bowled along to the brunch. He had texted to see if I was keen to sneak out for a pint the previous evening but when I'd asked if he could come along to the brunch instead he didn't hesitate to help out.

The prize also included pre-match drinks and Premium

tickets to the test match, and it was very much a match that tested us: a rollercoaster that dropped, surged and shuddered. The twenty-point margin at the final whistle was not an indication of how closely contested the match was. We had Tadhg Furlong and Iain Henderson back fresh, and Garry Ringrose slotted in as if he'd never been away, but the Scots created space and found holes that caused plenty of stress.

An early, easily kickable penalty was eschewed as we kicked to the touchline. The statement of intent fell flat as we lost the lineout and Scotland cleared their 22. Despite us dominating the first fifteen minutes, the Scots put a good ball in behind and earned a penalty, which they converted. Scotland grew in confidence but a long, lofted pass from Peter Horne toward the edge was pilfered by Jacob Stockdale. For the third time in as many matches, he raced in from long distance.

A great example of how we rattled and shuddered at times was in the twenty-eighth minute, when Finn Russell took a quick throw to himself. Scotland moved the ball wide to the opposite edge and Huw Jones's chip and regather looked certain to lead to a try as Stuart Hogg swooped in support with no one in front of him. But a poor pass allowed our defenders to get back and claim the bobbling ball. We were pushing our luck before, thankfully, a wayward lineout throw and good interplay created the scoring opportunity we needed. After being held up over the line, we put together a set play from the scrum. A square carry from Garry Ringrose, another from James Ryan. We actually got too far across the field, as we were setting up for a reverse play on the third phase. The strike play looked like it was done in slow motion. The Scots got off the line in numbers, but the play worked just well enough that Jacob Stockdale could step inside the last defender and add a crucial try out wide in the forty-second minute of the first half. It's a great time to score, to send our opponents into the changing rooms a little disheartened, while lifting our spirits. That was especially the case when Johnny nailed the conversion from a tough angle.

When we scored a try just after half-time I started hoping for a bonus point. Sean Cronin came on to replace Rory Best with fourteen minutes remaining, and three minutes later he lunged over from a maul to secure the bonus point and seal the victory.

I got a bit overexcited in the post-match interviews, stating that our ten-point advantage in the Championship table, with just one game remaining, meant that we could not be caught. In reality, if England got a bonus-point win later in Paris they could still catch us at the top of the table next week in Twickenham. I couldn't believe that I'd gotten so carried away, because I'm normally very circumspect. Standing among the coaching staff as the French ended the English chances with a 22–16 victory in Paris, I was mightily relieved: England couldn't catch us now. The Scottish coaches, Gregor Townsend and Dan McFarland, congratulated us on winning the Six Nations, but our celebrations were muted. It was a relief to have won, but we wanted more. We knew that after consecutive losses the England team would be hostile and focused on denying us the Grand Slam, just as we denied them last year.

Monday, 19 March, Dublin

Christy Moore is a legend! He's incredibly popular with the players, and they'd requested that he make a brief appearance at camp during the Six Nations if he was available. Christy chose to come in during the England week, and it dovetailed perfectly with what became the theme of the week. I know that some teams use themes to help them stay focused and collective, but this week's theme wasn't planned; it gathered momentum organically on the back of the community contributions the players had made a week or two earlier. Each of them was, in the words of one of Christy's songs, an 'ordinary man'. But when teaming up to play on match days, they were extraordinary. By the end of the week I was challenging these ordinary men to be the extraordinary team that they were and to deliver the 'exceptional deeds' that they were capable of.

In a very light week of training, we got ourselves organized with an indoor walk-through on Monday afternoon, which was ideal preparation to train on Tuesday morning at full speed. We enjoyed the brief respite and sense of companionship that listening to Christy engenders, and he sang a few favourites, including, of course, 'Ordinary Man'.

On Wednesday, footage emerged of Eddie Jones referring to the 'scummy Irish' during a corporate event last summer. He noted that we were the only team that had beaten England during his tenure and said he was 'still dirty about that game' but was adamant that 'we'll get that back, we'll get that back, don't worry, we've got 'em next year at home, we'll get 'em back . . .' The comments were obviously made with an assumption that they would never become public, and they washed over us. We had much more practical things we needed to focus on to be ready for the weekend, rather than be distracted by what was supposed to be light-hearted banter. The media thoroughly enjoyed Eddie's discomfort, but the issue was irrelevant to us.

What was relevant was how we were going to attack them and what we were going to need to do to repel their attacks and limit their supply of possession, particularly any loose or turnover ball. We do very little live contact in training, but on Thursday, prior to travelling to London, we crossed our fingers and did a close-up tackle drill. This involved a full tackle, with a second man assisting in the tackle and driving through the tackle or reloading into the first defender position. It was physical, and at one stage Rob Kearney got hit back a couple of metres and players barged through. We'd been exposed in the wide channels in the last three games so we knew that they might try to create opportunities to shorten our defensive line and attack us on the edges. We couldn't afford to waste players in the breakdown, when we needed as many on their feet as possible. The more players we had available, the more width we'd cover, which meant that we could be more forthright in our defensive line speed.

We shared our flight with supporters and there was a really positive energy among the players and those who were travelling with us. When I first started as Ireland coach, Mick Kearney, the team manager, had initiated a Thursday-evening meeting, to review the week and to problem-solve anything further that was likely to occur over the next two days. Mick, a top man and always keen on a quiet glass of red wine, would get two bottles organized along with a nice block of chocolate (or two). The meeting had been extended to include a one-hour game of Texas Hold 'em at the behest of Greg Feek. We'd probably played about forty games of poker over the past three or four years. We'd put a tenner in each, get our chips and play away, but in all that time I'd never won. On Thursday evening, in the Richmond Park Hotel, I got off to a good start but was copping flak, with the other coaches and Ger Carmody saying that I couldn't afford to win: it'd be bad luck. They needn't have worried, as I crashed out before the hour had finished.

Friday morning, I got an early call from the team doctor, Ciarán Cosgrave: there was a bug going around and he'd had it himself overnight. We later found that nobody was too badly affected, apart from James Ryan. He'd had a horror night and had been isolated in a separate room. Ruth Wood-Martin, our nutritionist, became host for James, delivering his meagre rations. This quickly became known as 'Ruth service'.

Prior to leaving for the captain's run we played a video. Vinny Hammond and I had worked feverishly to put it together, and Vinny's brilliant at synching images to soundtracks. To the five minutes and twenty-two seconds of 'Ordinary Man', we combined images from training and the arrival at the grounds, running out on to the pitch and warm-ups, followed by the best of our slow-motion match moments from the Championship thus far. We wanted the players to feel the special bond that comes from wanting something so much and working so hard to achieve it. The images and song ended together on a freeze frame of a full squad huddle and the words:

> Ordinary men
> Extraordinary team
> Exceptional deeds

Relieved that the illness hadn't spread to any of the other players or staff, we enjoyed the pleasant and sunny conditions at Twickenham, literally the calm before the storm. We did a light bit of defensive work, followed by an enthusiastic game of 'walk touch', where players are paired up and can only be 'tagged' by their partner. The backs played against the forwards, and the game was as giddy and chaotic as it usually is, allowing the players a bit of light exercise and stress release.

We knew the 'Son of the Beast' was going to chill the conditions for the following day, but it was still a bit of a shock to see the snow fall and feel the Baltic chill: an incredible contrast to the previous day. The other incredible contrast was that England had announced seven changes to their team from the twenty-three who'd played against France. The most significant saw Danny Care replaced by Richard Wigglesworth at scrum half, and Owen Farrell moving from No. 12 to No. 10, relegating George Ford to the bench. The powerful inside centre and Rugby League convert Ben Te'o, well known to many of our players because he'd played for Leinster for two seasons, was brought into the starting line-up at 12.

I was surprised that they'd dispensed with the Ford/Farrell combination. With the two pivots at 10 and 12, they would have been better able to attack with the width that had seen us look vulnerable at times during the previous three matches. The other significant backline changes saw the return of Elliot Daly and the shifting of Anthony Watson from the wing to fullback. The changes made me think that they were going to be more direct, but also mix their play up a bit to make the most of the very rapid pace of Daly and Watson along with the flyer on the right wing, Jonny May. A couple of injury-enforced changes in the pack meant that George Kruis and Sam Simmonds would add their fresh mobility to the England effort. For our part, James Ryan had recovered fully from his bug and was fit to play.

Bizarrely, we got a note from the RFU to say that they

had extended the in-goal areas by two metres at each end of the pitch. I thought back to the tries scored by Argentina and wondered whether this might be a ploy to allow a bit more space for the ball to be played into the in-goal for their chasers. We alerted the players, especially Rob Kearney and the wingers, that they'd have to be sharp to cover any ball that England slid through behind our defensive line.

Early on match mornings, I go for a walk to organize my thoughts, but I didn't have too much time to think on this morning. I walked out in my shorts and a thin jacket and was struck by the frigid air and snow flurries in Richmond Park. I turned back early and didn't get to organize too many thoughts, but felt comfortable that there wasn't too much more to be said. We received another note, this time to say that the pitch markings were going to be in blue, rather than white, because they would be more visible in case further snow fell.

On the bus on the way to a match, I usually receive a text from David Ó Síocháin updating me on the weather and pitch conditions. This time, David's news was that the referee, Angus Gardner, had arrived at the ground and the RFU had added white dashes on top of the blue line markings because Angus was blue/green colour blind and would struggle to see the blue lines. I showed the text to the coaches. We chuckled nervously and shrugged, knowing that there would probably be a few more surprises over the next four or five hours.

The Baltic conditions, with the wind gusting and spraying light snow across the ground, presented challenges for both camps. We got through the warm-up unscathed, but as we settled into the coaches' area, a gust of frigid air snatched up Simon Easterby's lineout sheets and distributed them among the crowd nearby. We were not far from the English coaches' area and feared that one of the sheets might have blown into their laps, because we only managed to retrieve two of the three. Thankfully, there weren't too many lineout hiccups after that.

The early try any team loves to get fell our way from an untidy four-man lineout win. Johnny Sexton put up a huge floating Garryowen and Rob Kearney chased, getting a hand into the contest. Anthony Watson couldn't control the ball and it spilled from his grasp. Garry Ringrose pounced and the TMO confirmed the try: 7–0 after six minutes. But it got better. A missed shot at goal was cleared by England but another four-man lineout play saw another seven points added.

This was a setpiece play with the timing and precision that you dream of seeing delivered on the big days. Tadhg Furlong slipped a deft offload to Bundee Aki, when it looked as if he was going to give the ball to Johnny on the wrap-around. Accelerating into space, Bundee looked to his right, toward Garry Ringrose, but then popped a superb pass to his left for C. J. Stander, who was running the ideal inside support line. C.J. was dragged down in front of the big Twickenham goalpost pad but reached out to force the ball against the base of the pad. Again, the TMO was called upon and again the try was confirmed.

At that point, my thought was, *We need to keep playing at them, we've earned what we've got on the scoreboard but we can't just defend an early lead: we've got to stay positive.*

Immediately, England seized back some momentum. Elliot Daly took a freakish catch to claim the kick-off and the English launched attack after attack for the next five minutes. Pete O'Mahony was sin-binned somewhat unluckily for a side entry when he appeared to be bound in the maul. We were under the pump and Elliot Daly scored three minutes later. With the half coming to a close and Johnny Sexton off the pitch undergoing an HIA, it would have been easy to put the ball into touch and take our 5–14 lead into the half-time break. But the lads played on and ninety-five seconds after the clock had ticked into the red, superb vision from Conor Murray, combined with an exceptional chip-and-chase finish from Jacob Stockdale, meant that we had added to our advantage before returning to the dressing rooms.

Ironically, Jacob grounded the ball just centimetres inside the dead-ball line, the line that had been extended by two metres. The old markings were visible on the pitch and the ball would have comfortably gone dead if the lines had stayed where they normally were. It was one of those days when things fell for us, and there aren't too many better situations for that to happen than in Twickenham, on St Patrick's Day, going for a Grand Slam . . .

For good measure, Joey Carbery, on as a temporary replacement for Johnny, calmly slotted the conversion.

England had to throw everything at us in the second half, and they were relentless in the first ten minutes after half-time. We were camped in our own half and, but for some committed defence, including a desperate diving ankle tap from Keith Earls when Elliot Daly looked to have got away down the left touchline, they would have scored. The fact that they didn't helped our belief and eventually we fought our way out of our own half.

In the fifty-fourth minute, the centre curse continued: Bundee Aki dropped awkwardly into a tackle and had to be replaced. Jordan Larmour, who had been training at wing and fullback, had to come on as his replacement. Garry

Ringrose moved to the inside-centre position and Jordan filled the outside-centre berth. We were starting to look a little frayed.

At the end of the third quarter, Conor Murray stepped up to chip over a penalty kick, and with less than twenty minutes remaining we led 24–5. It was now or never for England, who again threatened, sliding a dangerous grubber kick through close to the line, but Keith Earls, primed as ever, got back to the ball first. They were attacking in waves, and Daly finally got space on the outside to score, but time was running short for England and the margin was still fourteen points in our favour. Johnny, who'd been battered and bruised during the game, was replaced by Joey Carbery, whose first action in play was a courageous slide to field a ball on the ground despite the oncoming boots of the England replacement fullback, Mike Brown. Joey couldn't quite convert a penalty with ten minutes to go, but time continued to tick away for England.

Keith Earls had to be helped from the field, and our reserve scrum half, Kieran Marmion, replaced him on the wing. Kieran had been enlisted to do a similar job on a couple of other occasions, but the backline was now very piecemeal. With three minutes left Mike Brown got the ball down in the corner, but a desperate tackle from Sean Cronin had forced both of Brown's feet into touch prior to the grounding and we clung to the safe margin for a bit longer. Some great defence in the last few minutes of the game kept them out until they managed to get just enough space to score in the corner. But the clock was well into the red at the time and the result was secure . . . as was the Grand Slam!

Wow, it felt special. Really special for all sorts of reasons. Partly because we'd been so close to falling at the first hurdle and partly because we'd pinned our hopes on exactly this outcome from the very start of the Championship and we'd managed to produce such an emphatic first-half perform-ance, in Twickenham, on St Patrick's Day.

I was keen to catch my breath and slipped down the tun-nel into the changing rooms to drop off my radio and earpiece and to clear my head. I walked quietly back to the tunnel entry and watched the celebrations and the presentations from there. It was satisfying to watch and hear the crowd support and to see the players gain reward for what had been an incredible eight weeks.

Celebrations were hearty but not excessive. The squad, staff and sponsors gathered along with family and close friends back at the Richmond Park Hotel and we enjoyed the evening. It was the following morning that became a little complicated, trying to get back to Ireland while the stormy 'Son of the Beast' continued to interrupt flights.

At breakfast, Andy Farrell had shaved his beard to honour a bet that he'd made and he looked about ten years younger. Feeky had lost the same bet but reneged, claiming that he didn't have a good enough razor with him to have a clean shave. Everyone was pretty relaxed.

When the time drew close for us to depart for the airport, Ger Carmody said to me that the flight was delayed by about forty minutes so we might be better off staying where we were, rather than going to the airport and having extra time there. We relayed the message to the assembled players, neatly attired in their Eden Park suits. Just when I thought we'd got through the delay unscathed, a few pints started to appear and when we got news of a further delay, the pints merged into espresso martinis, but there was great banter and it was a fantastic few hours spent together.

Finally, we got word that a departure time had been confirmed and we needed to head for the airport. Ger got up to announce this to the gathered players and management. Just as he was about to speak, 'Radio Gaga' blared out on the sound system, linked suspiciously to one of the players' phones. It was hilarious as all the players got up and danced about. Then suddenly the music stopped again and everybody sat down, but as soon as Ger started to speak again, 'Radio Gaga' resumed and everybody sprang up in a repeat performance. Finally we got on to the bus and into the Aer Lingus lounge at Heathrow.

One further delay allowed time for a few more drinks in the lounge and a rousing rendition of 'The Fields of Athenry' led by Andy Farrell. It was a great impromptu singalong, crowded into a corner of the lounge surrounded by supporters holding their mobile phones aloft to capture the moment. A moment to savour.

PART FOUR
RWC Diary

Sunday, 19 March 2017, Dublin

The preparations for Japan 2019 started with individual player reviews, a few weeks after our exit from the 2015 Rugby World Cup. I visited each of the players in their provinces to get their feedback and to review their performances. For some of the senior players, like Paul O'Connell, 2015 was always going to be their last World Cup. But I encouraged the others to remain in Ireland and to keep working hard so that Ireland could be as well prepared as possible to get beyond the quarter-final stage of the 2019 World Cup.

For the coaches, while we are short-term focused in match weeks, we have also been trying to broaden our depth over the past year and a half, so that we have more players with the quality and experience to perform in the pressure cooker of a World Cup. We want to avoid the fate we suffered in 2015, when a spate of injuries in the lead-up to the quarter-final left us vulnerable. The reality is that it's difficult, with every test match being important and only about a dozen of them each year, but we have tried to include new players and to learn more about them, while giving them a chance to press their claims.

Coming into yesterday's final round of Six Nations matches, we were out of contention for the championship, but we wanted to retain our ranking among the top four teams in the world, ahead of the RWC pool draw in May.

This offers the advantage of avoiding any of the other top-ranked teams in the pool stage. It may seem odd that the seedings are confirmed more than two years prior to the tournament, but with all the organization that goes into the event it's understandable.

We've been ranked in the top four in the world since beating the All Blacks in Chicago, but if Wales had beaten France in Paris yesterday, they would have moved ahead of us, which would have meant that we'd have needed to beat England to reclaim our top-four world ranking prior to the seedings being confirmed for Japan 2019.

The game in Paris went well beyond the normal eighty minutes. France were awarded a scrum with seconds remaining, trailing 13–18. The scrum went down and the French tighthead prop Uini Atonio was removed for a HIA and replaced by Rabah Slimani. The Welsh questioned the veracity of the head injury, but the doctor was adamant that a HIA was necessary. The Welsh prop Samson Lee was sin-binned after a series of French attacks close to the line, and the French opted for another scrum. They got further penalties and the game continued until, in the 100th minute of 'normal' time, Damien Chouly got over the Welsh line to score.

It was one of the most bizarre finishes to any match that I'd seen, but at least it ensured that we would retain fourth place in the world rankings. Even better, we managed to beat England, denying them consecutive Grand Slams and preventing them from setting a new record of nineteen consecutive test match victories. We'd managed to stop the All Blacks' run of eighteen consecutive test victories last November, and this week I had plenty of texts from Kiwis pleading for us to beat the English so that the All Blacks could at least retain a share of the record.

The players responded really well to a couple of injuries to key men. Conor Murray was ruled out on Thursday after failing a fitness test, and Jamie Heaslip was ruled out when we returned to the dressing room after the warm-up. Kieran Marmion and Luke McGrath stepped up impressively in place of Conor, and there was a calm reshuffle of jerseys in the back row just prior to heading out onto the pitch. C. J. Stander switched from No. 6 to No. 8, Pete O'Mahony started at No. 6, and his No. 20 jersey was handed to Dan Leavy, who was called back from the showers.

Thursday, 11 May 2017, Kyoto

At the RWC draw yesterday, we got Scotland and Japan in our pool, along with two yet-to-be-determined qualifiers. Scotland, who beat us in the first round of the Six Nations a few months ago, will be challenging. Japan will also be difficult: they now have a team playing Super Rugby and a number of foreign-born players who will qualify to play for them in the next two years, which will add strength and depth to their side. As we entered the Kyoto State Guest House for the draw, highlights of Japan's victory over South Africa in the 2015 RWC were playing on multiple screens, underlining the threat that they will pose.

Should we make the quarter-finals, our likely opponents will be either South Africa or New Zealand: an intimidating proposition, whichever team it may be.

This morning we visited the former residence of the Tokugawa shoguns, Nijo-jo Castle. Surrounded by a moat and nestled amongst meticulously designed gardens, the castle is made up of multiple chambers connected by corridors, so that any fire could be contained. Our tour guide told us about the 'nightingale floors', which would squeak if there were intruders, and the cavities in the walls where samurai would be hidden ready to protect the Shogun. It was an intriguing introduction to some of the traditions and history of Japan.

Saturday, 6 October 2018, Tokyo

The reconnaissance crew of Ger Carmody, Jason Cowman and I have spent a busy week in Japan visiting training venues and accommodation options, and meeting local dignitaries – business cards always at the ready to exchange with a bow and *'Hajimemashite'* (nice to meet you). Between venues, we're either bundled into a minivan or riding the Japanese bullet train, the Shinkansen, which flies past the clutter of houses and concrete, punctuated by the occasional green field or market garden.

We've been calculating travel times and working out how we'll set up team rooms and timetables in various locations. Moving over fifty people and lots of equipment and baggage can present challenges between venues. We feel it's important to keep some consistency with the routines that are familiar to players, such as the team room layout, training times, food and recovery options. We're also trying to secure locations where there will be a range of activities available during their downtime.

The travel times are variable, depending on traffic, as we learned when we toured Japan in the summer of 2017. Getting from Hamamatsu, where we were staying, to Ecopa Stadium for the captain's run took forty minutes, but on match day it took sixty-five minutes. Ideally, we want to minimize disruptions and avoid spending too long on buses driving to match venues.

The squad will arrive at Haneda Airport in Tokyo on 12 September next year, then travel by bus to arrive at the New Otani Makuhari Hotel. A few days' training in the Ichihara prefecture will be followed by a midweek move to the Sheraton in Yokohama, not far from Yokohama Stadium, where we'll play Scotland in our first game.

Our second game is at Ecopa Stadium in Shizuoka versus the host nation. Finding the right accommodation here has been difficult, but we have opted for the Katsuragi Hotel. It's a risk for us, as the hotel is isolated and very different from what the players would normally experience, with a mix of traditional Japanese rooms and Western-styled rooms. The food is very Japanese, which will be a good experience, but we will need to organize a range of Western options as well. The breathing space, after the congestion of Tokyo, will hopefully help us to recover from the Scotland match on a six-day turnaround. There's no exact science to any of this, but there weren't too many other options, so we hope to get the best from our six days at the Katsuragi.

It's a logistical nightmare trying to get training venues close to hotels, with travel of thirty to forty minutes often required. Pitch sessions last for up to ninety minutes, including warm-up and individual skills, then we plan to timetable a break along with a snack, before players do a further sixty to ninety minutes in the gym. Adding in time for changing, strapping and individual preparation plus eighty minutes for travel – it drags out the training day, and being on a cramped bus is not the best way to prepare for sessions or to recover from them. It's far from the convenience of Carton House, where we have the luxury of a brief walk to the training pitches and the gym. It will be the same for all the teams, but getting the right venues and working around transfer times as best we can will certainly help.

Sunday, 23 December 2018, Carton House

For our Christmas camp, instead of our usual focus on the Six Nations, we have included some pre-planning for the RWC and a Mind Gym that is focused on mental and physical freshness. It's a shift toward a longer-term focus to be ready for next September, rather than the immediate focus on what will be our next game, at home to England in the Six Nations.

We explained to the players that the initial training squad for the RWC will be forty-two to forty-five players, and we gave them an idea of when the squad is likely to be reduced, and the cut-off date for the naming of the thirty-one-man RWC squad. We focused on recovery strategies and planning/periodization more than on performance in the twenty-four hours that we had together. We also included player visits to the elderly alongside the ALONE volunteers.

Monday, 17 June 2019, Carton House

Today was Day One of our RWC preparations. Looking to set a benchmark, we worked the forty-four-man squad hard. We emphasized the need to be 'ALL UP and ALL IN' when we got into the opposition 22. We piled a couple of players with pads on top of nominated players, who had to repeatedly fight to get up, then get forward, then be dynamic with their 'body/ball'. We went through three rotations, before doing pick-and-go drills against pads. It was all close-quarters work, and at the end of the session players were spent. There would be no excuse for being trapped on the ground or for being slow to get into position – the players ALL needed to get up and they ALL needed to get into positions to contribute. The RPEs (Rate of Perceived Exertion) reported by the players reflected their efforts, with 9/10s and 10/10s dominating.

Tuesday, 18 June 2019, Dublin

Today we visited EPIC, the Irish Emigration Museum. It was an opportunity to take some pride in what Irish people have done around the world and to understand some of the adversity that they've faced. The acronym EPIC is explained at the end of the journey through the museum: Every Person Is Connected. We want to connect as a group and also contribute a new benchmark at the RWC.

Tuesday, 25 June 2019, Carton House

This morning we got the players up at 6.15. They assembled in the team room with no clue about what was going to be required of them until the 'Commodore', Oddie Braddell, strode in. He was quick to capture the attention of the players with his booming voice and enthusiastic banter. The players were put into groups, and their challenge was to build a raft, then race it. It was an industrious but enjoyable activity, with players showing different aptitudes for leadership and practical skills as well as demonstrating their competitiveness when it came to the racing.

Jordan Larmour paddled feverishly to be on the pace in the first leg, but most of his backwash landed inside the raft so that when Sean Cronin took over, the raft slowly sank into the lake. There was a bit of chaos in the final race as some of those who were already beaten looked to capsize the more successful rafts. John Ryan raised his arms in response to the cheering when it appeared that his team would get a well-earned second place. That was until he realized that the cheering was for the players swimming behind him, trying to tip his raft over. He just managed to churn the water sufficiently to get to the bank before being set upon.

It's great to balance all the hard work with some competitive fun, so that players can connect up and enjoy working together.

Friday, 28 June 2019, Dublin

A few of the players are starting to show signs of wear and tear after an intense couple of weeks, so the upcoming recovery week will be ideal. Each Friday is 'competition day': the players compete in small-sided conditioning games. The games include plenty of passing and running and are strategic, so there's a crossover of rugby skills, but equally important are the competitive element and the ability to stay focused as well as the willingness to keep working. We want to test skills under fatigue and pressure, and I have cut a few video highlights and lowlights to offer feedback next week.

Friday, 12 July 2019, Galway

After the down week, the players assembled in Galway refreshed and ready to work hard again. On Tuesday we travelled to the Killary Adventure Company, in an absolutely beautiful spot on the shores of Killary fjord just outside of Leenane in Connemara. The fully fit players were put into groups for the assault course, while the others paddled about in kayaks and rafts. The assault-course lads ended up caked with mud and joined those on, or mostly in, the water to get the bulk of the mud off before showering and getting back on the bus.

On Thursday, Eric Elwood brought his Connacht Academy lads along to the Sportsground and gave us a really good hit-out. It's great to get involved with the young players, who bring so much enthusiasm to training and at the same time gain confidence from matching up with the international players.

A really positive week finished with a high-speed open session earlier today. There was plenty of support and a good amount of noise. Players worked hard in the small-sided competitive games mixed with some very physical ALL UP and ALL IN work.

The week also gave us a chance to spend some time catching up with the Connacht coaches, sharing a few thoughts and ideas as well as mapping out our plans for selection and the potential return dates for players.

Friday, 19 July 2019, Limerick

Another big week of pre-season training, this time using the superb facilities at the University of Limerick, Munster's home base.

On Wednesday, we spent the afternoon at Adare Manor, with the players trying their hand at archery, clay-pigeon shooting or playing nine holes of golf. We were looked after incredibly well, and it was an ideal opportunity for the players to recuperate for a few hours.

With each week, the reality that I will be finishing after the RWC comes more into focus for me. Presentations to acknowledge my time as Ireland coach – from Connacht at the open session in Galway and again today at the end of training in Thomond Park – were humbling. This job has been such a big part of my life for the past six years that it's difficult to think about stepping away, although at the same time I look forward to being free of the pressures of the role.

Friday, 2 August 2019, Dublin Airport

Our week at the very impressive new High Performance Centre in Abbotstown has been positive. We had a big session on Tuesday, and finished with a Japanese cooking lesson at KAL, where Fiona Uyema led a team of chefs to guide the players through a number of challenges. It's a fantastic set-up, and the friendly staff and delicious food were hugely appreciated by the squad.

After a tough conditioning session on Thursday that left many players bent over and gasping, Danny O'Reilly from the Coronas paid us a visit after dinner. He brought along a great group of musicians for an acoustic session. Danny's sister Róisín O and her bandmate John Broe, along with Alfie and Harry from Hudson Taylor, and the Dubs footballer Kev McManamon were all brilliant. Before the music started, I looked around the room and sensed that the group was exhausted, but once Róisín started singing 'Man in the Mirror' and the others started passing instruments around and singing different songs, the players livened up and the evening was great fun.

Abbotstown was an ideal base for the week, and there were plenty of positives as players committed to the work required. But there were also some tough conversations, as we released five players at the end of training on Friday.

Before finishing for the day, Richie Murphy and I had an hour-long session with a group of youngsters who had won the prize of a coaching session offered by our kit sponsor, Canterbury. Richie and I were both tired after a busy week, but it was a great reminder of why you end up coaching. We enjoyed the session, challenging the youngsters' skills and creating competitions for them before finishing with a modified conditioning game at the end. The enthusiasm of the kids certainly helped fuel the energy that Richie and I needed to keep up with them.

Unfortunately, this entry is being written while I'm waiting to board my flight to Auckland, where I'll catch a connection down to Palmerston North before heading straight out to the beach at Himatangi. The family are all scrambling back because my mum is dying. We can't get hold of my brother Jamie who is on holiday with his family in China, but there's real urgency now because the palliative-care people and my sisters, who have been caring for Mum, have said it's very close.

Thursday, 8 August 2019, Auckland Airport

This book started as a joint project between my mum and me. She loved offering her recollections and opinions over the past couple of years, especially on the first six chapters. Her enthusiasm was a big part of why I chose to write it, and we laughed about many of the memories and reflections.

Walking out through the arrivals hall in Auckland on Sunday, I was relieved to find Jamie and the rest of his family waiting for me. We bustled across to the domestic terminal and connected to our flight down to Palmerston North. Jamie explained that after getting a message from our youngest sister, Helen, when he and his family were in Hong Kong, he'd booked a new flight and they'd flown directly to Auckland. They'd got through Hong Kong International Airport just in time, because the following day there was mayhem, as protesters flooded the terminal and disrupted flights.

We were picked up by Helen, had showers at her place, then travelled out to the beach to spend a really good hour with Mum. She was lucid, though quieter than usual, and she needed a rest after our catch-up. She slipped away the next morning and we spent the next two days grieving, planning and organizing what had to be done. We said goodbye to her on the beach that she loved the following day, just the eight kids together.

I didn't stay on for the official service, and now I'm waiting for my flight back to Dublin for our game on Saturday. I'm sure the other coaches will have everything under control, but I'm also keen to have something else to think about, and to have something to do that will keep me busy.

Saturday, 10 August 2019, Dublin

In the lead-up to our game versus Italy, some players in our match-day squad will have been feeling uncertain about their prospects of making the RWC squad. With this in mind, the coaches emphasized that the best way to press for selection was to work hard to make the game easier for the other players – simply, to be proactive in getting to where they needed to be and then delivering what needed to be done.

Our first scrum was all power to win a penalty, but then the pass from the first lineout was intercepted, and the game continued a bit like that: we mixed some really positive play with some poor execution. After getting stepped early on by Carlo Canna, Joey Carbery grew into the game, scoring a try after sharp handling from Chris Farrell, and controlling play impressively with some pinpoint kicking. Our scrum continued to put us on the front foot and well-worked overlaps were finished off by the wingers Dave Kearney and Andrew Conway in the left and right corners, to give us a 19–10 half-time lead. An early second-half try from a driven maul made the game safe, and a charge-down late in the game from Kieran Marmion completed the scoring. The 29–10 win was a solid starting point for the summer series.

Unfortunately, in the forty-ninth minute Joey got wedged awkwardly when making a tackle and hurt his ankle. We're not yet sure about the extent of the injury but it's possible that there is ligament damage and/or a fracture. Injuries have already curtailed much of the season for Joey, so it's a real concern that he will miss vital time running the game for us.

Wednesday, 14 August 2019, Quinta do Lago

After a few days at home, I was still feeling jaded this morning as I got on the flight for our warm-weather training camp in Portugal. Here now at the Hotel Magnolia, I'm hoping that my mood lifts and that I can overcome the jet lag over the coming week.

Friday, 16 August 2019, Quinta do Lago – The Campus

Yesterday was very tough for the players, with two pitch sessions in very hot weather. We would usually avoid going onto the pitch twice in the day, but the warm-weather camp has been earmarked for some big sessions and hard work.

Sunday, 18 August 2019, Quinta do Lago – The Campus

Another very big 'double day' yesterday, with the conditioning session at the end of the day being particularly strenuous. The players are coping well, and making good use of the well-equipped gym to work on any small deficiencies as well as getting the big work done. The hot and cold contrast pools and sauna are ideal for recovery along with walking off the heavy sessions in the temperate outdoor pool.

While the players got this morning off, a small group of staff had the exhilarating experience of doing a tandem skydive. We jumped from 15,000 feet, with a freefall of about sixty-five seconds, before the parachutes were deployed and we eased our way down in arcing loops. It was on the bucket list, and I sent a photo back to my brothers and sisters, which at least gave us something different to message each other about.

I've just spent a couple of hours looking through the footage of the two games that England have played so far this summer against Wales. They looked especially menacing at Twickenham. I feel that we will need to be ready to go next Saturday, because England have already demonstrated that they're ready.

Friday, 23 August 2019, Richmond Park Hotel

The captain's run was very low-key today. Ross Byrne will start at out-half in the absence of Johnny Sexton, whose thumb injury has almost healed. With Joey Carbery's ankle injury ruling him out, Jack Carty will come off the bench, just as he did against Italy. There's uncertainty around Joey's recovery time, but we will see how he responds to a rehabilitation programme that should have him available for the Scotland match in the first pool game of the RWC.

This evening Matthew Syed came in and chatted with the squad. I've enjoyed his books *Black Box Thinking* and *Bounce*, and a number of his articles. He spoke about many aspects of performance, including committing to a team, using the example of Cristiano Ronaldo as an individual talent who realized that working harder to bring others into the game could make him an even better player.

Sunday, 25 August 2019, Churchtown, Dublin

We flew back from London last night and I have had time to go through the game. I believe the performance was out of character, and I described it in the post-match press conference as an aberration, because we'd never lost so many setpiece balls or been so disconnected. We looked fatigued, and after a tough training week in Portugal I think we were.

The first scrum came up, but we looked strong and went forward. The scrum was reset and again we went forward but we were penalized for a knee to the ground, allowing Owen Farrell to kick the first three points of the game. We responded with an excellent try by Jordan Larmour just a few minutes later, after Iain Henderson turned the ball over from an English lineout. We led 10–8 after twenty-eight minutes, but that was as good as it got for us.

The longer the game went on, the further off the pace we looked. A simple set-play try, and a string of lost lineouts and missed tackles by us, allowed England to build a 22–10 half-time lead. To make things worse, Conor Murray and Cian Healy picked up injuries toward the end of the first half. Another lost lineout in the forty-fifth minute saw Maro Itoje stroll through a gap close to the ruck, and the margin started to blow out. We created some opportunities, but poor handling let us down and a lack of sharpness meant that we struggled to sustain any real pressure.

Dev Toner came on with Sean Cronin, but the lineout continued to struggle. The only second-half score we managed was an excellent individual try by Bundee Aki, but the scoreboard was well gone at that point. The final ignominy was a lineout on our 5-metre line that we threw directly to their replacement hooker, Luke Cowan-Dickie, who finished the scoring.

The 57–15 loss is by far the largest that we've suffered in the last six years. But I know we can build our way back from this performance. It's one of the dilemmas of the pre-RWC period, when the pre-season workload spills over into a match week. That makes it challenging for players to perform at their best in the short term, but I'm hoping that it still fits with the longer-term goal of being ready to perform well when we arrive in Japan.

Saturday, 31 August 2019, Cardiff

With RWC squad selection due on Monday morning, many of the players who didn't play against England were given opportunities to press their claims today against Wales. It was great to have James Ryan back – his work rate and contact skills instil confidence in those around him. On the back of a more balanced week of training, the performance was more energized and accurate.

A line break from Dave Kilcoyne was followed up with a great inside ball from Jack Carty to Andrew Conway, who got into space and linked with Jacob Stockdale, who finished the score. Jacob then finished another when he pounced on a loose pass from Aaron Shingler.

Wales had more possession and territory in the first half, but carried only half as many metres as we did and missed twenty tackles. My feeling was that there had been some good work from our lads, but Wales had been below par.

Our scrum kept the Welsh under pressure in the second

half, eventually winning us a penalty try and the comfort of a 22–3 lead with just over a quarter of the game to play.

After concerted pressure Wales scored to close the gap, and would have added another but for a phenomenal try-saving tackle from Garry Ringrose and Luke McGrath. A late try by Rhys Patchell made the last few minutes a bit nerve-racking, but the performance and the 22–17 result were a step up from last week.

Sunday, 1 September 2019, Dublin

After the match, we returned to St David's Hotel in Cardiff. Our flight back was later in the evening, so we had time to review the game and to confirm selections for the RWC squad of thirty-one players, which has to be forwarded to World Rugby by 9 a.m. tomorrow.

We have been picking shadow squads during the summer series, tracking each player's training and match performances. As the decisions got tougher, there was more discussion, with comparisons being made and combinations considered.

In the front row, Jack McGrath has been a stalwart for us, but with injuries affecting him during the previous season he hasn't had quite the same sharpness, so Cian Healy and Dave Kilcoyne grabbed the loosehead spots. One of the hookers had to be left out, and Rob Herring had unfortunately played only fifteen minutes against Italy due to injury, so he was unlucky to miss out in a highly competitive position.

One very tough decision was leaving Devin Toner out of the squad. Dev had been late to get started in the pre-season due to an injury, but he was a known quantity for us. We had hoped that he'd solve a few lineout issues when he came on against England, but we were also realistic that one player cannot completely change something which has so many working parts. One issue for us was that we had been alerted that the citing commissioner was looking at an incident close to our line in the seventy-fifth minute, when Dev made shoulder contact with Rob Evans. We hadn't noticed the contact at the time, but we reviewed the footage and it didn't look good. We could see that there was nothing deliberate from Dev but that his shoulder had impacted directly onto Rob Evans's head. After Scott Barrett's red card and suspension over a shoulder charge in the Rugby Championship, we fretted that Dev would incur a similar sanction. We had been warned by Alain Rolland, in his presentation to us, that any shoulder-to-head contact was likely to have a starting point of a six-week suspension.

It was a difficult call, but we decided to select Tadhg Beirne, who can play both second row and back row, and Jean Kleyn, the only specialist tighthead-scrummaging second-row in the squad.

With Pete O'Mahony, C. J. Stander, Jack Conan, Josh van der Flier and Rhys Ruddock, we felt that we had good options in the back row, especially as Pete had played at No. 7 for us in Australia, when captaining the side. Jordi Murphy, a versatile and team-orientated player who started the 2015 RWC quarter-final, missed out, along with Tommy O'Donnell, who is such a good athlete but who has missed a lot of time through injury. Again, difficult conversations to have with good people and quality players.

Scrum half was especially difficult. It had already been a tough decision to leave out John Cooney, who'd had a great season for Ulster and had been with us through the Six

Nations. The medics were confident that Joey Carbery would be fit for the Scotland game, and we decided that he could provide emergency scrum-half cover, meaning that we would select only two specialists. That left us needing to omit one of the three scrum halves in the squad: Conor Murray, who has worked his way back into form after his layoff at the start of last season; Luke McGrath, who's been playing well and has a strong kicking game; or Kieran Marmion, who is not just an outstanding player but a great team contributor. It was very difficult to choose between Luke and Kieran, because they're both top-quality people and players, but we opted for Luke on the strength of his kicking game.

Ross Byrne had done a good job leading into the England game, and it was a big task to keep the team together on that day, but we leaned toward Jack Carty after his incisive display against Wales, for which he had deservingly won Man of the Match. His kicking had been smart and accurate, especially in the first half, and he had been a threat running at the line.

The four centres were already in the squad, so the other decisions were in the back three. Dave Kearney struggled last season with injury, but he had been robust in the preseason before picking up a soft-tissue injury following the Italy game. Will Addison has impressed every time that he's been involved with us, but he has missed a lot of time through injury and his calf tightened up during the Wales game. The outside backs tend to be more prone to soft-tissue injuries than others due to the high speeds they generate, so durability is a factor we needed to consider. We decided that Andrew Conway has played well, Jordan Larmour offers great versatility and footwork, while Keith Earls, Jacob Stockdale and Rob Kearney have all played big roles in big games for us in recent times.

In the end we finalized the squad of thirty-one before combining our notes on the players who missed selection, which formed the basis for my feedback when I spoke with them today. It's a day I dread and the players vary in their responses, with some having less expectation than others; but regardless of the reaction, I feel miserable for those who miss out.

Saturday, 7 September 2019, Dublin

It is still hard to believe that the final summer series fixture today against Wales is the last time that I'll coach at the Aviva Stadium. It was obviously Rory Best's last home game too, which held far more significance: he had made his test debut at the same ground, albeit not the same stadium, in 2005.

Both team line-ups were very strong, and it was great to get Johnny Sexton and Robbie Henshaw back involved. We dodged an early bullet when Rob Kearney won the race to a kick-through to deny George North an early score. The game was fast and physical, with plenty of early width and endeavour. Wales dominated the early possession, but we looked dangerous, with Bundee and Robbie linking up through the line and then Jordan Larmour getting space on the outside. We kept the pressure on and Rob Kearney scored after some good handling.

Breaking the offside line early from a lineout, Dan Biggar intercepted a pass from Johnny. A great chase dragged him down and he was held up over the line. Biggar cleverly let the referee know that he didn't get the ball down, so there was no need to go to the TMO. If the TMO had become involved, the offside was likely to have been picked up and we would have got a penalty seventy metres back down the field. Instead, Wales were awarded a 5-metre scrum and after a series of pick-and-goes, Hadleigh Parkes ran a strong reverse-angled line, received a flat pass and scored close to the posts. A super line break and offload soon after from Josh van der Flier came to nothing as Wales scrambled well and defended stoutly. It left us trailing 7–10 at half-time.

We got the squeeze on Wales in the first ten minutes of the second half and Tadhg Furlong burrowed over from close range to wrestle the lead back. James Ryan scored ten minutes later after some strong attacking phases and the margin went out to nine points, which is how it ended. The performance was a confidence booster for us, as we kept the pressure on and forced Wales backwards, whether we had the ball or they did. We missed a few chances to increase the scoreboard margin, and there were facets of the game that we will need to tidy up, but it was a nice way to finish at the Aviva, with a boisterous crowd and a well-earned win.

I feel that we have banked a good volume of work and are starting to build some momentum. The scrum has been strong throughout the pre-season and we have recovered well from the lineout meltdown against England. The main concerns are the lack of time some of the combinations have had together out on the pitch, and the injuries to Joey Carbery and to Keith Earls, who limped off earlier this afternoon. The view is that Joey and Keith might be available for Scotland, but will definitely be available for Japan. We think that's manageable with the rest of the squad in good heart and good shape.

It's now all about the World Cup.

Wednesday, 11 September 2019, Heathrow Airport lounge

After such a long build-up, there's a sense of anticipation in the group as we set off for Japan. It's already been a long day for many of the players, who travelled to Dublin Airport from their provincial centres. We assembled at the Radisson Hotel and worked our way through the last bits of organization and media commitments. Aer Lingus are our airline partner and do a great job of looking after us as we work our way through the airport.

There has been some media focus on our No. 1 world ranking, but as I explained to Michael Corcoran in an interview earlier this afternoon, the Rugby World Cup is not about being the No. 1-ranked team in the world. It's not even about being the best team in the world. It's about being the best team on the day, during those two confined forty-minute windows, when you have to be at your very best just to compete. I'm nervous, because those minutes have so many variables contained in them.

Friday, 13 September 2019, Chiba prefecture

We are settled into the Hotel New Otani Makuhari. Before we left Dublin, Kelly passed on a small birthday survival package, and at our coaches meeting yesterday, fine-tuning our organization for the next few days, we chewed through some of the chocolates that were enclosed. We completed a walk-through on the hotel tennis courts this morning. It was adequate, but I delivered some terse feedback a couple of times when players didn't get their detail right. We have just two trainings here in Chiba and we need to make the most of them in preparation for Scotland. We got through the welcome ceremony without anyone tripping up when stepping onto the stage – as happened in 2015 – so that was positive at least.

The highlight of the day was the spin class this evening. Players and staff walked down to a studio packed with spin bikes. It resembled a nightclub more than a workout space, with flashing lights and surround-sound. The players were giddy, giving plenty of boisterous feedback to the instructor during the twenty-five-minute session. There was plenty of energy and a feel-good factor at the end of what was a light but entertaining workout for both players and staff.

Saturday, 14 September 2019, Chiba prefecture

Because the training venue is thirty-five to forty minutes away by bus, we scheduled the pitch sessions and the gym sessions in the same training window, rather than travel back and forth twice in the day.

When I jogged across the pitch at Ichihara Suporeku Park, the cushion of closely knitted grass felt luxurious; but beneath the grass the surface seemed to be striated, with slightly uneven furrows.

In the backs unit session, before we even got up to speed, Rob Kearney put his hand up and left the pitch with calf tightness. Then Robbie Henshaw, running onto a pass, twisted and dipped, reaching slightly to his left, then grabbed his hamstring. He limped into the in-goal area at the end of the pitch and was attended by the physios. At that point the players were unsettled, and some of the staff looked dismayed:

we'd barely started our first training and already two players had picked up injuries. I quickly reshuffled the backline and advised the players to train within themselves and take a bit of extra care with the slight unevenness under the grass surface.

I was frustrated and concerned but tried not to show it. The weather is forecast to be wet in Yokohama over the weekend, and the prospect of losing two players who are so experienced and so good in the air is far from ideal. We already had Keith Earls and Joey Carbery sitting out the training, so we were left with very few options. Richie Murphy, Vinny Hammond and Andy Farrell stepped in to make up the numbers and we managed to get ourselves organized to complete a team run in rather tentative fashion.

Wednesday, 18 September 2019, Yokohama Bay Sheraton

The grass was trimmed a bit shorter after the injuries on Saturday, which seemed to make the surface feel a bit more stable. We were still treading a little bit gingerly but got what we felt we needed to get done during training on Monday and earlier today. Our captain's run is a day earlier than usual – on Friday, rather than Saturday, for a Sunday game – so we will use the time in the stadium to train, as we usually would two days out from the game. The coaches were able to make good use of the eighty-five-minute bus journey from Ichihara, going through the training footage and planning what we will show to the players and what we will focus on in Friday's training.

The Japanese are fantastic hosts, and we were greeted by a line of enthusiastic staff on our arrival at the Yokohama Bay

Sheraton this evening. We have now had a bit of time to get to know our liaison staff, Shino Kusunose and David McFall, who have already shown that they're going to add great value, pitching in and contributing to whatever is required. For me, it's a reunion of sorts with our interpreter Hiroyuki Hama-mura, who worked with David Nucifora and me as an analyst at the Blues many years ago. We have also worked with our security man, Kubaan Louwrens, before. He is calm and thorough, which offers peace of mind.

Saturday, 21 September 2019, Yokohama Bay Sheraton

Yokohama Stadium is impressive, and it was ideal to get a good hit-out and orientate ourselves there yesterday. The team naming was relatively simple as far as the backs were concerned: with only ten fit backs, we have just enough for the seven starting players and three reserves. The Scots have gone with a very experienced back row, and Duncan Taylor, after spending much of last season injured, is back in the mid-field alongside Sam Johnson, who was so impressive in the Six Nations. Their scrum-half, Greg Laidlaw, has a consistent kicking game, while the mercurial Finn Russell and Stuart Hogg are incredibly dangerous if offered any time or space.

We returned from the stadium to watch the opening game of the tournament, with Japan beating Russia. We know that they'll be watching our game tomorrow in preparation for next Saturday, but our full focus is on Scotland.

Today we restricted ourselves to a walk-through at a nearby school. We were on the roof, nine storeys up, in a space the size of a basketball court. Space is at a premium in Tokyo, and rooftop pitches and courts are common. We felt a bit exposed, being surrounded by high-rise apartments and hotels, and through his binoculars Kubaan spied a few people recording us, but we felt that they were likely to be interested locals or rugby fans, so we worked our way through the plays that we are keen to put into place tomorrow.

This evening the heavyweights New Zealand and South Africa went head to head. South Africa started with a line speed and brutality that stifled New Zealand, but two tries in four minutes just before the half-hour mark showed how dangerous the All Blacks are when the game breaks open. New Zealand's 17–3 lead was enough to keep them clear of South Africa for the remainder of the match, though there were a few close calls, especially when it looked like Cheslin Kolbe had got away, only to be dragged down short of the line and forced into touch by Richie Mo'unga.

Both of those teams are going to be very tough in the quarter-finals. For us, we need to win tomorrow to ensure that we put ourselves into a good position to reach the knock-out stage.

Monday, 23 September 2019, Katsuragi Hotel, Kitanomaru

Yesterday, we got the start we wanted and the result we needed. The first real chance we had to get onto the front foot, Iain Henderson charged through a gap close to the ruck and, after a few close carries, James Ryan barged over. It was the ideal confidence boost and momentum starter after just six minutes. Concerted pressure and an effective lineout drive added another try for Rory Best. Just ten minutes later, after some proactive defence from Chris Farrell, the ball bounced loose and Andrew Conway toed it through.

From the resulting 5-metre scrum, three quick close-in carries ended with Tadhg Furlong scoring and the score was 19–3 – as it remained until half-time, during which the weather deteriorated. The possession and territory stats at half-time were very even, but we had seized the opportunities to convert the pressure we'd exerted.

In the first ten minutes after half-time Scotland put plenty of pressure on, but the defence held firm and the rain was getting heavier, making it more difficult for them to chase the game. Andrew Conway contested well for a high ball in the Scottish 22, and it fell to Jordan Larmour; from the quick ruck ball, Conor Murray rifled a flat pass to the edge, where Andrew had repositioned himself, and he stepped inside the last defender to get over for the bonus-point try. Despite a few more line breaks and opportunities, especially after Chris Farrell charged through a gap from a scrum, we added just a penalty goal, but, importantly, we kept Scotland scoreless and consolidated a vital 27–3 first-up win.

The relief last night was tangible amongst the whole group. We had all been on edge since the first training, when we had lost two players before we'd even got started. Reviewing the game, there was still plenty to tidy up but there were plenty of positives. Johnny Sexton and Jack Conan have picked up niggly injuries, while Bundee Aki copped a head knock, but there is nothing too worrying from the game. Rob Kearney has made good progress and should be fit for the Japan game, but Robbie Henshaw is unlikely to be available until we play Samoa in the final pool match.

It was great to catch up with two of my brothers for a coffee this morning. I had grabbed about three hours' sleep after reviewing the game and doing plenty of research on Japan. We caught the Shinkansen south to Kakegawa, then travelled by bus to Katsuragi. I spent the time on the train running through the Scotland review and Japan preview footage so that, once we got to the hotel, we could have a quick meeting and turn our focus toward the dangerous Japanese side. I sensed that it was a bit of a hard sell after the two big wins we had against Japan in 2017, with many of the young players from that squad now more established, plus the return of many of the Lions players, especially in the forward pack. The Japanese had also been well beaten by South Africa prior to the tournament and had been made to work hard by Russia before winning that game comfortably enough in the end. If we're not quite mentally or emotionally right for the game we're at risk of losing, because the Japanese have some very dangerous players and they've shown it on a number of occasions, especially in Twickenham last November, when they led England at half-time.

Friday, 27 September 2019, Sakura-dono, Katsuragi Hotel

My room at Katsuragi is a self-contained dwelling, spacious and very traditionally Japanese. It is very quiet and nestled amongst trees and grass, which is a pleasant contrast to the concrete of Chiba and Yokohama. The one drawback is the size of the spiders. Called *Ashidaka-gumo*, which translates as 'tall-legged spider', some of the ones I have seen are the size of my hand and they're very fast, so it's difficult to chase them down. I think they're a type of huntsman spider, and the first time I saw one it was directly above my head as I was about to turn the light out. Thankfully, I'm not too anxious about spiders, but I chased it off to feel more comfortable about going to sleep.

The captain's run this morning at Ecopa Stadium went smoothly but the scan on Jack Conan's foot didn't, with a stress fracture ruling him out of the remainder of the tournament. It was very disappointing for us and for Jack. We had named him in the starting line-up and were keen to have him involved after he was so impressive against Japan at the same venue two years ago. Amongst the coaches, we discussed potential replacements but decided to wait until after the game tomorrow before making a decision.

Ulster are due to play later today, Irish time, so I spoke to Dan McFarland and he withdrew Jordi Murphy as a precaution. I also spoke to Leo Cullen, as we might choose to bring Dev Toner over and leave Tadhg Beirne in the back row. If we wait until tomorrow and see how players come through the game, then we can perhaps make the best decision.

Sunday, 29 September 2019, Kobe Bay Sheraton Hotel

It's 9.30 p.m. and we're now in Kobe, where we play Russia on Thursday evening. It's been a difficult twenty-four hours since losing to Japan. I haven't slept, apart from a nap on the Shinkansen, because I had such a knot in my stomach after the game. Once we got back to the hotel, I spoke to Tim on FaceTime for a while, and he passed the phone around to Ella and Luke, which was a positive distraction; but the knot tightened again as soon as I finished the call and I turned my attention back to what I needed to get done.

Reviewing the game overnight at least gave me the chance to get a fine-toothed comb through it. I have various sets of notes and clips ready: one set for the team as a whole, another for the backs, others for individual players, and finally a set for the match officials. With just a five-day turnaround, at least I'm ready for the review and mostly ready for the preview, having selected a few clips from the two games that Russia have played thus far.

On reflection, we started well enough in the game to lead 12–3 after thirty minutes. The two early tries we scored came after good interplay that led to line breaks, then sustained pressure. With the security of having a penalty advantage, Jack Carty put a cross kick into the corner, which Garry Ringrose took superbly to score. The second try followed soon after, when Jack chipped to himself and deflected the ball back for Rob Kearney to gather and scramble over the line. Directly from the kick-off, which James Ryan took superbly, we made another line break from a cross kick to Keith Earls, who linked with Rob; but a few positive phases later Rory Best was adjudged to have lost the ball forward when he clearly hadn't, and the opportunity came to nothing.

The match footage confirmed a few things that had frustrated us when watching the game live. There were four offside penalties given against us, which seemed very harsh. When Japan had the ball, the number of side entries missed at the breakdown, and players being taken out beyond the breakdown, was baffling – which made it incredibly difficult for us to turn the ball over or even to slow it down. The Japanese hold plenty of width in their attack, which means that they are sometimes light at the ruck, and we were keen to get pressure on their ball. When we couldn't impact on the security or speed of their ball, they showed the skill, power and pace that they have. Loose forwards Michael Leitch and Kazuki Himeno were often in the wide channels and they carried powerfully, but they also showed the passing and offloading ability they have, which brought the high-speed threats of Kotaro Matsushima and Lomano Lemeki into the game.

The Japanese had defended aggressively and attacked with the tempo and energy that we had lacked in the second half. Their passing skills and running lines were impressive, and they committed so few errors, despite playing at such a rapid tempo, that they continually kept us under pressure. From a neutral perspective, it was also a great result for World Rugby and for the tournament, with the host nation now leading the pool, and the passionate Japanese support has been magnified.

Watching the Wales versus Australia match this afternoon when we arrived in Kobe, the TMO intervened after Samu Kerevi, carrying the ball high in two hands, made contact with Rhys Patchell. The referee then penalized Kerevi for foul play. There is a danger that this sort of TMO intervention – calling the referee's attention to an infringement that is marginal or non-existent – causes the game to become disjointed. In our game, by contrast, all four officials missed Jack Carty being taken out in the air and Rob Kearney getting hit in the face by a swinging arm that forced him from the field.

We are still in control of whether or not we qualify, and we need to make sure that we keep it that way. The players will dust themselves off and commit to their recovery for the upcoming five-day turnaround.

Tuesday, 1 October 2019, Kobe

Our discipline was questioned in the press conference today, after the four offside penalties proved costly against Japan. In my frustration I revealed some of the feedback that we'd received from World Rugby: two of the offside calls were confirmed as incorrect, and a third shouldn't have been called because it had no effect on play and the player who stepped forward stepped back again. As well as giving Japan the advantage of the penalties, the decisions also made us more hesitant, which meant that our line speed was less than it needed to be and the Japanese attackers revelled in the extra space afforded to them.

I was actually disappointed with myself for mentioning the feedback from World Rugby, because it's delivered in confidence and it was a confidence that I had always respected – I should have just taken the criticism of our discipline on the chin. I thought that the Japanese had played tremendously well, and I could have defended our discipline and complimented the Japanese and left it at that.

It was good to get out on the pitch this morning and to focus on our performance rather than the Japan result. We had a useful session in searing heat with Kobe Steelers from Japan's Top League. Their group of young players tore into us with good skills, timing and running lines. We gave some players a rest while getting others back onto the pitch. Jordi Murphy only arrived from Belfast on Sunday evening but trained with plenty of positive energy today. Against Russia, Rhys Ruddock will make his first start of the tournament and Pete O'Mahony will play on the openside to allow Josh van der Flier a rest.

Kobe's coaches, Dave Dillon and Nick Holton, hosted us and organized the training, which was much appreciated. We had originally planned an open session to engage with the local community, but the logistics proved challenging for World Rugby and we were restricted to having a group of young students attend. They were enthusiastic and stayed around hunting for autographs and photos after the session had finished.

Russia have made a few changes to their team, so they will be a bit of an unknown for us, but we are very keen to get some rhythm back. We watched Scotland play against Samoa last night, and the roofed Kobe Misaki Stadium looked sweltering. People in the crowd were fanning themselves, while the players looked sodden, their limbs glistening and their jerseys darkened by sweat. In two games at the stadium thus far there have been sixty-five handling errors, which is inordinately high. We are hoping that Typhoon Mitag, due to hit Japan over the next few days, will lower the humidity. At least temperatures are forecast to drop from 30 degrees to about 25 degrees – but inside the oven that the stadium creates it will still be very hot and slippery.

Wednesday, 2 October 2019, Kobe Bay Sheraton Hotel

The conditions for the captain's run were stifling, but at least the windows at either end of the stadium were open, as well as a few along the sides. Unfortunately, they have to be closed for the match, so by the time 45,000 people pack into the stadium and two teams get up and running, stifling is going to be an understatement.

Joey Carbery was meant to cover out-half and scrum half from the bench, but he struggled with foot pain after the captain's run, so we'll replace him with Conor Murray, who we'd initially planned to rest. Conor is very keen to be involved and the week has been light, with just one training, so we're hoping that the players have plenty of fuel in their legs, because it's going to be very tough work tomorrow.

Thursday, 3 October 2019, Kobe Misaki Stadium

Well, we got what we needed with five points from the match, but we made hard work of it, and the conditions ensured that the work got harder the longer we played. Scoring a set-play try within two minutes was the ideal start, as Rob Kearney sliced through to score. Another score to Pete O'Mahony followed ten minutes later, but we missed a number of chances before Rhys Ruddock barged over later in the half. Two good late tries sealed the bonus point and pushed the differential out to 35 points to nil, but we made far too many handling errors, which left us frustrated.

Thankfully, that frustration didn't appear to be shared by the huge support that we had in the stadium. There were masses of green jerseys and plenty of raucous support, singing and cheering – which certainly helped to keep the players energized despite the heat. A number of the players after the game commented on the difficulty of getting a full breath into their lungs and on how slippery the ball was, but we weren't looking for any excuses in the review, where we made sure we stayed accountable for doing better regardless of the conditions.

Sunday, 6 October 2019, Grand Hyatt Fukuoka

A couple of days off, after the Shinkansen journey to Fukuoka, have made a very positive difference to the group. There's renewed energy and a readiness to go again, and I'm hopeful that that will be apparent in training tomorrow and in the off-pitch preparations for Samoa. They looked very dangerous at times against Japan yesterday evening, scoring a couple of good tries. They were also a bit ragged defensively and loose with the ball, so hopefully we can exploit a few opportunities against them next weekend.

Tuesday, 8 October 2019, Grand Hyatt Fukuoka

We have had two good training days. The Japan 2019 crew have done a great job with the gym at Shirouzuoike Park – it's the most spacious one we have had, and the air conditioning inside is a bit of a life-saver. Jason Cowman has been impressed by a few really good scores from the players on the counter-movement jump, which measures lower-body power. There have also been some really positive strength scores in the gym, so there is definitely a bit of a bounce evident from the weekend off. It's also been visible on the training pitch, with a sharper energy and willingness to work. We're managing the load for the players, trying to retain a freshness, but they're doing well to make that easier for us because they're preparing well, and the accuracy on the pitch has been good. It's also been helpful to have Robbie Henshaw back in the group, and he's slotted in well alongside Bundee Aki, with Garry Ringrose due a bit of a break after three big eighty-minute performances in a row.

We're all aware that a very powerful storm, Typhoon Hagibis, is due to hit Japan this weekend. Initially, we were in line to get the brunt of it, so we had informal discussions with JR2019 yesterday about potentially shifting the match to Tokyo. However, its course has shifted northwards and it is likely to strike further up the east coast, in Tokyo and beyond – which could threaten the Japan versus Scotland match. I know that the RWC staff are working behind the scenes on contingency plans, but hopefully all the matches survive the weekend.

Thursday, 10 October 2019, Grand Hyatt Fukuoka

With Typhoon Hagibis approaching, World Rugby have cancelled two of Saturday's games: England versus France and New Zealand versus Italy. The Japan versus Scotland game on Sunday is under threat too. It seems bizarre that games could be cancelled at a World Cup, but it was always a risk with the tournament being played during typhoon season.

England top Pool C and will be freshened for their quarter-final game against Australia. They have already left for a three-day break in Miyazaki, away from the path of Hagibis, where Eddie Jones says that they'll 'regenerate, refocus and put a bit more petrol in the tank, so we're really happy with it'. France miss the chance to top the pool but they will be freshened for their match against Wales, who had a very physical battle with Fiji yesterday evening.

If the Japan–Scotland game ends up being cancelled as well, that would put Japan on 16 points. We'll be on 16 too if we beat Samoa with a bonus point, but Japan would win the tie-breaker because of their victory over us. And Scotland would definitely be out unless we got nothing from the Samoa game. We need to be pragmatic and focus on getting the best performance we can against Samoa in what are likely to be windy conditions here in Fukuoka. The conditions have certainly presented plenty of challenges in the last four weeks – this time we'll contend with the wind, instead of the rain we had against Scotland or the heat and humidity in the Japan and Russia games.

I spoke to the Italy coach, Conor O'Shea, this afternoon. He was gutted, as were his players, that their game against New Zealand has been cancelled. Their long-serving hooker, Leonardo Ghiraldini, broke down in tears when the news came through, and their captain, Sergio Parisse, said: 'It is ridiculous that a decision of this nature has been made, because it isn't like the fans arrived yesterday. It is ridiculous that there was no plan B, because it isn't news that typhoons hit Japan.' Meanwhile, if their match versus Japan is cancelled on Sunday, Scotland are threatening legal action under the 'Terms of Agreement' for the tournament, which state that in the event of a 'force majeure' a game may be shifted or postponed. It seems that with some contingency planning, especially prior to the tournament, the Saturday games could have been brought forward by twenty-four hours – even if they had to be played in closed stadiums – which would have been fairer for all concerned.

It will be interesting to see if the teams that are getting a week off will be better prepared and fresher when the quarter-finals are played. For any team, after a number of intense and competitive weeks, getting the chance to freshen is a huge advantage. It's evident to all of us in Fukuoka, where the players have bounced back with plenty of energy after having a two-day break. As a result, I think that we will be ready to perform better against Samoa.

Friday, 11 October 2019, Grand Hyatt Fukuoka

When we arrived at Fukuoka Hakatanomori Stadium for the captain's run, we were surprised by the patchwork appearance of the pitch. Segments of the turf could be lifted up and were unstable at the edges, which may cause issues tomorrow. It's a bit of a concern, because we're very keen to put some pressure on the Samoan scrum but the surface may compromise that; and if the segments shift at all, that instability may heighten the risk of injury.

For entertainment this evening, Vinny Hammond and Colm Fuller put together 'Fukuoka Big Brother', a six-minute spoof. Vinny photoshopped various players into different shots and Colm did impersonations of them in voiceover. It was hilarious and eased the tension. Tomorrow's match weighs heavily on those selected, because we need to win to be sure of staying in the tournament. To give ourselves the best chance of topping the group, we need to win well and claim a bonus point, then see what happens – if anything – between Japan and Scotland.

Sunday, 13 October 2019, Grand Hyatt Fukuoka

I think the Samoans were struggling a bit by the time they got to our game. They had suffered a few injuries and suspensions, and it probably helped us quickly take control of the game with three early scores. Samoa got one back before we lost Bundee Aki to a red card. The ball bounced up between him and U. J. Seuteni, with both players keen to win possession. Seuteni got to it first, leaving Bundee hardly any time to adjust from trying to field the ball to making a tackle. Seuteni was off balance and wasn't able to get up and running before colliding with Bundee, and while Bundee dropped slightly, he didn't have time to get into a tackle position. His shoulder made contact with Seuteni's jaw and the referee decided that there was not enough mitigation to avoid the sanction of a red card.

Johnny Sexton scored a good try on the short side from an attacking scrum and we had the bonus point by half-time. Jordan Larmour danced his way through a few gaps and Joey Carbery came on for a confidence-boosting thirty minutes, along with the rest of the bench, without the team losing cohesion; but concern about Bundee's red card has taken the shine off the 47–5 win. The Samoa coach, Steve Jackson, was outspoken about Bundee being unlucky and said he hoped that the sending off would be deemed sufficient punishment. I chatted afterwards with Steve and we shared the same concerns about the inflexibility of the 'High Tackle Framework' and the reality of split-second decisions on the pitch.

One concern as the match continued was player safety, with the pitch lifting up in places and uneven in others. Fine gravel was seeping up through the seams and a number of players finished the game with abrasions. We discussed the state of the pitch in the coaches' box and sent a message to Paul Dean to request that the match be called off early. Deano approached the match manager and a message was sent on to the referee, via the fourth official. The referee chose to continue, but chatting to the Samoans and our players later, we thought it was incredible that two teams at rugby's premier tournament had to play on a pitch as badly cobbled together as that one was.

I spent most of last night reviewing the game. Late kick-offs are always a bit frustrating because it means that reviewing the match goes deep into the early hours of the morning. David Nucifora, Vinny Hammond and I discussed Bundee's red card, and we considered what mitigating factors could have been taken into account but weren't. In the 'High Tackle Framework' there are five mitigating factors, and we felt that one of these – 'Reactionary tackle' – applied. We had timed it: there was just a fifth of a second between Seuteni grabbing the ball and the contact with Bundee, making it more an unplanned collision than a tackle, and we agreed that that would be the basis of our defence at the judicial hearing.

Despite the devastation caused by Typhoon Hagibis, Tokyo was calm this evening and the Japan versus Scotland game went ahead. There was a minute's silence prior to the match, due to the rising death toll from the typhoon, which puts a few things in perspective. Scotland started well and Finn Russell scored early, but for the remainder of the first half Scotland struggled to contain the speed and width of the Japanese attack, with Kenki Fukuoka and Kotaro Matsushima combining to even up the scores in impressive fashion.

I had received a text from the All Blacks assistant coach, Ian Foster, before the match asking which team I thought would win. I replied that I hoped it would be Scotland, so that we could top the group; but the Japanese were irrepressible in the second quarter. They scored under the posts through their loosehead prop, Inagaki, and a superb grubber down the left edge was gathered by Fukuoka, who raced away to score. 21–7 at half-time became 28–7 just after half-time when Fukuoka ripped the ball off the Scotland centre Chris Harris and streaked away for his second try. Scotland rallied with two quick tries, but Japan held on and topped the pool, leaving us to meet the All Blacks in the quarter-final.

Monday, 14 October 2019, Tokyo Bay Hilton

We arrived back in Tokyo this evening. We have had meetings and a walk-through to set up our attack and defence for the week, and we will train tomorrow and Thursday in preparation for the quarter-final. We know that New Zealand trained today and haven't had to travel or to recover from a match during the weekend, but we feel that if we can get a couple of good trainings done, we can be competitive.

Prior to the quarter-final in 2015, I spent hours preparing for Sean O'Brien's defence after he was cited for swinging an arm and partially closed fist into the sternum of Pascal Papé, who was holding him back, but the judiciary suspended him for a week. There has been a guilty-until-proven-innocent climate to all of the disciplinary hearings that I have prepared for or attended, and the feedback from Bundee's hearing this evening was no different. Despite one of the assistant referees stating that he 'thought that the collision/tackle was unusual because the ball had become dislodged in a previous tackle and then was bouncing along the ground with the collision/tackle happening quickly after Samoa #10 had gathered the loose ball' – which was exactly what we had argued – the judiciary dismissed the 0.2-second reaction time as a mitigating factor and issued a six-week suspension, reduced by half due to Bundee's good disciplinary record. It meant his World Cup was over.

Thursday, 17 October 2019, NTT Communications Shining Arcs

We have kept trainings short, but they have been sharp. The players have finished doing their post-training extras and individual work. We have had a few injury scares, and Tadhg Furlong and James Ryan won't train tomorrow, but we're hopeful that they'll be fit for the match. There is an edge, but whether it will be enough is hard to assess. The All Blacks have not been challenged since their first match against South Africa, and Italy would certainly have forced them to work hard, but they'll be fresh and there is no way that we can sneak up on them any more.

We have decided not to go to the stadium for the captain's run tomorrow. The travel time to Tokyo Stadium was listed as 45 minutes by JR 2019, but Kubaan has done a dummy run and it took 65 minutes. When we questioned the time discrepancy, JR 2019 said that we should actually allow 75 minutes to get to the stadium. It is far from ideal to spend two and a half hours on a bus the day before such a big test match, as well as spending 75 minutes the following day to get to the stadium. We will do a short captain's run at NTT instead, although the kickers will go into the stadium after lunch to familiarize themselves with the ground and to work through their kicking routine.

Saturday, 19 October 2019, Tokyo Bay Hilton

Yesterday's captain's run went well, and we're still hopeful that all those selected will be fit to start the match, but we won't be sure until they get through the warm-up this evening. We had Risteárd Cooper in after lunch yesterday and he shredded me with plenty of quips and impersonations, as well as having a good shot at a number of the players and a few other staff. Before dinner Shane Lowry and Joe Canning called in and chatted to the squad.

It's been a long morning. Waiting for an evening game can be stressful. My son Tim arrived to collect his tickets along with Robbie, one of his mates from Terenure. He had a card for me from my mum, with a message she wrote when she realized that she wasn't going to live long enough to see the World Cup. I walked away from him to read the card, because I knew I was going to well up. She wrote that she was 'so proud of what you have achieved but even more proud of who you have become'. I had to take a few minutes, then wandered back to the two lads, and we passed a bit of time before I was due to meet the coaches to discuss the last few messages prior to catching up with the players.

Sunday, 20 October 2019, Tokyo Bay Hilton

Sport can be brutal at times, and I'm feeling beaten up this morning. I got a bit of sleep from 5 a.m. until 7 a.m., before going down to say farewell to some of the staff who are on flights back to Dublin this morning.

The All Blacks flew into us from the start, and we helped them along, making too many errors. I think our confidence slipped once we conceded the ball a few times and conceded scores that were far too easy for the All Blacks to convert.

The game as I saw it unfolding and on review:

From the first kick-off, we don't adjust to a change in their set-up and it allows them to get up above us into the contest for the ball. We're lucky that they knocked it on, but it's an indication that we are not seeing things as early as we need to. There is good space for Keith Earls on the cross kick from the ensuing scrum, but it goes too far forward.

On exactly four minutes, Garry Ringrose and Robbie Henshaw both go low in the tackle on Ardie Savea and there is a clash of heads that causes both of them to spend time off the field in the blood bin. Garry Ringrose gets eighteen stitches. (This is one of the reasons that World Rugby need to keep their eyes open. We had a low-tackle focus after Bundee's red card, but it contributed to two head injuries in one play. In the past, two-man tackles would tend to have one player going high and one low, but that's now a risk that has potential red-card consequences if you get it wrong.)

At four minutes and six seconds Jacob Stockdale is inches away from an intercept and a potential seven points, but the ball goes to ground and the penalty produces the first three points for the All Blacks.

We play some quality rugby as Jacob leaps to catch the kick-off, despite contact from Sevu Reece, who tips him off balance. Through a number of front-foot phases and two partial line breaks, an overlap is created, with Jordan Larmour in great space and Rob Kearney with no one in front of him on the inside pass. Unfortunately, Keith Earls hesitates and the ball is knocked out of his hands by the All Black centre, Jack Goodhue. Jordan scrambles back well, but we end up in our own 22.

Missed tackles start to count against us, even when we look to have good defensive numbers. The players are working hard around the fringes, but Brodie Retallick's clean-out opens great space for Aaron Smith to dart through to score, and we're 10–0 down.

A penalty kick for touch, inches away from being perfect, is batted back into the field of play by Richie Mo'unga. It's hard not to think about what could have been if this kick had been a fraction wider, but the awareness and skill from Mo'unga is first rate. We knock the ball on from the lineout back in our own half, and the All Blacks score from the scrum with a sharp set play that we defend poorly. Handling errors and some poor decision-making keep offering access for the All Blacks, and they don't need too many invitations to make the most of opportunities.

A lineout set play in the 32nd minute creates great space on the outside and inside of Johnny on the second phase. Rob Kearney makes his run a bit early, though an early pass might have given him a bit of space. There's an overlap for Jacob Stockdale, but with the timing slightly awry, Johnny hesitates and gets hit. The ball is dislodged, and a really good attacking opportunity turns into a try for them, as the ball is kicked ahead by Mo'unga, then by Beauden Barrett, who scores out wide. We are not playing well, but we're probably creating more than the 22–0 suggests.

We finally get real pressure on the All Black line and have a penalty advantage just metres out – but then the penalty is reversed because Pete O'Mahony has led with the shoulder when trying to make a clean-out. It's an action that occurs numerous times in every game. There's no room for Pete to get an arm underneath Joe Moody, who is stopping the ball from coming back. I watch the replay in the dressing room and get a feeling that it's not our day.

That's not what I say to the players at half-time. I get them to pause and take a 'big breath of belief'. I focus on the opportunities that we have created. If we create a couple more in the next quarter, and at the same time just hold our run a fraction and keep our confidence, we can make the right pass and get back into the game. We talk about a couple of good options that we can use to attack from lineouts. Faz looks to stir the players, urging them to get off the floor and to get off the line. He tells them that we've had some good defensive sets and we can be better this half. We need to stick our tackles. He doesn't mention it, but at this stage we've missed ten tackles and they have missed just one.

The second half starts as the first half did, with an early error. Richie Mo'unga overhits his clearing kick and it's headed into touch on the full, but Jacob loses his bearings and catches the ball as he steps onto the sideline. The All Blacks get to start the half with an attacking lineout.

After ninety seconds defending our line, an offload from the floor by Kieran Read puts Codie Taylor in enough space to get through and score. In the coaches' box, it's time to make some changes, because we'd hoped to build our way back but now we have to gamble on flat-out chasing the game.

A good half-break from Keith Earls comes to nothing as the All Blacks continue to tackle well. A high ball is contested by Robbie Henshaw ten metres from the All Black line, but it slips out of his hands. The All Blacks, knowing that we have to chase the game, start to use angled kicks to put us deep into our own half. They back their defence to create opportunities if we start to overplay. From our clearing kick they counter-attack and the players defend bravely before winning a penalty on the floor after eleven physical phases.

On the cusp of the final quarter, another penalty kick doesn't find touch and we are running short of time, having squandered the opportunities we've created. The players have kept working and it's now very tough for them to stay task-focused and not allow the frustration and disappointment to cloud their thoughts, because the game has gone and our World Cup is all but over.

A great kick and spectacular regather from Beauden Barrett sets up another attacking platform for the All Blacks. A cross kick and quick ruck and Matt Todd scores. The score has blown out to 34–0. The players are still trying to make things happen, but the harder we try the less cohesion we have. We make most of the substitutions that we have left and Rory Best leaves the field to a standing ovation. It's not the finish he deserves, but there's no compassion from opponents when big matches need to be won.

A great ball through from Joey Carbery slips through Robbie's hands as he attempts to ground the ball in-goal. Robbie is a quality individual and class player, and quickly makes amends with a good line and strong finish after receiving an inside transfer from C. J. Stander to score under the posts. The Irish in the crowd are fantastic, and cheer as if we are still in with a chance, despite trailing 34–7.

Again trying too hard, a poor clearing kick invites the All Blacks back onto the front foot and the game becomes manic, with very little structure – just the way the All Blacks like it to be. A turnover from Ardie Savea and an offload from Dane Coles put George Bridge over. We get a penalty try as Matt Todd stops C.J. from scoring, but with defenders trying to force an error or grab an interception, we end up conceding a final try from a 5-metre scrum. It's irrelevant as far as the result is concerned, but it dents the pride of the team just a little bit more to finish at 46–14. The All Blacks were all class against us and incredibly difficult to contain.

I returned to the dressing room after the pitch-side interviews and thanked the players and the staff for the last six and a half years. I acknowledged their disappointment and mine at the way the World Cup had finished for us, but I also encouraged them to take confidence from their many achievements and expressed the pride I have in them as people. I thanked them for the privilege of having worked with them and wished them, Faz and all the staff the very best for the future.

And that's the last game. Not the fairy tale I hoped for, or that I felt Rory or the senior players merited. For me, I hope that I can look back in time and get some perspective – that it is not only the end that counts but the path that's been travelled and the moments that money couldn't buy. Not the trophies but the triumphs, the moments where we broke new ground or made a difference.

Sunday, 3 November 2019, Churchtown, Dublin

Since the quarter-final, I have spent plenty of time thinking about the tournament and what we could have done differently. There is no perfect formula, but if I could change a few things I think I would focus less on the RWC and more on what we do well and what we can keep working at. We attempted to taper and then peak for the World Cup, but it's not as simple as that. Even the best players are human beings. We don't work with straight lines or predictable circumstances and confidence can be fickle.

We didn't prioritize this year's Six Nations and I think that was a mistake. It doesn't mean that we didn't prepare and focus on each game, but we had a longer-term priority and I think it diluted the rhythm that we'd built over the previous five years. What we were good at was building behaviours and committing to the habits that helped us to be accurate and connected on the pitch.

I received a text after the game from one of the key people involved with the All Blacks' RWC programme in 2007. They put more resources into RWC preparation that year than ever before, with a conditioning window, periodization and planning, but they suffered their worst-ever exit, losing to an unfancied French team. They didn't get a lot of luck in the match, but after three big pool-match wins, NZ were suddenly out of the cup at the quarter-final stage. In the same World Cup, Ireland were also fancied but were well beaten by France and Argentina and scraped past Georgia 14 points to 10.

The following World Cup, the French lost to the All Blacks by twenty points. A week later they lost to Tonga by five points, but still scrambled into the quarter-finals. After a win over an England side that had also struggled at the tournament, they beat Wales in the semi-final by a point after Sam Warburton was red-carded for Wales after just eighteen minutes. Nothing suggested that France would get close to upsetting an All Blacks team, playing at home, that had already comfortably beaten them a few weeks earlier. But in the end, anyone watching the final felt that France were incredibly unlucky not to topple the All Blacks, who survived with a very narrow 8–7 victory.

The Rugby World Cup is very difficult to predict and just as difficult to prepare for. At the start of the 2019 tournament, I said in an interview that it wasn't about being the best team in the world but about being the best team on the day. If anything, this year's tournament would support that belief. Our performances did not have the consistency of 2018: our levels of accuracy and cohesion fluctuated from game to game, and during games. On reflection I don't believe that you can afford to taper and peak: you have to be building all the time, and that is done training by training, and performance by performance.

You only have to look at the unpredictability of the knock-out stages of RWC 2019. The three teams that got a week off all dominated their quarter-finals, with England and New

Zealand big winners and France seemingly on their way to winning until they received a red card. Wales are always tenacious, but after fifty minutes, with France leading 19–10 and driving toward the Welsh line, the red card not only reduced the French to fourteen players but also relieved the intense pressure on the Welsh line.

The way that England dominated the All Blacks and the pressure they applied to win with a bit to spare suggested that they were going to be very hard to beat in the final. Meanwhile in the other semi-final, South Africa just managed to squeeze past Wales in a poor game of rugby.

Losing Kyle Sinckler early in the final didn't help the English, but South Africa's twenty-point win was hard to argue with. Five scrum penalties and some accurate kicking allowed them to keep the pressure on England, while England didn't look to be the same team as they had been the week before.

I guess what it consolidates in my mind is that the margins are very fine and repeatability of performance is key in any competition. Our level of performance slipped as we started to look too far ahead, and we couldn't just step back onto the pitch and play with the same level of accuracy, cohesion and confidence. I think the players will build their way back from the defeat to a very good All Blacks team. But when looking more broadly at the RWC, I think there's a danger in becoming too focused on delivering one-off performances at the end of four-year cycles: that it is more about having a growth mindset on a weekly basis to improve player capability, build team cohesion and strengthen the squad's identity.

Acknowledgements

This book has been a long-term project, and I've found the process both enjoyable and exasperating, but I couldn't have written it without the support and guidance of a number of people.

Firstly, to the IRFU, the staff and the players: thank you for the confidence you have invested in me and the work you have done to deliver so many special days – without which, there wouldn't really be too much to write about.

Thanks to my mum and my siblings for their contributions, corrections and good humour in helping me to put together the early chapters. Thanks also to Kelly and my children, for their proofreading and for giving me the time and space so that I could organize my thoughts.

Ciarán Medlar has been pivotal, and his contribution to managing the project is hugely appreciated.

At Penguin, many thanks to Brendan Barrington, whose input has been invaluable.

Finally, thanks to all those undying supporters who watch enthusiastically from a distance, or plan their holidays to coincide with tours, or get along to the home matches to roar the team on. It matters, and you make it memorable.